The Redmans Of Levens And Harewood : A Contribution To The History Of The Levens Family Of Redman And Redmayne In Many Of Its Branches

Greenwood, William

Nabu Public Domain Reprints:

You are holding a reproduction of an original work published before 1923 that is in the public domain in the United States of America, and possibly other countries. You may freely copy and distribute this work as no entity (individual or corporate) has a copyright on the body of the work. This book may contain prior copyright references, and library stamps (as most of these works were scanned from library copies). These have been scanned and retained as part of the historical artifact.

This book may have occasional imperfections such as missing or blurred pages, poor pictures, errant marks, etc. that were either part of the original artifact, or were introduced by the scanning process. We believe this work is culturally important, and despite the imperfections, have elected to bring it back into print as part of our continuing commitment to the preservation of printed works worldwide. We appreciate your understanding of the imperfections in the preservation process, and hope you enjoy this valuable book.

THE REDMANS OF LEVENS AND
HAREWOOD.

ALTAR-TOMB IN ELY CATHEDRAL.

Dr. Richard Redman, Bishop of St. Asaph, Exeter and Ely.

Photo. by Rev. H. R. Campion.

The Redmans of Levens and Harewood.

A CONTRIBUTION TO THE HISTORY OF THE LEVENS
FAMILY OF REDMAN AND REDMAYNE IN
MANY OF ITS BRANCHES.

BY

W. GREENWOOD, F.S.A. *Scot.*, ETC.,

BARRISTER-AT-LAW.

Kendal
Titus Wilson, Publisher
Highgate
1905

1199524

TO
MY WIFE AND DAUGHTER.

NOTE.—*It should, perhaps, be mentioned that there are families of Redman (and its variants) which are entirely unconnected with the Redmans of Levens and Harewood, with whom alone this History professes to deal.*

CONTENTS.

CHAPTER.		PAGE.
I	Norman Origin of the Redmans	1
II.	Norman de Redman and the Knights Hospitallers	8
III.	Henry I., Sheriff and Seneschal	14
IV	Sir Matthew I , Sheriff of Lancashire, and Henry II.	29
V.	Sir Matthew II , Warden and Sheriff of Dumfries	38
VI.	Yealand	48
VII.	Sir Matthew III , Governor of Carlisle Castle	53
VIII	Sir Matthew IV., Governor of Roxburgh and Berwick	57
IX	Levens—Manor and Hall	70
X	Sir Richard I., of Harewood, Speaker of the House of Commons	78
XI.	Sir Matthew V , Sir Richard II , Knight of the Shire for Westmorland , and Sir William, Knight Banneret	90
XII.	Sir Edward, Esquire to King Richard III	98
XIII.	Sir Richard III. and the Pilgrimage of Grace , Matthew VI , and Cuthbert	107
XIV	Redmans of Bossall The Bishops of Ely and Norwich	117
XV.	Harewood Manor, Castle and Church	127

CHAPTER.		PAGE.
XVI.	Redmans of Thornton-in-Lonsdale	157
XVII	Redmans of Ireby	186
XVIII	Redmans of Twisleton	195
XIX	Off-shoots from the Thornton Colony.—Kirkby Lonsdale and Ireland, Fulford, London	206
XX.	Tunstalls of Thurland Castle	219
XXI	Unidentified Redmans	228
XXII	Redman Arms	236
	Appendix	245
	List of Authorities consulted	266
	Index	270

PEDIGREES.

	PAGE.
Redman of Levens and Harewood ... ... facing	1
D'Avranches origin of Redmans	5
De Lancaster, Barons of Kendal	10
De Camberton	47
Lambert, of Calton	111
Redman, of Bossall	118
Early Lords of Harewood	128
Redman, of Thornton ... . facing	157
Redman, of Ireby ... ... ,,	186
Redman, of Twisleton	196
Redman, of Fulford	215
Tunstal, of Thurland	220

LIST OF ILLUSTRATIONS.

	FACING PAGE.
Altar-tomb in Ely Cathedral Dr. Richard Redman, Bishop of St. Asaph, Exeter and Ely (Photograph by Rev. H. R Campion)	*frontispiece*
Charter, temp. Hen. II., granting Levens to Norman de Redman. By permission of the C. & W. A. & A. Society	2
Levens Hall—front view By permission of Mr. John F. Curwen, F.S.A.	16
Charter of 1 Ric. I. exempting Lords of Levens from payment of Noutgeld	28
Gardens of Levens Hall By permission of Mr. John F Curwen, F S.A	38
Plan of Levens Park (made about 1720). By permission of Mr John F Curwen, F.S A	50
Ground-plan of Levens Hall. By permission of Mr. John F. Curwen, F S A.	72
Ruins of Harewood Castle	78
Arms, Aldeburgh and Redman Redman quartering Aldeburgh, formerly in the Great Chamber of Harewood Castle	84
Altar-tomb in Harewood Church Sir Richard Redman, the Speaker, and his wife, Elizabeth, daughter of the first Lord Aldeburgh	88
Altar-tomb in Harewood Church. Sir Richard Redman and his wife, Elizabeth, daughter of Sir Wm Gascoigne	94
Altar-tombs in Harewood Church	100

LIST OF ILLUSTRATIONS.

Ruins of Harewood Castle. (From drawing by Herbert Railton)	106
Section of Altar-tomb of Sir Wm. Ryther. By permission of Mr. H. Speight	112
Arms formerly in Harewood Castle and Church By permission of Mr. H. Speight	127
Ruins of Bolton Priory. (From drawing by Herbert Railton)	130
Altar-tomb of Sir William Ryther, in Ryther Church. By permission of Mr. H. Speight	136
Window in Harewood Castle, with Arms of Baliol and Aldeburgh	144
Sideboard in the Great Hall of Harewood Castle	146
Harewood Church	151
Altar-tomb of Chief-Justice Sir William Gascoigne in Harewood Church. By permission of Mr H. Speight	156
Redman Arms in window of Thornton Church	164
Tombstone of the Lady Sarah Redmayne, at Thornton	174
Altar-plate of Thornton Church, made from silver bequeathed by Ralph Redmayne, Esq.	181
Ingleton Church (from drawing by F. C. Tilney)	186
Font, Ingleton Church	194
Thornton Church	206
Thurland Castle	219
Arms of the Earl of Strafford	236
Arms, Redman and Aldeburgh By permission of the C & W. A & A Society	244

PREFACE.

WHEN first I began to study Redman history a few years ago my only thought was to prepare a few notes from which my little daughter, in years to come, might perhaps care to learn something of the doings of her ancestors in past centuries.

I had not, however, proceeded far in this labour of love before I began to realize what an amount of work was involved in anything like a thorough exploration of the available evidences, and to wish that someone in a previous generation, who had traversed all this ground before me, had been considerate enough to hand on the fruits of his research, thus saving a needless repetition of labour for all who should follow in his footsteps.

Prompted by this feeling I now venture to place on record the substance of what I have been able to learn of the history of this old and historic family, so that those who have not the time or facilities for independent research may have the advantage, such as it is, of my work; and also that any future historian may have a foundation ready prepared on which he can build a structure more worthy of its object. Thus I shall have the satisfaction of knowing that the efforts of later students will be more profitably employed in adding to the present knowledge of Redman history than in acquiring it *de novo*, as has so often and needlessly been done.

My book has been written under a handicap of ill-health and limited leisure; and all I can claim for it is such credit as may be due to an earnest effort to be accurate. I have tried, with what success I cannot say, to infuse a little life into the dry bones of the evidences, in a wish to avoid the dreary progression of charters, inquisitions, and so on, which, however dear to the scientific genealogist, are well calculated to scare the greater number of readers who are no less keenly interested in the stories of our old families.

I have also endeavoured, as far as possible, to present only such features of the Redman history as are of general interest or are really necessary to illustrate descents and the connection of different generations and branches of the family. All other material, and there is a great quantity of it, which is of interest only to a limited few who may wish to trace their own connection with the Redmans, I have not thought it right to introduce into a book which only professes to present a general view of the family story. I shall, however, always be very happy to place such information of this character as I possess at the service of anyone to whom it would be of use.

No-one can be more conscious than myself of the limitations of this book. There is a large field of history which still remains unexplored, and in which later seekers will, no doubt, find much that is of value. Some of the branches with which this volume deals are but superficially treated; other important branches remain untouched. But in spite of its incompleteness I hope my book will find acceptance as a useful contribution to the stories of our old English families.

If it gives to any reader a small fraction of the pleasure I have derived from its writing, and if it spares labour to or in any way smoothes the path for a future teller of the Redman story, I shall feel that I am more than rewarded for work which has been to me a delight.

My work has been much simplified by the generous and valuable assistance I have received, for which I wish to express my sincere thanks. Gratitude is especially due to Colonel Parker, of Browsholme Hall, who in the most courteous and ungrudging way has placed his unrivalled knowledge of Redman history at my disposal, and among other gentlemen who have also been most kind and helpful are Colonel Bagot, M.P., of Levens Hall; Mr. William Farrer; the Rev. James Wilson, M.A., my brother-in-law, Mr. J Harper Scaife, LL.B., who has helped me most generously throughout, and others whose courtesy I acknowledge in later pages. I am also greatly indebted to the kindness of Mr. Curwen, F.S.A, the Rev. H. R. Campion, M.A., Mr. H. Speight, the Cumberland and Westmorland Antiquarian Society, and Messrs. Jack, of Edinburgh for several of the illustrations which appear in the book.

W. G.

Spring Grove,
    Middlesex,
        3rd November, 1904.

Redman of Levens and Harewood

ADAM D'AVRANCHES, lord of Yealand and Silverdale
|
NORMAN DE REDMAN ob circa 1184, lord of Redman, Yealand, Levens &c
Dapifer of Warinus Minister of the Holy Hospital of Jerusalem

---

SIR HENRY I = Dau. of Adam, Dean of Lancaster (son of Waldeve of Liverston)
ob circ 1225, lord of Levens, Selside, Lupton, Trantherne &c, Seneschal of Kendal and co-Sheriff of Yorkshire

NICHOLAS

BENEDICT ob v p, one of the hostages of Gilbert Fitz Reinfrid, Baron of Kendal, 1216

SIR MATTHEW I = AMABEL (dau of Nicholas, Lord Stuteville, or of William Lord Greystoke)
ob circ 1250, Sheriff of Lancashire &c, Roll of Arms 1243-6

NORMAN ob ante 1247, benefactor of Shap Abbey

THOMAS vix 1247

HENRY II = —
ob 1278, Lord of Levens, Yealand, Lupton, &c

INGRAM vix 1254

RANDLE vix 1254

NICHOLAS vix 1278

JULIANA vix 1254

AGNES vix 1254

NORMAN = **MATILDA** = (2) **WM DE BRETBY**
vix 1277, a co-heiress of Camberton, ob ante 4 Jan 1300-1

SIR MATTHEW II = **GODITHA** of Camberton,
ob 1319, Knight of Shire for Westmorland and Lancashire, Commanded forces against Baliol and Bruce
a descendant of Gospatric Earl of Dunbar and of Kings Ethelred II and Malcolm II of Scotland

HENRY, benefactor of Cockersand Abbey (1300)

THOMAS next heir of Alan de Camberton (1307)

---

(1) = — **SIR MATTHEW III** — (2) **MARGARET**
ob 1360, Sheriff of Cumberland, Knight of Shire for Westmorland, and Governor of Carlisle Castle
ob May 1374, widow of Hugh de Moriceby (ob 1348-9)

HENRY = **MARIOTA**
(eldest son) ob circ 1359

ADAM of Yealand, ob ante 12 Feb 1338

WILLIAM, ob ante 1318

---

(1) **LUCY** = — **SIR MATTHEW IV** — (2) **JOAN** dau of Henry, Lord Fitzhugh
ob circ 1390, Governor of Roxburgh and Berwick, Fought in France and Spain under John of Gaunt and at Otterbourne
and widow of William 4th Lord Greystoke and Anthony, 3rd Lord Lucy

JOHN

MATTHEW vix Apr 1 1369 ob v p

(1) **ELIZABETH** = —
dau and co-heiress of William 1st Lord Aldeburgh and widow of Sir Bryan Stapleton

SIR RICHARD — (2) **ELIZABETH**
ob 1426, lord of Harewood, Levens &c, Sheriff of Yorkshire and Cumberland, Knight of Shire and Speaker of House of Commons (1415)
dau of Sir William Gascoigne Chief Justice of England (See Appx pp 249-50)

FELICIA = **SIR JOHN DE LUMLEY**, son of Ralph Lord Lumley, ob 1421

SIR MATTHEW V = **JOHANNA**
ob v p 1419, dau of Sir Thomas Tunstall of Thurland Castle

RICHARD of Bossall vix 1471

JOAN = **SIR THOMAS WENTWORTH**

A quibus Earls of Scarborough &c

SIR RICHARD **MARGARET**, dau of Thomas Middleton, Esq, a descendant of the Lords Berkeley, De Ferrers, &c (See Appx pp 249-50)
ob 1476-7, Knight of Shire for Westmorland

RICHARD, ob 1505, Bishop of St Asaph, Exeter, and Ely

A quibus Earls of Strafford &c

SIR WILLIAM = **MARGARET** dau of Sir W Strickland of Sizergh Castle
ob 1482, Knight Banneret, MP for Westmorland

SIR EDWARD = **ELIZABETH**
ob 1510, Sheriff of Cumberland &c
(inq p m 1529) dau of Sir John Huddleston of Millom Castle

RICHARD

WALTER (vix 1482)

ELIZABETH = **JOHN PRESTON** Esq of Preston Hall and Levens

HENRY = **ALICE PILKINGTON** ob v p

(1) **ELIZABETH** dau of Sir William Gascoigne, inq p m 1544

RICHARD = (2) **DOROTHY**, dau of Wm Layton Esq of Dalmain

MAGDALEN

JOAN = **MARMADUKE** b 1507, son of Sir Wm Gascoigne

MATTHEW VI = **BRIDGET** dau of Sir W Gascoigne, of Gawthorpe
b 1528, vix 1600

WILLIAM vix 1600

FRANCIS vix 1544

CUTHBERT = **ELIZABETH** vix 1589, dau of Sir Osw Wilstrop
vix 1589

ANN = **JOHN LAMBERT** Esq, of Calton

GRACE = **RICHARD TRAVERS** of Nateby (Lancs)

MAUD = **CHRIS IRTON** of Irton (Cumb)

MARY = **THOMAS GARGRAVE** of Bolton in Craven

A quibus
GENERAL JOHN LAMBERT

THE REDMANS OF LEVENS.

CHAPTER I.

NORMAN ORIGIN OF THE REDMANS.

THE North of England has been the nursery of many a knightly family which has borne itself gallantly through the centuries, has sent its sons, generation after generation, to fight for their King, and has mated its daughters with husbands as well-born as themselves.

A few of these families, like the Penningtons and Stricklands, have maintained their position in defiance of "time and tide," and to-day live in castles built by their ancestors in far-off feudal days and own lands which were theirs under Plantagenet kings, or even before Domesday Book was compiled. Others have helped to fashion history for four, five or six centuries until, through forfeitures of estates and divided and subdivided inheritances they have lapsed from their position, and, for a time at least, have been largely lost to view.

Of the latter and less fortunate class is the family of Redman, of Redman in Cumberland, of Levens in Westmorland, of Harewood in Yorkshire, and of a score of other manors scattered over five counties north of the Humber and Mersey. An offshoot of one of the most eminent of noble Norman stocks, the Redmans were men of substance and position in the north before John came to his throne; and from the twelfth to the early years of the eighteenth century they took a prominent place in the land of their adoption. They furnished, in long succession, knights for her shires, bishops for her church, and sheriffs for her counties. They fought gallantly from the borders of Scotland to the borders of Spain; they were governors of important castles and arrayers and leaders of armed forces; and, in short, for all these centuries there were few spheres of useful activity in which they did not bear an honourable and often a conspicuous part.

Although the records are full of references to the Redmans, and although many a skilled antiquary has made a painstaking study of their history, the origin of the family successfully eluded discovery until a few years ago, when an old charter which had escaped the notice of the Historical MSS. Commissioner, when examining the muniments at Levens Hall, and was brought to light by Mr W Farrer, the learned editor of Lancashire Records, supplied a clue to the mystery.

This old charter, so fortunately discovered, is the original grant of Levens by William de Lancaster (II.), Baron of Kendal, to the founder of the Redman family at a time when the name had not yet been adopted. The deed, the date of which is probably circa 1170, runs thus —

Notum sit omnibus, tam presentibus quam futuris, clericis et laicis, quod ego Willelmus de Lancastra, dedi et concessi Normanno de Hieland, pro suo homagio et servicio, Lefnes, per suas rectas divisas, in Bosco, in plano, in pratis, in pascuis, sibi et suis heredibus, de me et meis heredibus, tenere libere et quiete et pro suo libero servicio, scilicet, pro octo solidis inde annuatim reddendis, salva piscaria et aqua de Kent usque ad Sandpol et salvis austurconibus et cervo et cerva, et apre et lea. Hiis testibus domina Helewisa, sponsa sua, Simone de   , Anselmo, huctredo, filio Osolf, Rogero, filio Ade, Roberto Mustel, Ricardo, filio Alardi, Jurdano, Gileberto, fratre suo, Gilberto de Croft; Johanne clerico, et aliis pluribus audientibus, hoc

Noverint tam presentes quam futuri quod ego Willelmus de Lancastre dedi et concessi Bernardo de Bielard pro suo homagio et servicio suo et pro recta servicio in Roseto in plano juxta in pratis. In falenijs. Silvis et in heredibus de me et meis heredibus tenere libere et quiete ... Juxta servicio scilicet p[ro] octo solidis reddendis sibi assisam et aqua de Kere usque ad Sanspol annuatum reddendis sibi assisam et corno et terra et apro et lea. his testibus et aliis auctoritatibus. Simonis de ... Radulfus de ... nepotibus huiusque filio Officio. Rogero ... Rogero multis ... abbatis. Jordano. Gilberto fratre suo. Gilberto de Croft. Jocelino et aliis plurimis audientibus hoc...

It will be seen that the name of the grantee in this charter appears as Norman de "Hieland," or, as it was known in later days, "Yealand"; and in this word lies the clue which enables us to assign on unassailable grounds, a Norman origin to the Redmans.

This family of Hieland or Yealand was founded by one Adam d'Averenge, or Adam of Avranches, to whom William de Lancaster (I), Baron of Kendal, gave lands in Yealand and Silverdale. In a boundary deed of Yealand:—

Willelmus de Lancastre dedit Ade de Yeland et heredibus suis, pro homagio et servicio suo, villam de Yeland cum Selredale, cum omnibus pertinentiis suis, quas Willelmus de Lancastre, vetus, dedit *Ade de Averenge*, avo ejusdem Ade, pro homagio et servicio suo, scilicet unam Karucatam terre et dimidiam per servicium militare; Testibus, Gilberto de Lancastre, Rogero de Lancastre, Thoma de Bethom, Ricardo de Coupland, Matheo de Redeman, &c.

(In cartis Thome Midleton de Leighton, armigeri, 28 July, 1629, apud Sizergh, in custodiâ Roberti Stirkland, Armigeri).

From this charter we see that William de Lancaster gave to Adam de Yeland and his heirs the vill of Yeland with Silverdale, which William de Lancaster, *vetus*, gave to Adam d'Avranches, grandfather of the said Adam. Thus we have the Norman Adam receiving lands in Yeland and Silverdale from the Baronial house of Kendal, and founding a family which was to be identified in the future as the family of Yealand, of whom Norman, of the Levens charter, and Adam of this Yealand deed, were members. This Adam de Yeland is specifically identified as grandson of the first settler, Adam d'Avranches. Who then was Norman, who is of such great interest to us as founder of the family that was to be known for so many centuries by the name of Redman? He was clearly of an older generation than Adam of Yeland, the grandson, who indeed was a contemporary of Norman's son, Henry, and of his grandson, Matthew; and there can be little doubt that he was a son of Adam of Avranches.

Having seen that Norman (de Redman) originally bore the name of the family founded by this Norman soldier, let us see what further evidence there is to identify him with this family. And for this purpose I may be pardoned for quoting Mr. Farrer's views as stated to me in a letter:—

> The strongest confirmation of your suggestion that Adam de Yealand and Henry de Redman were cousins is the reference to a plea in 1246, where Alice, wife of Robert de Conyers, and Matthew Redman are defendants, and their *ancestors* are said to have been seised of common &c (Alice was daughter of the Adam de Yealand of the charter). Then there are the following charters which, as they say in Lancashire, are "ungeto'erable"—
>
> (1) Know that I, Roger de Yeland, by the love of God and for the health of my soul &c. by the advice of Sueneva, my wife, have given six acres of land and a toft of my demesne of Yeland in pure alms (to the Canons of Cockersand) to hold fully &c. I also will that the said brethren have easements belonging to the said land (f. 1476).
>
> (2) Know &c. that I, Henry son of Norman de Redeman, have given &c. 23 acres of my land in Yeland, to wit of my demesne around Hildriston in pure alms (to the Canons of Cockersand) with common right and easements of the said vill, as much as the said alms can bear, for the health of my soul &c. (f. 1476).
>
> These charters from the Cockersand Chartulary prove that Roger, son of Adam de Avranches, and Henry de Redman were severally possessed of demesnes in Yealand, and I should imagine that the first charter passed between 1190 and 1205. These references seem to make your suggestion re the relationship of Norman to Adam de Avranches as likely as anything of this kind can be made, and probably the pedigree which I have sketched out may be considered correct.

ADAM DE AVRANCHES,
1st grantee of Yealand and Silverdale.

- ROGER DE YEALAND = SUENEVA, dau of
  grantor of lands in Yea- Grimbald de Ellel
  land to Cockersand Abbey
  circ 1190-1205, d. before
  1207
  - WILLIAM,
    Dods MS.,
    cxlii, f. 18.
  - SIR ADAM DE YEALAND,
    Sheriff of Lancashire,
    12-17 Hen. 3
    - ALICE, dau = ROBERT DE
      and heiress, had   COINERS,
      one moiety of   or CONYERS
      Yealand

- NORMAN DE HIELAND,
  or REDMAN,
  Lord of Levens, &c.
  - SIR HENRY DE REDMAN = dau of Adam,
    Lord of Levens and one   Dean of Lancaster,
    moiety of Yealand, grantor m circa, 1184.
    of land near Hilderston,
    in Yealand, to Cockersand
    Abbey, 1190-1220.
    - SIR MATT DE REDMAN,
      lord of a moiety of Yea-
      land in 1242-3, Sheriff of
      Lancashire 1245-8, plain-
      tiff re common in Yealand
      1246, final concord 12th
      November, 31H3, 1246.
    - BENEDICT,
      ob s p

Having thus, as I hope satisfactorily, established Norman's identity as a member of the family of Adam d'Avranches it may be well to glance for a few moments at the great Norman family of that name, of which there can be small reason to doubt that Adam was a cadet.

According to Collins, the family of the Vicomtes d'Avranches "flourished in Normandy with great dignity and grandeur from the time of its first creation into a sovereign kingdom, A.D. 912, to the conquest of England in the year 1066, having been always ranked among the foremost there, either for nobleness of blood or power, and having had the government of many castles and strongholds in that Duchy."

Without following Collins to his ancestral goal in an uncle of Rollo, the piratical pioneer of the Norman Dukes, there is no doubt that the d'Avranches family was of considerable importance in the Duchy, and was not considered unworthy of an alliance with its reigning House. The most notable of its members was perhaps that Hugh d'Avranches (Lupus), to whom his uncle, the Conqueror, gave so many fat manors and the earldom of Chester, and who, in his power and splendour, almost rivalled William himself.

It was but natural that members of this family should find the seductions of England, with its promise of rich spoil, irresistible, and should join the army of Norman invaders which flocked over, both at and after the Conquest. To Hugh, the Conqueror's favourite, fell the choicest plums; Roland d'Avranches became Lord of Folkestone, and founded a short line of Barons by Tenure; Robert d'Avranches had a grant of the Barony of Okehampton; and no doubt there were other members of the family who had substantial pickings, and had good reason to be grateful for William's enterprise in crossing the Channel. Here we may leave the Avranches progenitors of the Redmans, and consider Norman, who, born a d'Avranches, grew to manhood as a de Yealand, and in later years identified himself and his descendants for ever with Redman, a Cumberland village between the rivers Derwent and Ellen.

CHAPTER II.

NORMAN DE REDMAN AND THE KNIGHTS HOSPITALLERS.

NORMAN, the first of his line to bear the name of Redman was probably born *circa* 1140, at a troublous time, when Stephen found the Empress Maud and the most powerful of his Barons arrayed against him, and for a time England was in the clutch of anarchy, bloodshed and famine. The Battle of the Standard was but a two-year-old memory, and people were still talking in awed whispers of the massacres and rapine King David and his Scots had left behind them on their raid into the Northern Counties.

In his early manhood it is not improbable that Norman, who is described as " Dapifer of Guarinus, Minister of the Holy Hospital of Jerusalem," may have fought in the Holy Land as a Crusader, although of this there seems to be no direct evidence. In this connection, however, it is interesting to record that there may be seen at the church of Thornton-in-Lonsdale " two fine linen cloths with the Temple of Jerusalem woven thereon," which were bequeathed to the church by Ralph Redmayne, in 1703. These cloths, to which evidently great value was attached, may or may not be memorials of some early Redman crusader.

Guarinus, whose "dapifer" Norman was, also presents difficulties. I had thought that he was probably William de Warren, the third Earl of Surrey, who accompanied Louis, King of France, on his expedition against the

Saracens, an adventure from which, by the way, he never returned; but a more plausible suggestion perhaps is that he was Warinus, of Lancaster, brother of William, first Lancaster Baron of Kendal, who was a Crusader and who, without any great stretch of probability, might have chosen as his *dapifer* the son of his neighbour Adam d'Avranches, of Yealand.

In these very early years, where records yield such scanty evidence, one must of necessity fall back to a certain extent on reasoned conjecture; and before we emerge from this nebulous stage into the clear atmosphere of established facts it may not be unprofitable to indulge in a little speculation as to the connection between the families of de Lancaster and Redman. That the connection of these two neighbouring houses was exceptionally close, admits of no question. The Redmans gained their first territorial footing in the north through William de Lancaster, the first, who, as we have seen, gave lands in Yealand and Silverdale to Adam d'Avranches. Later, as we shall see, the Redmans were further enriched at de Lancaster hands by the manors of Levens and Selside and other goodly lands.

One cannot think that in these olden days, any more than now, men were in the habit of giving away land by thousands of acres merely out of friendly impulse. Such an act argues either a close family tie or some commensurate return. Feudal services from one family would scarcely call for the sacrifice of no inconsiderable sections of two counties; one might think such rewards would ensure the loyalty of a small army of knights, while the rents reserved were little more than the proverbial peppercorn.

The inference which is irresistibly suggested is that

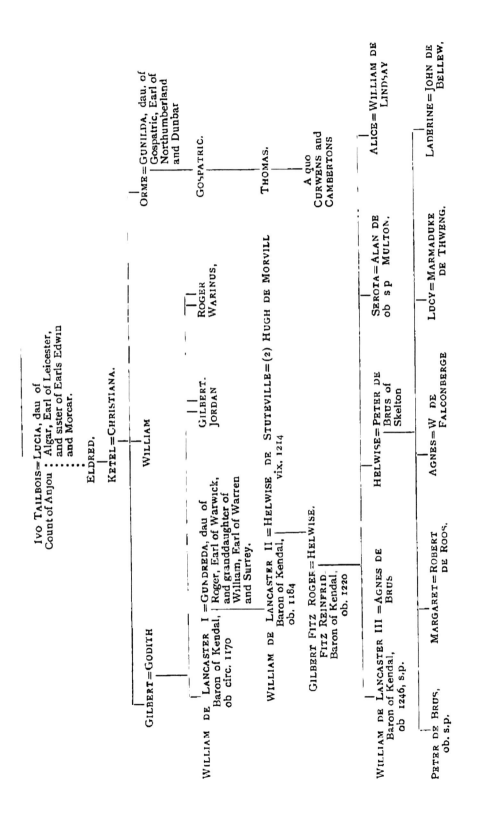

these broad acres came to the Redmans through a marriage alliance or alliances with the family of de Lancaster; and it seems to me possible that it was the bright eyes and rich dower of a de Lancaster heiress that lured Adam of Avranches into the north of England and led to his settlement there. However this may be, on no other than a supposition of this kind can one understand the very intimate relations between the two families; but, the probability conceded, many circumstances otherwise difficult to understand, become intelligible.

But enough of conjecture, which is often misleading in proportion as it is alluring. Norman seems to have transferred his duties as dapifer from Guarinus to William de Lancaster II., for when he witnesses a Confirmation of lands by William de Lancaster to William, son of Roger de Kirkby-Irleth, he is described as *Normannus Dapifer* (Farrer's *Lancashire Pipe Rolls*, &c., p. 443); and again as "Norman, the dapifer," he witnesses a grant by William to Hugh, the hermit, "pro salute animae meae et Helewisiae sponsae meae" (Ex Registro de Cockersand, f. 112; Monasticon vi., 909). As Norman de Redeman (Red*e*man, by the way, appears to be quite a favourite early spelling of the family name, of which we find something like a dozen variants) he witnesses the grant by Thomas, son of Cospatrick, of five acres of arable land in Hailinethait, one toft, pasture for ten cows, and an acre of meadow (*Cartae Miscell.*, vol. ii., fo. 2).

Norman, who, as we have seen, had already inherited and acquired large estates adds to them the Manor of Tranton (variously called also Tranetherne, Trenterne, &c.) granted to him by Stiffinus, son of Dolphin de Trimble (near Lowther, in Westmorland). In the grant it is described as

Totam terram de Tranton videlizet, quae propinquior est apud villam de Trinbe &c. cum omnibus pertinenciis suis in aquis et in agris et in pratis et in pasturis et cum communa pastura de Thrinbe . . . reddendo annuatim octo Sollida (sic) pro omnibus serviciis &c.

The witnesses to this grant are Robertus de Morisbe, Garnacius de Huencuite, Adam Morisbe, Huctredus, filius Osulfe, Willelmus de Lowdar, Willelmus et Thomas . . . filius Adam de Morland, Adam Sillcet (Selside) &c.

We make further acquaintance with these Trantherne lands in a Confirmation (1201) to the Church of St. Mary, of Kildeholm, " ex dono Normañ de Redeman t'rā de Tranethern cū omibz ptiñ suis."

"Now what," is the interesting question asked by Colonel Parker, of Browsholme Hall, who, I may be allowed to say, is beyond comparison the chief living authority on Redman history, " could possibly interest Norman de Redman in a remote nunnery in a distant part of Yorkshire to such an extent that he should help to endow it ? He had no Yorkshire lands. Now Nicholas, the name of one of Norman's sons, is a Stuteville name and the name of the grandson and heir of the founder of the nunnery, Robert de Stuteville (temp. Henry I.) Is it not a reasonable presumption that Norman married a daughter of Robert de Stuteville or of William, his son ? The connection of the Stutevilles with Carleton and Drigg is interesting in this connection. I find that Hugh de Morville, Lord of Kirk Diomed (temp. Henry II), married Hawisia daughter of Nicholas de Stuteville; so, at any rate, we have a Redman neighbour closely allied to the family."

That Norman's interest in the Knights Hospitallers was a practical one is proved by the fact that he gave of his lands to the support of the Holy Hospital of Jerusalem. Some years after his death, we find a confirmation by Gernat (e), Minister of the Hospital of Jerusalem, " with the common and unanimous consent of the brothers of the order," of four acres of land in Levens, to Henry, son of Norman, " which we had of the alms of (Norman) the Dapifer, his father, 'tenendas de nobis in feodo et hereditate, libere et quiete, ab omni seculari servicio quod ad (elemosinam) pertinet, reddendo annuatim Domui nostrae XII^d in assumptione beatae (M) Virginis.'"

At what time and for what reason Norman discarded the name of Yealand in favour of that of Redman I have been unable to discover. It is clear that he reached manhood a Yealand and that he lived for some time and died "de Redman." The change appears to have come towards the end of his life, and was probably inspired by the laudable wish to found a family of his own, distinct from that of his brother, Roger of Yealand; and for this purpose he identified himself with his Cumberland property and elected to be known as "de Redman." How these Redman lands came to him is another problem awaiting solution.

Norman probably died circa 1184, while Henry II. was still on the throne, and left behind him two sons, both under age, (1) Henry, his heir and successor, and (2) Nicholas, whose only legacy to posterity is his name.

CHAPTER III.

Henry I. Sheriff and Seneschal.

WITH Henry, Norman's successor, we reach firmer ground, where there are few will-o-the-wisps to seduce us from the well-marked track of history; although it is inevitable that in the story of a family covering more than seven centuries one must at times encounter gaps which the records do not bridge for us.

When Norman died, comparatively a young man, his heir was still in his 'teens, and probably had three or four years to wait for the full fruits of his inheritance. At any rate he must have reached manhood in 1187-8 when he proffered a mark in order that the Fine levied between himself and Ketel, son of Ughtred, concerning the territory of Levens in Westmorland, should be inscribed upon the Roll of the Curia Regis. By this agreement Ketel granted to Henry and his heirs the whole of the Manor of Levens, one moiety to be held by the said Henry in his demesne, the other to be held by Ketel of the said Henry by an equivalent service to that which Henry rendered to the chief lord for the same. Levens was parcel of the Barony of Kendal, and from that day to the present time has continued in two moieties called, respectively, Over and Nether Levens. (Farrer's *Lancashire Pipe Rolls*, p. 71).

The different transactions relating to Levens at this time are not a little confusing; and it will be well to give them in detail. We have, in addition to the Fine above mentioned, the following grant to Henry, by Gilbert Fitz Reinfrid, Baron of Kendal and Henry's overlord:—

GRANT OF LEVENS TO HENRY REDMAN.

Sciant tam praesentes (quam futuri quod) ego Gilbertus, filius Rogeri, filii Ranfridi, con(cessi) et mea praesenti carta confirmavi Henrico, filio Nor(manni), Levens per suas rectas divisas, scilicet, etc, tenendum de me et haeredibus meis in feodo et hereditate, libere et quiete etc, in bosco, in plano etc, salva aqua mea de Kent, etc, reddendo mihi et haeredibus meis, Henricus et haeredes sui, annuatim xvj solidos de firma et quinque solidos et denarios de cornagio pro omni servicio. Hiis testibus :—Ricardo , Adam decano, Gilberto de Lancastre, Radulfo de Arrundell, Willelmo , Radulpho de Beethome, Rogero de Beethome, Rogero de (Bur)thon, Matheo Garnett, Willelmo de Kellet, Hugone de Poplington, Henrico de (I)nsula, Ormo de Irebie, Thoma de Torenthorn, Rogero de Kelland (Yelland), (Dav)id de Memecestre, Adam Garnett, Adam de Manser, Ricardo de me, Gilberto, fratre suo et multis aliis.

Then there is another grant, recorded by Dodsworth—this time of Selside as well as of Levens—by Gilbert Fitz Reinfrid to Henry de Redman:—

Notum sit omnibus, tam presentibus quam futuris, quod ego Gilbertus fil' Rogeri, fil' Reinfredi, concessi et hac presenti carta mea confirmavi Henrico de Redman, quod ipse et heredes sui teneant Levenes et Selesete (Selside), cum pertinentiis de me et heredibus meis in perpetuum. (Dodsworth, MS. 159, fo. 180).

And finally we have the following grant by Henry to Ketel of a moiety of Levens. (Nether Levens.)

Notum sit omnibus tam futuris quam presentibus quod ego, Henricus, filius Normanni de Readmane, concessi et hac carta mea confirmavi Ketello, filio Uthrid, medietatem de Levens, exce(ptas) acras, scilicet (Cros)thwaite et quindecim in Levens conces( ) Ketelli modo ut an(tecessores) nostri haereditalis scilicet predictam medietatem ei et heredibus suis tenendum de me et meis heredibus cum omnibus pertinentiis in divisis racionalibus quae pertinent praedictæ villae, libere etc, excepto quod ego Henricus et haeredes mei habebunt proprios porcos de Yelland quietos de Ketell et haeredibus suis de pannagio in bosco praedictae villae de Levens, et iste predictus Ketellus habebit proprios porcos domo Uthred de Kirkabia quietos de pannagio in praedicto Bosco etc Reddendo annuatim XXX denarios de cornagio   etc (et faciundo quod) pertinet ad capitalem Dominum salvo forensico servicio Hiis testibus (Adam) decano Lancastriae, Benedicto Gernet, Mathaeo Gernet, Adam , Rogero, parsona de Heversham, Willelmus de Kellett etc

The net result of these confusing transactions was to place Henry de Redman in full possession of Levens, (which, as we have seen, was granted to his father), and also of Selside, manors which were to remain in Redman hands for several centuries.

Some years before Henry entered on his patrimony his matrimonial fate was taken into the capable hands of a local cleric, "Adam, the Dean," who, in 1184, when the prospective bridegroom was still in his teens, proffered one hundred shillings for permission to marry his daughter, who was in the King's gift, to the son of Norman de Redman (Farrer's *Lancashire Pipe Rolls*, p. 52). This transaction would probably take place shortly after the death of Henry's father, Norman It has been thought that this Adam, who proposed to become Henry's father-in-law, was Adam, dean of Kirkham, whose name appears so frequently on the Pipe Rolls and as a witness to charters; but there can be little, if any, doubt that he was Adam, Dean of *Lancaster*.

"I am quite satisfied," Mr. Farrer writes to me, "that Henry de Redman married a daughter of Adam, Dean of Lancaster, and through her had Lupton and probably some other lands." He thus reviews the different evidences:—

By permission of Mr. John F. Curwen, F.S.A.   LEVENS HALL—FRONT VIEW.

(1.) Adam, the Dean, proffers 40 marks for ward of his nephew, with ½ carucate of land, and for his mother's marriage, Mich 1182. (*Pipe Rolls*, p. 47).

(2.) Adam, the Dean, proffers 100^s that he might marry his daughter, who was of the King's donation, to the son of Norman de Redman, Mich 1184. (p. 52).

(3.) Adam de Lancaster proffers 10^{li} for ward of land and heir of Richard, son of Waldieve, by pledge of Benedict Gernet (Chief Forester of Lancs.) Mich 1198. (p. 102).

This I believe to have been the thanage estate of Tatham and Ireby.

(4.) Henry de Redman renders 2 marks to the aid of scutage of King John for an estate *held in thanage*.

(5.) Adam, the Dean, 2 m. for the same, Mich 1202. (p. 152).

This, I think, refers to Tatham and Ireby. Vide notes, pp. 157-8.

(6.) Henry de Rademan proffers 40 m. for ward of land and heir of Roger de Heton, and to have the marriage of the same heir to his own daughter. Mich 1206. (204).

Adam de Kirkham, decanus, pp. 347, 361, 366, 402, 409, and 439.

I think there can be no doubt that there were two Adams, both Deans, one of Kirkham or Amounderness, the other of Lancaster or Lonsdale.

(The references are to Mr. Farrer's *Lancashire Pipe Rolls*.)

Mr. Farrer, whose opinion on such a point is of the highest value, identifies this Adam, Dean of Lancaster, as a son of Waldeve, Lord of Ulverston, and thus brother of Augustine, from whom the line of Heaton sprang; and of Richard, founder of the family of Tatham; both families of considerable importance and interest. The following pedigree, supplied by Mr. Farrer, will explain these relationships:—

18 REDMANS OF LEVENS AND HAREWOOD.

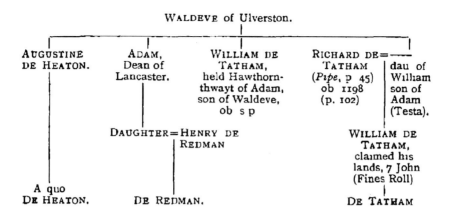

This pedigree, which is most interesting and valuable, disposes of the mystery of the following grant for lights by Henry to the Abbey of Furness which has probably puzzled every student of Redman history.

Henricus Redman, concessu uxoris suae et haeredum suorum dat nobis redditum ius annuatim ad luminaria in ecclesia abbatiae nostrae, scilicet ii. s. quos W(illelmus) filius Wa(l)thevi, avunculi mei, mihi reddit pro terra de Herthornthwaite, quae fuit Adae, avunculi mei, scil: xii. d. ad Pasca et xii. d. ad festum S. Michaelis et xii. d. quos Gamellus, filius Levin, reddit mihi pro terra de Middlethwayt. (*Furness Coucher Book.*—Chetham Society. Vol. ii., p. 509).

The William, son of Waldeve, of this grant would thus be William de Tatham, son of Waldeve of Ulverston, and "Adam, my uncle," could be none other than Henry's father-in-law, the Dean. To understand these identifications it is important to remember that "avunculus" was a term of wide application, covering, as Mr. Farrer informs me, "almost any relation of a man's mother, or who came through his mother. It may be mother's uncle or stepfather &c; and I think it is used by a man of his wife's uncles or his father-in-law"—a most serviceable kind of word indeed.

The records are full of evidences of Henry de Redman's varied activities, as Seneschal of Kendal, as Co-Sheriff of Yorkshire, as soldier, and in the many duties that would naturally fall to a man of his position. Unfortunately the dates of many of these evidences are not available; so that it is impossible to make the record of Henry's doings reliably consecutive.

Henry witnessed a grant by Gilbert Fitz Reinfrid and his wife, Helwise, to the Church of the Holy Trinity of Kirkby-in-Kendal; and, as a witness to Gilbert's grant of Coneswic, he appears as "Henrico de Redman, his (temporibus) senescallo." He was also a witness, with his son Matthew, to a grant by Gilbert, son of Robert, to the Hospital of St. Peter, at York (Hist. MSS. Commission. Rep. 10. Pt. 4. Levens Hall Papers); and to Robert de Veteripont's grant to the Abbey of Shap, in 1212 (*Burn and Nicolson*, vol. i., p. 203).

He makes frequent appearances on the Lancashire Pipe Rolls and Charters, a few of which may perhaps be given. The references are to Mr. Farrer's volume. He pays 20 marks, in 1198-9, for the custody of the land and heir of William de Kelled (p. 107); in 1205-6 he proffers 40 marks for the custody of the land and heir of Roger de Heton, and for having the marriage of the said heir to his daughter (p. 204); and in 1211-13 he gives a third part of 10 marks for having a writ for his debt against Helwise de Estutevill, widow (1) of William de Lancaster II., and (2) of Hugh de Morvill (p. 247).

"Henricus de Radman, Seneschal of Kendal," is among the witnesses to the confirmation by Honorius, Archdeacon of Richmond, to the Canons of Conishead, of the Church of Ulverston (p. 365); to a release, in 1205, by Hugh Bussel to Roger, Constable of Chester, of the Barony of

Penwortham (pp. 379-80); to a release by Robert Bussel to Roger de Lacy, Constable of Chester, of the same Barony (p. 381); to a grant by Gilbert Fitz Reinfrid to Reiner de Stiveton of the land of Medlar &c (pp. 441-2); and to several other agreements and grants.

We get a glimpse of Henry in his Judicial character in connection with the release by Matilda, daughter of Elias de Stiveton, to Gilbert Fitz Reinfrid of estates which Matilda had mortgaged to him. "The Transaction," Mr. Farrer says, "took place in Gilbert's Baronial Court of Kirkby Kendal, before Henry de Redman, the Seneschal, and the suitors of the Court, viz:—Lambert de Bussey, lord of Lambrigg; Adam, son of Roger, lord of Yealand; Gilbert de Lancaster; William de Windsore; William, son of Waldeve, lord of Tatham &c, and others."

Henry, like most of the members of his family, was a man of practical piety and figures as a benefactor of the religious houses. We have already seen that he gave lands for lights to Furness Abbey. In 1199 he granted a moiety of Silverdale with fishing and other rights to the Canons of Cartmel (Rot. Chart. in Turr. Lond. Asservati). To the Abbey of Shap he gave lands in Lupton:—

Sciant omnes quod ego, Henricus de Rademan, dedi domui S'cae Marie Magdalene de Hepp, et Abbati et canonicis ibidem Deo servientibus, pro salute animae meae, et uxoris meae, et omnium antecessorum meorum, in puram et perpetuam eleemosinam quandam partem terrae meae in Villa de Lupton. (Dods. MS. 159.)

And in conjunction with Matthew, his son, he confirmed a gift to the monks of Byland (Hist. MSS. Comm. Rep. 10. pt. 4); while in 1200 he confirmed his father's gift of "Tranetherne" to the church of St. Mary, of Kildeholm. The *Furness Coucher Book* (Chetham Society, vol. II., p.

453) contains a record of an amicable settlement between the Convent and Sir Henry de Redman, "miles," concerning certain lands belonging to the Church at Urswick negociated by John, Abbot of Caldre. (Burn gives 1212 as the date of this settlement.) This, so far as I have been able to discover, is the only occasion on which Henry is described as a knight.

These records are prosaic enough, dealing as they do with the commonplace acts of any man in Henry de Redman's position; but there was at least one stimulating epoch of his life, in which we find him taking an active part in concerns of historical importance; but before dealing with it, it may be well to devote a few lines to Gilbert Fitz Reinfrid with whose life that of Henry seems to have been closely linked.

Gilbert was a man of great wealth and importance in his day. The son of Roger Fitz Reinfrid, justicier and sheriff for Sussex and Berkshire, and of Rohaise, his wife, niece of the powerful Ranulph, Earl of Chester, and great-great-niece of the Conqueror, Gilbert started life under excellent auspices; and he crowned the good fortune of his birth by wedding the only daughter and heiress (Helwise) of William of Lancaster II, Baron of Kendal, becoming possessor through his wife of vast properties in Westmorland and Lancashire. To these possessions, a small kingdom in themselves, Richard I, soon after he came to his Throne, added "the whole forest of Westmorland, Kendal and Furness, to hold to him and his heirs, as fully and freely as William de Lancaster and Nigel de Albini had held the same."

On the death of his father-in-law in 1184, Gilbert succeeded him in the Barony of Kendal; and from this point in his career became constantly and closely associated with Henry de Redman. It has been seriously stated that Gilbert married Helen, the only daughter and heiress of William de Redman, and that King Richard 1. had a finger in this matrimonial pie (Jones's *History of Harewood*, p. 40.) But as the Records not only refuse to disclose any such person as William de Redman in these early days or to lend any assent to this wedding, we must conclude that, if Helwise de Lancaster had a successor (or predecessor) in Gilbert's affection she was not this nebulous Helen, daughter of a non-existent William. Jones was a man of excellent intentions; but he has committed many sins of misrepresentation against dead and gone Redmans, and this is one of them.

According to Dodsworth, Fitz Reinfrid and Henry de Redman were joint-Sheriffs of Yorkshire from 12 to 16 John (Gilbert was also Sheriff of Lancashire and Westmorland and Custos of the Bishopric of Durham); and thus were closely connected officially in the year of their joint disaster. There can be little doubt that both Gilbert and Henry were in sympathy with the Barons who, on that June day, in 1215, compelled their treacherous and shifty sovereign to sign the Great Charter on the field of Runnymede; and it is certain that they were among the Barons on whom John so adroitly, if dishonourably turned the tables a few months later.

It will be remembered that almost before the ink of his signature was dry, John set to work to repudiate his act. He whined to the Pope and induced him to issue a bull annulling and abrogating the Charter, and at the same time he enlisted foreign mercenaries by the thousand to wreak his vengeance on his subjects. The Barons, who might have known their King better from previous experience, were caught napping, and one hundred and eighty of them with their retainers were trapped in Rochester Castle and compelled by hunger to surrender.

John's "bag" was rich enough to gratify even his greed of revenge; for among his prisoners were William de Albini, the finest soldier among the rebellious Barons and the soul and centre of their cause, Gilbert's son, William de Lancaster, and many another knight whose ransom was a fortune in itself. William de Albini, William de Lancaster, William de Avranches, Osbert Giffard, Alexander de Pointon, Alan de Multon and others were delivered into the safe keeping of Peter de Maulay; Roger de Leyburn and Simon Fitz Simon were among the prisoners entrusted to the custody of John Marshal; and Henry de Redman, Michael de Fossa and Robert Fitz Geoffrey went to the keeping of Robert de Courtney.

This was an exceedingly bad business for our two Sheriffs. Fitz Reinfrid recovered the Royal favour and the release of his son, with that of his knights, Ralph de Aincourt and Lambert de Busay, by payment of a fine of 12,000 marks, an enormous sum in those days, and in its amount a striking evidence of his exceptional wealth. And he was also compelled to provide hostages for the future loyalty of himself and of William, his son. These hostages were Benedict, Henry de Redman's son and heir; the heir of Roger de Kirkby (Gilbert's son-in-law); the son and heir of William de Wyndesore, who had married Gilbert's niece; the daughter and heir of Ralph d'Eincourt; the daughter or son and heir of Roger de Burton; the daughter and heir of Adam de Yeland; the son or daughter of Thomas de Bethun; the son or daughter and heir of Walter de Strickland, who is said to have wed Christina, Gilbert's sister (*Sizergh Castle*, by Lady Edeline Strickland, Gen. Notes); the daughter of Richard de

Coupland; and the son of Gilbert de Lancastre. (Rot. Finium, Pt. I., m. 6). Rymer gives the date of this as in August, 1215.

It will be seen that of these youthful pledges, the cream of the rising generation in Gilbert's district, four at least were of his own family—his grandson, his great-nephew, his nephew and the son of Gilbert de Lancaster. It is interesting to note that Benedict Redman comes first in a list which appears to be arranged partly in order of nearness-of-kin to Gilbert; a fact which might suggest a closer connection between Gilbert and the Redmans than is capable of proof. There may be nothing whatever in this precedence of Benedict Redman over Gilbert's own grandchild among pledges whose importance was gauged by the nearness in blood to the man who provides them, but at least it is material for the speculative.

Henry seems to have spent the Christmas of the Great Charter year as a prisoner; for on 12th December, 1215, Robert de Courtenay is ordered to keep Henry de Redman and others in safe custody (Rot. Lit. Claus. Turr. Lon.); and, whenever he recovered his freedom, it was not until John had given place to Henry III. that Henry was in possession of his lands again. In 1217 the Sheriffs of Cumberland, Westmorland and Lancashire were directed to restore Henry to his possessions.

This misadventure at Rochester Castle appears to have brought Henry's prominent activities to a close. In fact he only makes one later appearance of any interest in the Records,—in 1220, on a list of Inquisitors for Lancashire, in company with Michael de Furness and others (Pat. Rolls. 4, Henry III.). He held no public office after 1217, his loyalty possibly being somewhat under suspicion, and the closing years of his life were spent in quietness and a discreet obscurity.

Henry had at least three sons, in addition to Matthew, his successor :—

(1) Benedict, Gilbert Fitz Reinfrid's hostage, of whom nothing more appears to be known, and who probably died during his father's lifetime.

(2) Norman. (3) Thomas.

Norman, like his elder brother, Benedict, had to play the unpleasant *rôle* of hostage, and seems to have had a particularly unhappy experience of it. In Rot. Lit. Claus 6, Henry III. (16 May, 1222), I find the following :—

THE KING TO PHILIP, THE MARSHALL, GREETING.

It has been represented to us by our dear and faithful brother, William of Lancaster, that in the time of King John, our father, in his rebellion he brought forth with him from his district Norman, son of Henry de Redeman, Richard, son of Roger de Kirkeby, and the son of William de Windsor, to place them as hostages for his redemption, you, when returning towards those parts took the same three and up to the present have detained them according to your will at Nottingham. Wherefore we command you, if it be so, that you cause the said three sons of the aforesaid Henry, Roger and William to be liberated without delay.

Norman must have died before 1247, in which year his brother, Thomas, made the following confirmation to the Abbey of Shap :—

Thomas, son of Henry de Redeman, for the health of his soul and of the souls of his father and mother and ancestors and posterity, confirms to the said Abbey of Shap, two oxgangs of land in the vill of Apelby, which Norman, his brother, bequeathed with his body to the said Abbey, which said lands Norman had by the gift of John de Veteripont, and into which he, the said Thomas, after the death of Norman, had entry as next heir, rendering for the same to him, the said Thomas, his heirs and assigns, three barbed arrows, one penny yearly at the feast of St. Lawrence, and doing for the same foreign service. (Machel—from the evidences at Helbeck.)

Thomas, son of Henry, was the founder of a branch of the family identified with Cumberland; the lands at Redman in which county seem to have fallen to him. His son, Norman, increased the family stake in the county by winning for wife Matilda, a daughter and co-heiress of Camberton, whose sister and co-heiress, Jennet, found a husband in Thomas de Culwen. Matilda brought to Norman as dower half of the manor of Camberton, and a quarter of the manor of Graysouthen, in addition to lands in Workington and Waverton, estates which were the cause of family dissension after his death.

Matilda, when Norman was no more, became wife to one William de Bretby, who in 1301, after her death, claimed from his stepson, Thomas de Redman, Jennet (Matilda's sister), late wife of Thomas de Culwen, John Redman, William, son of Waldeve de Redman and others, a moiety of the manor of Camberton, and a quarter of the manor of "Greysuthen," which Matilda on her marriage had settled on him for life. William made his claim good and recovered the lands. Norman was living on 6th June, 1277 (A.R. 1235); and his widow was wife of William de Bretby on 2nd September, 1295, and was dead before 4th January, 1300-1, the date of the above claim.

Six years later (1307) we find Norman's and Matilda's son, Thomas, appearing as next heir to one Alan de Camberton, his mother's kinsman, as evidenced by the following Inquisition, 35 Ed. I., No. 143:—

Mary, who was the wife of Alan de Camberton deceased, concerning the lands which she held in dower, on the day on which she joined the Scots, the King's enemies, of the inheritance of Thomas de Redman and John le Venour, cousins and heirs of the aforesaid Alan.

The jurors say, upon their oath, that the said Mary on the day on which she joined the Scots, held in dower of the inheritance of the aforesaid Alan, formerly her husband, a third part of two carucates of land, with the appurtenances, in Camberton, &c., and that the aforesaid Mary died at Frerton, in the county of Fife, in Scotland, about the feast of the Nativity of St. John the Baptist, in the 32nd year of the reign of the King that now is, &c., and they say that the aforesaid Thomas de Redman and John le Venour are the next heirs of the said Alan. (Roberts' *Calend. Geneal*, ii., 745.)

It was probably the same Thomas who was a juror on the Inquisition post mortem of Thomas de Derwentwater made at "Assepatrick" in Cumberland on May 15th, 1303 (Inquisition post mortem, 31 Ed. I., n. 15). In 1319 a Thomas de Redman was appointed one of the collectors of the scutage of 34 Ed. I. in the county of Cumberland in the place of Wills de Mulcaster (deceased). Commission tested at York, 24th May, 12 Ed. II. (Fine Roll, 12 Ed. II., m. 3.)

Five years later, in 1324, Thomas de Redemane, man-at-arms, was returned by the sheriff of the county of Cumberland, pursuant to writ tested at Westminster, 9th May, as summoned, &c., to attend the great Council, &c., 17 Ed. II.; and in the same year we find Thomas Redman unable to act as collector of the scutage on account of illness, and another (Alexander de Bastenthwayt or John de Skelton) appointed in his place by Commission tested at Westminster, 22nd May. (Fine Roll, 17 Ed. II., m. 4.)

Henry died *circa* 1225, at about the age of sixty, seized of Levens, a moiety of Yealand, of Lupton and Redman, and possibly of lands in Overton and elsewhere. He was succeeded by his son Matthew, whose age at the time of his accession would be approximately thirty-five.

Among many interesting charters preserved at Levens is one of 1 Richard I (renewed 10 Richard I) exempting Gilbert Fitz Reinfrid and his heirs from noutegeld (or cornage rent) "throughout all his lands of Westmerland and Kendale, and from suit to the shire, hundred or trithing courts and from aid to the sheriff or his bailiffs." This charter of which, through the courtesy of Colonel Bagot, I am enabled to give a reproduction, dates from Henry de Redman's time and was probably in his possession. It is still in good preservation, more than seven centuries later, and runs thus —

Ricardus Dei gratia etc. Sciatis nos concessisse et dedisse et presenti charta confirmasse Gilberto, filio Rogeri, filii Reinfredi, et heredibus suis post eum, quietantiam per totam terram suam de Westmerland et de Kendale, de noutegeld, scilicet de 14^l 16^s 3^d, qu' ipse Gilbertus solebat reddere per annum pro noutegeld de prefata terra. Concessimus etiam eidem Gilberto et heredibus suis quietantiam per totam prefatam terram suam, de schiris, et de wapentac', et de trithinga, et de auxiliis vicecomitum, et omnium ballivorum suorum, etc. Teste Willelmo comite Arundel (et multis aliis).

CHARTER OF 1 RIC. I. EXEMPTING THE LORDS OF LEVENS FROM PAYMENT OF NOUTGELD.

CHAPTER IV.

Sir Matthew I., Sheriff of Lancashire, and Henry II.

HENRY'S second son and heir, Matthew, who was the first of seven Redman knights bearing that name and linking the twelfth with the seventeenth century, was probably born about 1190, three years after his father came into possession of Levens, Yealand, Silverdale and the other family lands.

He would thus be a boy of nine when John came to his throne, and would spend his boyhood and youth amid the constant alarms, the seething discontent and appeals to arms which marked the reign of that weak-kneed monarch. At the crowning time of family trouble, when his father was taken prisoner at Rochester Castle and his elder brother, Benedick, had to leave his home as hostage for Fitz Reinfrid's good behaviour, Matthew would have reached man's estate and had not improbably made his début on the battlefield. His lot, however, fell in more peaceful times than that of his father; and his days appear to have been mostly spent in discharging his duties as sheriff and seneschal, and in the peaceful pursuits of a country gentleman of the time.

In 1229, a few years after he succeeded to his inheritance, Matthew, in company with Richard de Copland, William de Yeland and Roger Gernet, was appointed a justice " for taking the assize of novel disseisin at Lancaster on the Thursday before the purification of the Blessed

Mary against the Abbot of Leicester concerning a tenement in Cokersand" (Cal. Pat. Rolls, Hy. III. 1225-32). He was probably the Matthew de Redman who, with Walter de Strickland and Alan le Boteiler, witnessed a grant by Thomas de Hastings to the Hospital of St. Peter at York. He was among the witnesses to the confirmation by William de Lancaster, the third, of a grant of lands in Furness to Alexander de Kirkby (Farrer's *Pipe Rolls*, pp. 442-3); to a grant in 1247 by Ralph de Ainecurt to Roger Pepin, a parson of Kirkby in Kendal, of land in Natelunt (MS. Dods. 149 fo. 142—"Natland Box"); and again, in his capacity as Seneschal of Kendal, to a deed of confirmation to Patric, son of Gospatric, by the third William de Lancaster (Burn).

In 1242 a fine was passed between Matthew de Redman, son and heir of Henry de Redman, and William de Lancaster, the third (Dods. MS. 159 fo. 180); and in the same year he was a tenant of the Barony of William de Lancaster for lands in Yealand, holding with Robert de Coniers one-eighth of a knight's fee (*Testa de Nevill*, pp. 398-9).

In 1243 Matthew "appeared on the fourth day against William de Lancaster in a plea to hold the fine levied in the Court of the King, before the Justices itinerant at Lancaster, between him, the said Matthew, complainant, and the said William, impedient., concerning the manors of Levenes, Skelesbolt (? Skelsmere), Quenefeld (Whinfell) and Lupton, with app'. whereof a cyrograph was made. William did not appear, and he was attached by Ralph de Ayncurt, and Richard de Heysham. Therefore, because the fine was of recent date the sheriff was commanded to distrain the said William by his lands to appear at three weeks from Trinity." (C. R. Roll No. 128. m. 2 dorso.)

In 1245 Matthew was appointed sheriff of Lancashire, holding the office with William de Lancaster; in the two following years he served alone; and in 1248 he had for colleague Robert Latham (Baines i. 58).

In 1246 he was concerned (with Robert de Coniers and Alice, his wife and Matthew's kinswoman) in a dispute with Thomas de Betham about common of pasture in Levens; and a similar dispute is revealed in C. R. Roll 64. m. 1. dorso — Thomas de Bethum versus Adam de Yeland and Matthew de Redman in a plea to shew by what right they claimed common-right, by Walter, son of Robert, pledged to sue at fifteen days after Easter.

These are all trivial incidents enough in the life of a doughty knight, who would have figured more appropriately on the field of battle than in witnessing signatures and squabbling in law-courts; but they are landmarks, however insignificant, and must serve where more stimulating records are absent.

The following petition gives one a vivid glimpse of the perilous times in which Sir Matthew lived, when almost every day brought a fresh alarm, if it did not, as in this case, actually bring disaster. The petition is by the second Matthew, who explains that when his grandfather (Matthew, the first) was one of the King's coroners in the county of Lancaster, the Scots came to his manor of Yealand Redmane and took from him all his goods and chattels, as well as the Rolls of his office of coroner, and committed Yealand Redmane and all the country to the flames. The petitioner expresses the pious aspiration that the King will not be incommoded at the time of the Eyres by the loss of these stolen Rolls, and assures him that his grandfather, the coroner, was not to blame in the matter.

A nre seinr le Roi et a soun counseil prie soun liege vadlet Maheu de Redmane si lui plest que come Mons Maheu de Redmane son Ael que dieux assoille qi heir fut un des coroners le Roi en le comite de Lancastr graunt temps dedens quen temps les Escos venierunt en le dit comite de Lancastr ces est—au manor de Yeland Redmane qe fut au dit Mons Maheu et qe est en Lonesdale en le dit comite, pristerunt de lui toutz ses biens et chatteuz ensemblement oue toutz les Roules tochanz l'office de Coronner et aiderunt la dite ville et tout le pays entour parquoi le dit Maheu prie la grace nre seignr le Roi qil ne soit empeche en temps de Heyr pur les Roules avantdits desicome tout le pays set le mischief et qe la defaute qe les Rules furent perdutz ne fut la defaute de Coronner. (Ancient Petitions, Bundle 136, No. 6799.)

In connection with this Petition Colonel Parker writes (Lancashire Assize Rolls, Pt. i., p. 10 of Introduction):—
"As Matthew Redman, the grandfather, died before 1254 and Henry, his son and successor, lived until the autumn of 1278, the absence of the coroner's Rolls seems to have passed unheeded for many years, and the Justices in Eyre during that period must have overlooked them. In 1292, however, the Justices held a very strict enquiry into every detail connected with the county and to this we probably owe the above petition."

Perhaps the most interesting event in Matthew's life to the student of Redman history was his marriage to Amabel, who brought as dower lands in Dreg and Carleton in Cumberland, which, with her assent, he gave to Furness Abbey. " Ego Matheus de Redman, voluntati et assensu Amabilie uxoris mee, dedi Deo et beatae Marie de Furnesia, terram meam de Dreg et de Karlton, quam accepi in liberum maritagium cum prefata Amabilia, sponsa mea." (Beck's *Annales Furnesienses* lxxx.)

In Farrer's *Lancashire Fines*, Pt. i., pp. 71-2, I find the following fine:—At Lancaster, on the morrow of the Ascension of Our Lord, 19 Henry III (18th May, 1235).

Between Robert, Abbot of Furneys, plaintiff, and Matthew de Redman and Amabel, his wife, impedients, respecting the fourth part of the manors of Carleton and Dreg, with the appurtenances. A plea of warranty of charter had been summoned between them. Matthew and Amabel acknowledged the fourth part of these manors to be the right of the abbot, and of his church of ffurneys, as that which he and his church have of their gift; to hold to him and his successors, and to his church in perpetuity, performing to the chief lords of that fee for Matthew and Amabel, and Amabel's heirs, forinsec service belonging to that fourth part, for all service and exaction. And Matthew and Amabel and the heirs of Amabel will warrant the said fourth part to the Abbot and his successors, and to his church, by the said service. For this acknowledgment the Abbot gave them forty marks of silver.

Who was Amabel? This is a question which provides ample scope for interesting speculation and divergent opinion. Mr. Farrer, who speaks on such matters with authority, says in a note on page 72 of his *Lancashire Fines*, Part i.:—"I have not been able to discover the parentage of Amabel. These manors (Carleton and Dreg) were members of the Stutevill fee in Cumberland, which Joan, daughter and co-heiress of Nicholas de Stutevill, lord of Liddel, conveyed by marriage to Hugh Wake. Amabel was probably a Greystock or a Harrington, as these families had held the two manors between them temp. Henry III. and Edward I."

According to John Denton, "William, the son of Thomas de Graystoke and the Lady Adingham in Fourness, in the tenth year of Edward I. (1282) held a knight's fee between them in Dregg; and in the twenty-ninth

Edward I. (1301) the Abbot of Caldre, Patrick Culwen, and the Lady Margaret Multon held Dregg of John de Graystock, and of John, the son of Robert Harrington, and they over of John Wake."

Here then we have, if we accept Denton's authority, lands in Drigg (to use its modern name) and Carleton in the hands of both Greystokes and Harringtons, but in both cases at a time when both Matthew and Amabel had long been dead. It is probable, however, that the Greystoke interest in these manors was of a much earlier date than that assigned by Denton. William de Greystoke (son of Ranulf), who died in 1209, wed Helwise de Stuteville, the only alliance between these two great north-country families; and it is not improbable that it was this union that brought Stuteville lands into the family of Greystoke. It is suggestive, too, to note, since we are endeavouring to discover Amabel Redman's identity, that William de Greystoke who married Helwise de Stuteville, was the son of an Amabel, and was not unlikely to give this name to a daughter. The following pedigree will perhaps make this point more clear:—

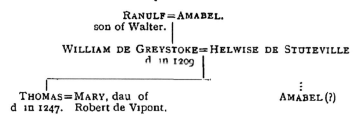

(Article on the Greystokes by the Rev. James Wilson, M.A., in the *Ancestor*, vol. vi.).

It is thus quite conceivable that Amabel, wife of Matthew de Redman, was a daughter of William de Greystoke and Helwise; in which case both the name and the dower-lands would be intelligible.

If she were a Stuteville (and after much thought on the subject my own speculation leans strongly to the Greystoke identification) she was probably a daughter of Nicholas de Stuteville, and aunt of Joan who married Hugh le Wake, of Blisworth, and from whom the " Fair Maid of Kent" and her son, King Richard II., directly derived their descent.

Which of these two suggested identifications is correct is a point which will possibly never be satisfactorily decided; but that Amabel was either a Greystoke or a Stuteville seems reasonably certain.

Amabel outlived her husband, and after her death had a legal dispute with Henry de Redman, Matthew's heir. There is a petition by Amabel (the date of which is not given) to have a special Court to take the Assize of Novel disseisin, brought by her against Henry de Redman, Roger de Cornthwayt and others concerning tenements in Yeland. Amabel describes herself as " Amabel q̄ fu la femme maheu de Redman gest du Comtee de Westm^d," which had lately been burnt and destroyed by the Scots, so that she cannot live there; and because the Justices of Assize so rarely come to those parts, she asks for a special Court, to consist of Edmund de Nevill, Adam de Skelton, Gilbert de Syngelton, and Robert de Shyreburne, " ou deux de eux."

Matthew appears to have died during his period of office as Sheriff in 1248, or very soon after—at least before Ascension Day, 1254, when his son Henry appears as owner of Levens. He had four sons and two daughters at least:—Henry, his heir; Ingram and Randle, who occur in 1254 as sons of Matthew de Redman; Nicholas, who appears in 1277-8 in a suit with the Abbot of Cockersand; and Juliana and Agnes, who also occur in 1254.

His arms appear in the Roll of Henry III., known as Glover's Roll (1243-6),—*de goules . . . . . trois horeilers (cushions) d'or.*

Henry II.

Of the second Henry the Records tell us little. He appears to have led a singularly retired and uneventful life, in striking contrast to the Redmans who came before and after him. In 1267—at least thirteen and possibly nineteen years after his father's death—he received a grant of free warren in Levens, Yealand, and Trenterne.

Rex concessit Henrico de Redman liberam warennam in omnibus dominicis terris de Lyvenes, Yeland et Trenterne in Com' Lanc' et Westm'land. (Dodsworth MSS. 159 f. 181).

In the same year (12th June, 1267) he received an exceptional mark of favour from Henry III., in whose "good books" he must have been, in the form of an exemption from the duty of serving on assizes, juries, &c., and of filling the offices of sheriff, coroner, eschaetor, &c., for life. (Patent Roll, 51 Hen. III., m. 15.) This exemption from holding prominent public offices no doubt accounts for Henry's rare appearances in the records of his time.

He was probably but a child when the headship of his family fell to him, and though he certainly held it for more than twenty years, there is little to record of him beyond the facts that he lived, married, and died. In the last year of his life he was a defendant, on June 22nd, 1278, in a case at Appleby Assizes; and on the 22nd of the following September his case against Roger de Lancaster was struck out because he was then dead, "eo quod predictus Henricus obiit" (Assize Roll, 1238 m. 13).

That he had a son and heir, Matthew, is conclusively proved, as will be seen later under Sir Matthew II.; and it is probable that he had also another son, Henry, for in 1300 we find among the benefactors of Cockersand Abbey the name of "Henry, son of Henry de Redman" (MSS. of W. C. Strickland, Esq., of Sizergh). It may be the same Henry who appears on the roll of Humphrey de Bohun, Earl of Essex and Hereford, containing the proffers of military service made at Carlisle:—

Dominus Johannes, Baro de Greystock, recognovit et offert servicium duorum foederum militum et dimidium, fac' per Henricum Redman, Ad' de Colewell &c cum v equis co-opertis. (Palgrave's *Documents Illustrating the Affairs of Scotland*, p. 209.)

CHAPTER V.

Sir Matthew II., Warden and Sheriff of Dumfries.

THE second Sir Matthew Redman, Henry's successor, was evidently a man of more enterprise and activity than his father. Like all of his stock he dearly loved the clash of arms, but while indulging his passion for hard blows he did not neglect the more peaceful obligations of his position. As Knight of the Shire for three counties he was constantly turning his back on the Borderland, and riding south to Westminster; and he was zealous in the discharge of his varied duties as magistrate, and Commissioner for one purpose or another.

Sir Matthew must have succeeded to his inheritance when quite a child. For in 1292 a Westmorland Jury found that he had a whole knight's fee, and that although he was of full age he still remained unknighted; and so Matthew had to pay a 20^s fine for his negligence. As it is not likely that he would be allowed much margin after reaching his majority before the question of knighthood would be raised, it is fair to conclude that when his father died in 1278 Matthew had not reached his teens and was probably not more than eight years of age. In fact, if we put down the date of his birth as 1270 we shall not be far wrong.

In 1291 Sir Matthew, who was now of age, was called upon to answer the King " by what warrant he claimed to have free warren in Levens, Yealand, and Trenterne"; whereupon he produced the grant made to his father by

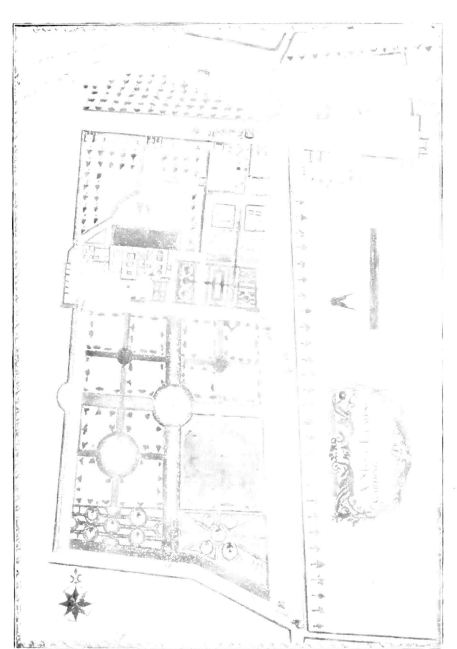

GARDENS OF LEVENS HALL.

Henry III. in 1267, "by which the King granted to Henry de Redman, father of the said Matthew, whose heir he is, that he and his heirs for ever shall have free warren in all his lands in Levens, Yealand, and Trenterne in the Counties of Lancashire and Westmorland. (Placita de quo warranto, 20 Edw. I.)

In 1292 he was engaged in a little legal dispute with a distant cousin who charged him with appropriating a wood in Yealand Coniers which she claimed. The following is a resumé of the case as given in *Lancashire Assize Roll* 410 m. 5 (20 Edw. I.)

The dispute was as to whether Matthew de Redman had unjustly disseised Isolda, late wife of William de Croft, of her freehold in Yeland Coygners—a wood, &c. Matthew comes and says that he and one Robert de Coygners hold the said wood and he asks for judgment.

Isolda says that one William de Lancaster was lord of the vill of Yeland Coigners and Yeland Redmayn, which William gave to the ancestors of the said Matthew, Yeland-Redmayn, and to the ancestors of the said Robert de Coigners, Yeland-Coyners, *except* the said wood, which he gave to one Adam de Yeland, and of which Adam died seized. After his death one Alice entered as daughter and heir and enfeoffed the said Isolda, who was so seized until Matthew unjustly disseised her; and she says that the said Robert neither had nor claimed any interest in the said wood except what Gilbert, his bailiff, took. Matthew won the verdict; whereupon Isolda, unwilling to accept defeat, applied for and obtained a jury of twenty-four on the ground that the jury of twelve made a false oath. But the ungallant two dozen confirmed the verdict of the dozen, and Isolda lost her case.

Three years later Sir Matthew entered on a long period of varied activities, the story of which is revealed largely by Parliamentary Writs and Writs of Military Summons, and which must have left him little time for the amenities of life. In 1294 he was Knight of the Shire for Cumberland, and was also engaged, with John de Cornubia, in assessing and levying tenths of moveables granted to King Edward I. to help him to pay the expenses of his numerous and costly wars (Pat. Rolls, 22 Ed. I.). In the following year, 1295, we find Sir Matthew, who had been returned Knight of the Shire for Lancashire, faring forth on his long ride to Westminster, to the Parliament summoned to sit "on Sunday next before the feast of St. Martin (the 13th of November) and prorogued to the second Sunday after. His fellow knight was John de Ewyas, Lord of the Manor of Samlesbury, in the parish of Blackburn.

It is interesting to note that the name of Sir Matthew Redman is the very first on the long roll of members sent by the County of Lancashire to Parliament. It is true that the return of knights summoned to Parliament by writ commenced thirty years earlier; but no original return made by the Sheriff for this county is found among the records until 1295. On this occasion Sir Matthew's sureties, who guaranteed that he "would come on the day contained in the writ," were his kinsman Thomas, son of Thomas de Yeland, Thomas FitzHall, William FitzAdam and William, son of Dake. (Baines's *History of Lancashire*, i., 91.)

When one considers the long journey from these northern counties to Westminster,—a journey which under favourable conditions must have taken at least a week,—and the risk of unpleasant encounters with bands of robbers on the way, the payment of four shillings a day which the Knight of the Shire received, could scarcely be regarded as an extravagant honorarium.

In 1297 Sir Matthew de Redman was summoned to appear with horses and arms at a Military Council held in London by the Prince of Wales, who was acting as his father's deputy during the latter's absence in Flanders; but he does not appear to have stayed long in the south, for a little later in the year more active employment was found for the Lancashire Knight. He was discharged from attendance at the Council and ordered to proceed forthwith to Scotland, in company with John de Lancaster, Robert de Clifford and others, to join the forces under John de Warrenne, Earl of Surrey and Sussex.

Warrenne, it will be recalled, entered Scotland at this time with an army of forty thousand men, bent on breaking the power of Wallace once for all; but he had counted without his enemy, and was defeated at Cambuskenneth, near Stirling. In this battle, and the subsequent retreat into England, it is more than probable that Sir Matthew took a part.

In this same year he appears to have been Warden of the Castle of Dumfries, for in this character he is mentioned in the Index to Petitions to the King in Council; and that he spent some time in his own part of the country is evidenced by his witnessing two grants, one of Skelsmergh by William de Lancaster (III) to Robert de Leyburne, and the other, a grant of lands at Old Hutton and Holmescales, by John de Culwen to Patric de Culwen, his brother.

In 1299 our knight was busy, with Robert de Clifford, defending the marches; for the Scots, in spite of their crushing defeat at Falkirk the year before, had soon plucked up courage again and were already raiding our northern counties. Military employment was still filling Sir Matthew's days in 1300, when he was Commissioner of Array in two counties, Lancashire and Westmorland. In the former county, in conjunction with Robert de Holond, he raised two thousand footmen to serve against the Scots in defence of the border-counties, which Edward's retiring army had left at their mercy. (Pat. Rolls, 28 Edw. I.)

While Matthew was away on the King's service in 1301 some evil-disposed persons had taken a mean advantage of his absence by destroying a mill belonging to him at Lupton; a proceeding which roused his indignation and led to the Commission of Oyer and Terminer disclosed by the Patent Rolls of this year. Three years later (April, 1304) Sir Matthew was Warden and Sheriff of Dumfries, with his son Adam as his "valettus," and in this capacity a complaint was laid against him of oppression (Docts. relating to Scotland).

In 1305 he accompanied Sir Henry de Percy to Scotland on the King's service. He had for companions John and Thomas de Tunstall, and was possibly engaged on some diplomatic service; and in 1306-7 he raised three hundred men of Westmorland, chiefly in his own district of Kendal, "to pursue Robert Bruce," on whom the mantle of Wallace's patriotism had fallen, with more than Wallace's luck.

The year 1307 was no restful one for this energetic Redman knight. Part of it he spent in legislative duties at Northampton, as knight of the shire for Lancashire. From Northampton he was sent post-haste to keep watch and ward again over the Marches; and in addition to these activities he was a conservator of the peace for his native county, Westmorland, as well as one of its magistrates.

The next year found him equally busy. He was employed in raising and leading Lancashire troops and in defending the Marches once more against the Scots, who under Bruce's skilful handling were becoming more than ever a menace. He was also one of the Justices appointed for Lancaster to hear complaints of prizes taken contrary to the Statute of Stamford.

The Scots furnished liberal employment again for Matthew in 1310, when Edward II. appointed "our beloved and faithful Robert de Leyburn, Matthew de Redman, and the sheriff of Lancashire," to raise three hundred foot-soldiers in Lancashire, whom Matthew was to lead to Berwick, where the King then was with his army, in order "to set out thence with us against the hostile and rebellious Scots." He was also in this year a commissioner for the conservancy of the peace.

The next year saw him again raising troops in Lancashire and leading them off to Scotland. A Matthew Redman figures among Clifford's knights on the Border in 1311, in company with Nicholas de Vipont, Thomas de Mounteney and others. It is scarcely likely, however, that a man of Sir Matthew's age and military eminence would be serving on the staff of another knight engaged in small border frays; and it is more probable that here we have another Redman who may conceivably have been the third Matthew, son of the knight we are considering. Clifford's small force, which numbered but fifty lances, was engaged in a scrimmage "apud Faringley," just over the Border, and ten knights and as many troopers lost their mounts. (Exchequer accounts, 14-15.)

In 1313 Sir Matthew was returned Knight of the Shire

for Westmorland, and obtained his writ "de expensis" for attending Parliament at Westminster in July; and we find him back again on legislative duty in London in the following September. He seems to have taken an active part with the Earl of Lancaster and other nobles and knights in getting rid, once for all, of Edward's insolent favourite, Piers de Gaveston. He was probably in that army of Lancaster which chased Edward and his offensive friend from York to Newcastle, and from Newcastle to Scarborough, where the young Gascon surrendered himself a prisoner—the prelude to the loss of his head at Warwick Castle. Matthew's name figures in the list of the Earl of Lancaster's adherents who, in 1313, were pardoned "for their participation in the death of Gaveston and the disturbance occasioned thereby."

It is possible that in the following year (1314) he took part in the famous battle of Bannockburn, in which Bruce so signally defeated an English army more than three times as large as his own, and thus secured independence for Scotland and an assured throne for himself. The name of Matthew Redman figures in the Scotch Roll, 7 Edward II. in a list of knights who were fighting in Scotland under Clifford in this year—but again doubt assails us as to his identity with the second Sir Matthew. It should perhaps be explained that at this time there were living three Matthew Redmans all capable of bearing arms; the Sir Matthew we are writing of, his heir and namesake, and a third Matthew who died in Cumberland in 1356. There are thus obviously occasions like this on which it is unwise to be too precise in identification. In this year of Bannockburn he was in the commission of the peace for Westmorland.

For the next four years he seems to have been resting

on his laurels; and in fact he only once more emerges, with any certainty, in a military character, when, in 1318, he was empowered, with others, to "raise all subjects, between the ages of twenty and sixty, capable of bearing arms in the county of Westmorland."

In 1324 a Matthew de Redman was returned "as man-at-arms by the sheriff of Westmorland pursuant to writ tested at Westminster, 9th May, as summoned by proclamation to attend the great Council at Westminster after Ascension Day, 30th May"; and again in the same year a Matthew was one of the jurors on the inquisition on Ingelram de Gynes; but it is impossible to identify these Matthews with this second Redman knight of the name, whose active career had probably come to an end some years earlier.

Sir Matthew makes many appearances in the records in characters perhaps less interesting than those so far considered. He was engaged as defendant, with Henry, his son, in a suit brought by Walter de Strickland:—

Appelby, 2 January, 1300-1.
Walter de Stirkeland v. Matthew de Redmane, Henry, his son, Henry, son of Robert and David, his brother, re obstruction of a way in Lupton. Matthew and Henry, his son, appear & say that Strickland's holding is in Helsington, and not in Lupton. Strickland, however, obtained his verdict. (A.R., 1321, m. 14 dorso.)

In 1318 the Close Rolls disclose "an order to cause a tally of the Exchequer to be levied in the names of Matthew de Redman and John de Cornubia, collectors of the 10th and 6th granted to the late King by the community of the realm, for the arrears of their account in the possession of Adam de Redmane, for the arrears of wages of William de Redmane, his brother, now deceased, of whose will he is executor"; Matthew was directed to pay the arrears. The Adam and William Redman here mentioned were Sir Matthew's younger sons.

In 1296 we find two charters of William de Camberton made to Matthew de Redman and Goditha, his wife, of his lands in Camberton and Dymouthe (Workington). (Placit. Abbr., 24 Edw. I.) These charters disclose the name of Matthew's wife, who was not improbably William's daughter. William de Camberton was a member of the family of Camberton who derived their descent, through Orme, from the old barons of Kendal and (although on this point there is a divergence of opinion) from Ivo de Tailbois, Count of Anjou, whose wife was Lucia, daughter of Algar, Earl of Mercia and sister of Edwin and Morcar, the historic earls. Through Gunilda, Orme's wife, there is a distinguished descent for the Cambertons from King Ethelred II. and from Malcolm II., King of Scotland

Matthew had, in addition to his successor of the same name, at least three sons, (1) Henry, (2) Adam, and (3) William, with the latter two of whom the next chapter deals. As to Henry, I cannot do better than quote Colonel Parker's views:—

I am not at all sure that Henry did not succeed his father Matthew. The first note of Matthew III. is his summons to Westminster in 1324. Six years later his son, the fourth Matthew, was born. Whether Henry succeeded and died between 1319 and 1324 may never be discovered; but his widow, Mariota (styled Maria), was seized of a tenement in "Lupton in Levenes" in 1334, which was claimed by John de Birton (A.R., 1364, m. 9); and on her death, about 1359, this property, described as 1 messuage and 9 oxgangs, &c., passed to Matthew III. (Patent Roll, 33 Ed. III.)

Sir Matthew (II.) probably died in 1319, in which year, on the evidence of the Close Rolls, the Sheriff of Lancaster was ordered to cause a coroner to be elected for that county in place of Matthew de Redman, deceased.

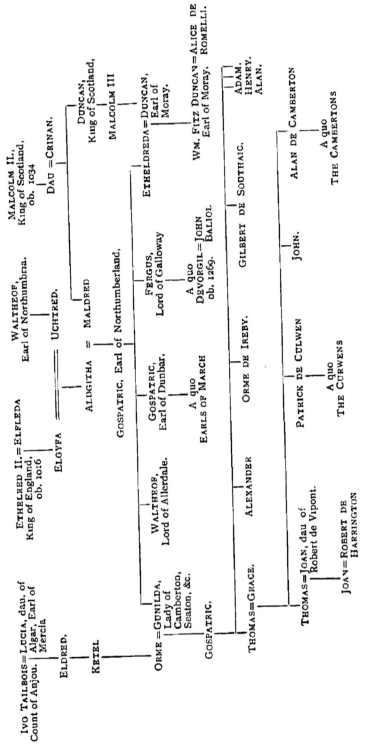

Descent of the Cambertons.

CHAPTER VI.

Yealand.

THE appearance on the scene of Adam, Sir Matthew's second son, affords an appropriate opportunity of reviewing and finally closing the chapter of Yealand, and especially the Redman connection with that manor.

As we have already seen, on the death of Adam d'Avranches, Yealand appears to have descended in equal moieties to his two sons, (1) Roger, who continued the senior Yealand line and the name, and (2) Norman, who founded the collateral family of Redman. Let us dispose of the senior section first, and as briefly as possible. Of Roger, Norman's brother, litttle seems to be known. As Roger de Yelland he was one of the witnesses to Gilbert Fitz Reinfrid's grant of Levens to his nephew, Henry de Redman; and, as mentioned before, he was a grantor of lands in Yealand to Cockersand Abbey sometime between 1190 and 1205. He probably survived his brother Norman more than twenty years, dying sometime before 1207.

Roger's son, Sir Adam de Yealand, was sheriff of Lancashire 1227-32 (Baines's *Lancashire*, vol. i., 58); and in 1216 he was commanded to deliver to the constable of Chester immediate possession of Lancaster Castle, with the county and all its appurtenances, to ward during the Royal pleasure (Rot. Lit. Pat. 17 John m. 9 & m. 3); and in the following month the King committed the castle of Robert de Gresley of "Mainecestr'" with all its appurtenances, and all the said Robert's lands within Lyme, to

Adam, to hold during the King's pleasure (Ibid. m. 9). Sir Adam had two younger brothers, Nicholas and Robert. In 14 John (Feb. 12), there was a grant from King John to Philip de Ulest of certain lands, among the witnesses to which were Adam de Yeland and Nicholas and Robert his brothers (Charter Roll, 14 John m. 2). There are several grants in the Close Rolls to these two brothers of Adam, who seem to have been of the King's personal retinue. Nicholas survived Robert, and in 1227 had a grant of the custody of his lands and heir (Cal. Pat. Rolls, Hy. III). This was probably the Nicholas de Yelaund who held one-and-a-half fees of Nigel de Munbray in Welford, in Northampton (Red Book of Exchequer).

On Sir Adam's death this moiety of Yealand went to Alice, his daughter and heiress, who wed Robert de Conyers. Alice and her husband were co-plaintiffs with Matthew de Redman in a suit against Thomas de Bethum, re right of common in " Yholand."

"The defendant exacts common in plaintiff's land, while they have none in his, nor does he make suit for this right. Defendant says that his ancestors since the Conquest, and for time without mind, have wont to common in the lands of the *Ancestors of Alice and Matthew* in the said vill, without any reciprocal rights. Later, he says he has never commoned in plaintiff's land, that put in view being as much his own ground as plaintiff's; but none of them knows his own separate part as the land has never been divided up between them." (Lancashire Assize Rolls, 30-31 Henry III., m. 12—Colonel Parker—p. 47). It was Isolda, daughter of Alice and Robert de Conyers, who had the legal dispute with Sir Mathew de Redman described *ante*-p. 37. But with the transfer of this moiety of Yealand to the Conyers family our immediate interest in it ceases.

The Redman moiety of Yealand descended from father to heir until, as we have seen, it fell to Adam, second son of Matthew II., who in 1327 had a grant of free-warren in his lands of Yealand (Cal. Rot Chart) Adam, who is described as the "King's Yeoman," probably held some Court appointment In 1327 we find (Close Rolls, 20 Edw. III.) an order to John de Lancaster, keeper of certain lands in the King's hands in the county of Lancaster, to pay Adam Redman, the King's yeoman, £100 out of the issue of the said lands, to be brought by him to the King and to be delivered to Robert de Wodehous, keeper of the wardrobe.

In the same year (Pat. Rolls) appears a grant to Adam de Redman, King's yeoman, for service to John de Eltham, Earl of Cornwall, the King's brother, that he shall hold for life rent-free the custody of the lands in "Tibbere and Runnerthwayt," Co Westmorland, of the lands in "Kirklevyngton and Kirk Andres." (There was a confirmation of this grant in 1331)

His brother William had died several years earlier, for in 1318 we find Adam acting as his executor and there was a direction for the payment of arrears of William's wages. (Close Rolls, 11 Edw II)

In 1328 the sheriff of Westmorland was ordered to take into the King's hands lands in Tybay and Ronnerthwayt, and deliver them to Robert de Sandford, to whom the late King, in the seventeenth year of his reign, granted custody for seven years, and afterwards granted the same to Adam de Redeman during pleasure (Close Rolls, 21 Edw: III.) In 1331 Adam acknowledges that he owes to Robert de Sandford five marks to be levied in default on his chattels and lands in Co. Westmorland, and, seven years later, he too was sleeping with his forefathers, for on February

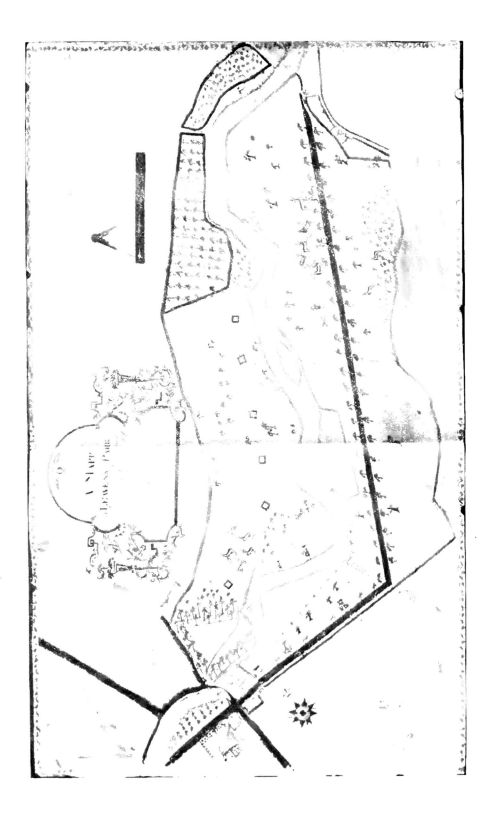

REDMANS OF LEVENS.

12th, 1338, William Langleys received a grant of his lands in Tebay, &c., (mentioned above) "coming into the King's hand on the death of Adam de Redeman."

Adam left a son and successor, John, and two daughters, Margaret and Elizabeth. For thirteen years John, who seems to have led rather an unenterprising life, retained his hold of the Yealand moiety, and then, on the 4th April, 1351, he too died, leaving not a chick behind him; and his estates went to his two sisters and co-heiresses, (1) Margaret, born 1335, who, according to Dodsworth, (108, f. 114) married John Boteiler, of Merton; and (2) Elizabeth, born 1336, who found a husband in Roger de Croft.

In his post mortem inquisition (MS. Dods. 108, f. 114) the jurors found that John, son of Adam de Redman, held on the day on which he died two-thirds of the manor of Yeland Redman, together with a reversion of the other third part on the death of his mother, Elena; that John died on the 4th day of April last, and that Margaret, aged sixteen, one of his sisters, and Elizabeth, aged fifteen, wife (at that tender age) of Roger de Croft, are his heirs.

The following pedigree may help to make things clear:—

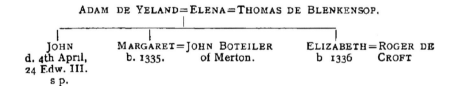

According to the editor of Townley's *Lancashire Inquisitions* (vol. i., p. 141), Margaret married John le Boteiler, and made a settlement out of the inheritance of her mother, Elena, on John le Boteiler and his daughter, Elena. This Elena married Nicholas de Croft, who was aged thirty in 1420.

Thus, nearly two centuries after Yealand was granted to Adam d'Avranches by William de Lancaster, the moiety which descended to Adam Redman's offspring passed into other hands; and the other moiety had long passed from the Yealands to the Conyers; but to this day the separate moieties bear the names respectively, of Yealand Redmayne and Yealand Conyers, in memory of their owners of so many centuries ago.

CHAPTER VII.

SIR MATTHEW III., GOVERNOR OF CARLISLE CASTLE.

THE third Matthew, who now comes on the scene, does not seem to have played quite as prominent a part as his father on the stage of his time, although he shirked none of the responsibilities of his position. He ventured beyond seas to fight for his King, he was usefully employed in keeping the Scots in check, sat in Parliament for one county, was sheriff of another, and filled one of the most anxious and responsible of military positions as governor of the castle of Carlisle.

In 1325 he was a juror on the inquisition post mortem of Robert de Clifford, one of his father's comrades in arms; and six years later we find him embarking for Ireland with Anthony de Lucy, whose widow, Joan, his son Matthew was to marry many years later. On this journey he had for companion, a kinsman, Roger de Redmayne. (Pat. Rolls, Edw. III.)

In 1337, when Edward III. began to pour his soldiers into France to enforce his absurd claim to the crown of that country, Matthew was among the knights to whom protection was granted on going beyond seas with William de Bohun, Earl of Northampton (Pat. Rolls, Edw. III). Bohun was one of Edward's sturdiest warriors, and we may be sure that if Matthew had not all the fighting he desired during the next few years, it was not the fault of his leader.

It is not until some years later that our knight emerges into view after his spell of warfare on the Continent. In 1344 he was back again in his own country, for in that year Edward appointed him " receiver and guardian of all the King's stores of victuals which were then at Carlisle " (Abbr. Rot. Orig., vol. ii., p. 165); and in the same year the responsible duty was added of seeing that no supplies reached the Scots from any port in Cumberland and Westmorland.

The climax of his career as a soldier was reached in 1359, the year before his death, when we find a letter of the King addressed to the Bishop of Carlisle on the subject of receiving the oath of Sir Matthew de Redman on appointment to the offices of sheriff of Cumberland and governor of Carlisle Castle (Hist. MSS. Com. 9th Report p. 191).

These military records are tantalizing in their scantiness; but it does not require much imagination to see that in a fighting career which covered twenty years of one of the most bellicose periods in our history, including the great battle at Crecy, Matthew must have seen enough fighting even to satisfy the warlike enthusiasm of an early Redman.

Sir Matthew appears in the Records in many other characters, of a peaceful nature. About 1344 he was witness to a grant by Sir Walter Strickland to his son John, of lands in Whinfell and elsewhere, and in 1351 John de Nyandsergh granted to Matthew all his lands and tenements, &c., of Nyandsergh (the present Ninezergh, which is about half-a-mile south of Levens Hall). Among the witnesses to this grant were Richard de Preston, his neighbour, and Thomas de Redman. Five years later he witnessed a grant by Ralph, son of John de Palton, to Ronald de Thornburgh, of lands in Sleddall in the vill of

Stirklanketill (His. MSS. Com. Report 10, pt. 4); and in 1358 William, son of Thomas de Icconshaw, appointed Thomas Banes as his attorney to deliver possession, in his name, of his tenement of the Holehows to Sir Matthew de Redemane, knight (Dods. MSS. 159 fo. 159b).

Sir Matthew's parliamentary work seems to have come late in life, for it was only in 1358, two years before the end came, that he was elected a knight of the shire for Westmorland. In the following year (1359) Matthew de Redeman and Margaretha, his wife, gave twenty marks for the custody of the manor of Twysleton, which belonged to John de Twysleton, and for the marriage of his daughters (Grossi Fines, p. 256). This little transaction, unimportant as it may seem, had far-reaching consequences; for it is exceedingly likely that in the alliance of one or more of Matthew's sons with the daughter or daughters of John of Twisleton, the colony of Redmans which flourished for three centuries in the district of Thornton-in-Lonsdale had its origin.

There is no difficulty in identifying Margaret, Matthew's wife, as the widow of Hugh de Moriceby—in fact she is specifically identified for us in the following entry in the Patent Rolls (33 Edw. III., pt. 1, m. 3):—"Matthew de Redman and Margaret, his wife, late wife of Hugh de Moriceby." I am indebted for the following interesting Moriceby notes to the courtesy of the Rev. James Wilson, M.A., the learned editor of the *Victoria County Histories of Cumberland and Westmorland*:—

(1) Hugh de Moriceby died in January, 1348-9, leaving Christopher (of full age) his heir. (Inq. p. m. 22 Edw. III. 1st nos. 32). As he held Brabanthwayt jointly with Margaret, his wife—was she an Ireby, of Ireby? Embleton and Brackenthwaite were held by the Irebys early in the 14th century. The suggestion is, of course, conjectural.

(2) Christopher, son of Hugh and Margaret, was in possession in 1355 (Inq. p. m. 28 Edw. III. 2nd nos. 4), and died in 1370, leaving his son Christopher his heir, a lad of 12 years (Inq. p. m. 44 Edw III 1st nos. 42).

(3) Margaret, who is styled as formerly the wife of Hugh de Moriceby, died in May, 1374, leaving Christopher, son of her son Christopher, as her heir. (Inq. p. m. 48 Edw III, 1st nos 49).

From these most useful references it is clear that Margaret, whose first husband, Hugh de Moriceby, died in January, 1348-9, could not have been the mother of Matthew's heir, who was born in 1330; and thus she was not Matthew's first wife. Her marriage to Redman could scarcely have taken place before 1350, at which time she had a son of full age.

This third Sir Matthew's will was proved in April, 1360, at Carlisle. In it, after commending his soul to God and to the blessed Mary, and all saints, and directing that his body should be buried in St. Peter's Church, Heversham, he leaves his personal estate to his wife Margaret, with power to dispose of it as she willed after her death. He appoints as executors Christopher and Hugh de Moriceby, both probably sons of Margaret, and his own stepsons. (See Appendix).

The village of Heversham is but a mile or two south of Levens, Sir Matthew's Westmorland home; and it was also in Heversham Church that Sir William Redman, of Harewood, was buried nearly a century and a quarter later.

Four years before the death of this third Sir Matthew, of Levens, there died another Redman of the name of Matthew, of Carlisle, whose connection with the main line I have been unable to discover. By his will, after leaving certain legacies to the church and to his brother-in-law, Robert D'Eyncourt, he bequeathed his personal estate, including money owed to him by William, Baron Greystoke, to his wife Emmot. (See Appendix).

CHAPTER VIII.

Sir Matthew IV., Governor of Roxburgh and Berwick.

THE fourth of these knightly Matthews was no less valorous than his predecessors, while the range and prominence of his activities were even greater than theirs. Wherever hard blows were to be exchanged, whether in distant Spain or on the family fighting ground, the Border, his stout arm could always be relied on. He raised armies and led them gallantly; he was governor of important castles; he proclaimed truce to the King's enemies, and conducted delicate negotiations with them. And what time he was able to sheathe his sword, he filled the peaceful offices of sheriff and knight of the shire with credit, and even found odd hours for the less exalted, but useful work of a magistrate in three counties.

Sir Matthew appears to have made his presence as a fighter felt on the Continent early in the sixties of this fourteenth century; for in 1362, when King John of France was handing over the hostages in the custody of his son, the Dauphin, he refused point-blank to surrender Matthew de Redman, "who has inflicted much damage on the said Duchy (Burgundy); and him we do not desire to be in any way included in our present quittance."

For some years after this enforced residence in France the records yield little evidence of Matthew's military activity, but in 1370 he appears to have been with the army of Sir Robert Knolles who, a little later, swept the whole of the northern provinces of France, from Calais to the walls of Paris (*Foedera*, vol. iv., p. 899). Three years later Sir Matthew was at the Court of the King of Portugal, probably on some diplomatic mission; and in the same year (1373) we find him taking part under John of Gaunt, in France, in that disastrous campaign which resulted in Edward III. finding himself stripped of almost all his ancient possessions, except Bordeaux and Bayonne, and of all his conquests save Calais.

During this campaign Sir Matthew had the narrowest escape from capture by the French and Burgundians, at Ouchy le Chasteau, near Soissons, when foraging in company with Thomas Lord Archer, Sir Thomas Spencer, and other knights. Two years later, when a truce was concluded with France, Sir Matthew was ordered by the King to proclaim it in Brittany (Rymer's *Foedera* iii., p. ii., p. 1034). In 1376 the good genius who had rescued him from the clutches of the French at Ouchy le Chasteau seems to have deserted him; for we learn from the Rolls of Parliament (ii., 343 a.) that he was taken prisoner, and, unable to redeem himself, was compelled to ask Parliament to petition for his release.

In 1379, when his sword was no longer needed in France or Spain, where he seems to have spent several years in incessant fighting, chiefly under John of Gaunt, he was appointed, with Roger de Clifford, joint-warden of the West Marches and commanded to hasten, with all despatch, to the defence of Carlisle (Rot. Scot. v. 2., pp. 21, &c.); and he was one of several commissioners (including his fellow-warden, Clifford, John de Harrington, Hugh de Dacre, and other knights) empowered " to array and equip with arms all the men in Cumberland capable of defending it, so as to resist hostile invasion and the destruction of the English tongue, with power to compel people to contribute thereto" (Pat. Rolls Ric. II.).

Amid all the bustle and responsibility of these Border duties, Sir Matthew, who seems to have been tender of heart as well as stout of arm, found time for acts of friendliness and charity; for on the 26th September of this year (1379) the King, Richard II., at Matthew's supplication, pardoned Thomas de Denethwayt for slaying one Elias Addison on the Sunday before St. Mark's day; and in the following March he offered himself as one of the pledges for Thomas de Catreton, who, whilst keeper of the castle of St. Sauveur in Normandy, was charged with a treacherous betrayal of his trust in surrendering it to the French for money (Pat. Rolls, Ric. II.).

A few days later more work was thrust into Sir Matthew's willing and capable hands; for, with Roger de Clifford, he was empowered to compel, by distress and imprisonment if necessary, all lay persons having lands and rents of inheritance in the counties of Cumberland and Westmorland of the value of one hundred marks and upwards, to remain upon them; and also to see that all the castles and fortalices within three or four leagues of the frontier are fortfied, repaired, suitably manned, and provisioned (Pat. Rolls, Ric. II.).

One might reasonably think that Sir Matthew's time was at last fully occupied with these manifold duties; but as the busy man always seems to have the most leisure, so he added to his activities magisterial duties in Cumberland and Northumberland. In 1381, in addition to being appointed sheriff of the county, he was entrusted with the responsible post of governor or captain of Roxburgh, "from the 1st of May," in succession to the Earl of Northumberland; and we find protection granted "for John Gregory, chaplain, going to Scotland under Matthew de Redmane, warden of the castle of Roxburgh." By an ordinance of the same date he was appointed sheriff of the county of Roxburgh. (See Appendix).

In this year, too, although it is possible that Grafton has assigned a wrong date to the incident, he seems to have been for a time captain of Berwick, and in this capacity he had the audacity to turn away the redoubtable John of Gaunt and his army from the gates.

In the 4 Richard II (1381), Grafton says:—

Sir Mathew Redmayn, Captain of Berwicke, refused to allow the Duke of Lancaster into the town. The Duke of Lancaster and his people went to Barwike wenyng to the Duke to have entered into the towne, for when he passed that way, he left all his provision behind him. But the capteyne of the towne, Sir Mathew Redmayn, denyed him to enter, and closed in the gates against him and his, saying he was so commanded by the Erle of Northumberland; and when the Duke heard these wordes, he was sore displeased and sayde "Howe commeth this to passe, Mathew Redmayn? is there in Northumberland a greater sovereign than I am, which should let me passe this way where all my prouision is with you? what meaneth these newes?"

"By my fayth, Sir," sayde the knight, "this is true that I say, and by the commandement of the King; and Sir, this I do to you is right sore agaynst my will, but I must nedes do it and therefore for Goddes sake holde me excused for I am thus commanded upon paine of my life, that I shall not suffer you nor none of yours to enter into the towne." Then the Duke, not saying all that he thought, brake out of this matter, and sayde, "Sir Redmayn, what tydyngs out of England?" and he sayde, he knew none, but that the countries were sore moued, and the King had sent to all this country to be in redinesse whensoever he should send. Then the Duke mused a little, and sodainly turned his horse, and bid the knight farewell, and so went to the castell of Rosebourgh, and the constable receyved him. (Grafton's *Chronicle* I., pp. 247-8).

Sir Matthew appears to have stayed at Roxburgh no longer than a year; for in 1382 he is described as *late* warden of the castle, and, at this time, it may be interesting to note, as some evidence of his growing importance, that he had "fifty-seven serjeants in his retinue." He still, however, remained actively employed in the north of England, where the Scots provided ample exercise for many an English knight; and in 1382 Sir Matthew, with John de Nevill, of Raby, and Roger de Clifford, was empowered to arrest and imprison certain persons who had broken truce and had "brought into England the goods of divers men of Scotland; and to enquire in the counties of Northumberland, Cumberland, and Westmorland, who are their accomplices and cause restitution to be made."

In the following year (1383) he was called away from the Border to the scene of his earlier exploits in France, where he commanded a section of the Bishop of Norwich's army against the supporters of Pope Clement; and, after a stout defence, was compelled to surrender Bourbourg to the French King. This appears to have been the last of Sir Matthew's warlike adventures over the sea, in which he seems to have had at least his share of the ill-luck which at that time pursued our armies.

In 1386 we find him actively engaged again in his own land where, with the Bishop of Bath and Wells, the Earl of Northumberland, John, Lord Nevill, and other joint-commissioners, he was empowered to treat with the Scots for peace. (See Appendix). Sir Matthew's fighting days are now rapidly drawing to their close, though, as we shall see, he was still a right doughty knight. In 1388 he was commissioner of array for the county of Northumberland, as well as governor of Berwick. In the latter capacity it fell to his lot to take a conspicuous part in the battle of Otterbourne, the fight in which the hatred and jealousies of two nations found such fierce vent, and which minstrels and chroniclers alike have conspired to invest with a romantic interest which scarcely any other battle fought on British soil can claim.

Sir Matthew was one of the first to whom news was brought of that famous feast at Aberdeen where the Scottish lords and knights arranged that "they should all meet, with their puissance on the frontiers of Cumberland, at a castle in the high forest called Jedworth," for such a raid into England "as should be spoken of for twenty years after"; and he took a leading and energetic part in raising the forces which assembled at Newcastle to resist the incursion.

Of the battle itself, fought with such tragic fierceness "by the fitful light of the moon," of its varying fortunes, its dramatic incidents and of the final rout of the English, the story is too well-known to need recital. That Sir Matthew bore himself right gallantly we know on abundant evidence. "And on the English party," Froissart says, "before that the Lord Percy was taken and after, there fought valiantly Sir Ralph Lumley, Sir Matthew Redman, Sir Thomas Ogle, Sir Thomas Grey, Sir Thomas Helton, Sir Thomas Abingdon—and divers others."

Sir Matthew was one of the leaders, with Sir Thomas and Sir Robert Umphreville, Sir Thomas Grey and Sir Robert Ogle, of the troops whom Hotspur, designing to catch the Scots in a net and effectually cut off their retreat, sent to sweep round northward from the position occupied by them, and "hold them in y^t they fled not awaye."

That this movement failed of its purpose was not in

any way Sir Matthew's fault—the tide of fortune flowed finally and overwhelmingly against the Englishmen, and their leaders were captured or slain, "saving Sir Matthew Redman, captain of Berwick, who, when he knew no remedy nor recoverance, and saw his company fly from the Scots and yield them on every side, then he took his horse and departed to save himself."

But he was not to escape so easily; and what later befell him is best told in Froissart's own words:—

I shall shew you of Sir Matthew Redman, who was on horseback to save himself, for he alone could not remedy the matter.

At his departing Sir James Lindsay was near to him and saw how Sir Matthew departed, and this Sir James, to win honour, followed in chase Sir Matthew Redman, and came so near to him that he might have stricken him with his spear, if he had listed. Then he said, "Ah! Sir Knight, turn; it is a shame thus to fly; I am James Lindsay; if ye will not turn I shall strike you on the back with my spear."

Sir Matthew spake no word, but struck his horse with the spurs sorer than he did before. In this manner he chased him more than three miles, and at last Sir Matthew Redman's horse foundered and fell under him. Then he stepped forth on the earth and drew out his sword, and took courage to defend himself; and the Scot thought to have stricken him on the breast, but Sir Matthew Redman swerved from the stroke and the spear-point entered into the earth.

Then Sir Matthew struck asunder the spear with his sword; and when Sir James Lindsay saw how he had lost his spear, he cast away the truncheon and lighted afoot, and took a little battle-axe that he carried at his back, and handled with his one hand quickly and deliverly, in the which feat Scots be well expert; and then he set at Sir Matthew, and he defended himself properly. Thus they tourneyed together, one with an axe and the other with a sword a long season, and no man to hinder them.

Finally Sir James Lindsay gave the knight such strokes, and held him so short, that he was put out of breath in such wise that he yielded himself and said, "Sir James Lindsay, I yield me to you."

"Well," quoth he, "and I am to receive you, rescue or no rescue?" "I am content," quoth Redman, "so ye deal with me like a good companion." "I shall not fail that," quoth Lindsay, and so put up his axe.

"Well, Sir," quoth Redman, "what will you now that I shall do? I am your prisoner; ye have conquered me. I would gladly go again to Newcastle, and within fifteen days I shall come to you in Scotland where ye shall assign me." "I am content," quoth Lindsay, "ye shall promise by your faith to present yourself within these three weeks at Edinburgh, and wheresoever ye go, to repute yourself my prisoner" All this Sir Matthew sware and promised to fulfil. Then each of them took their horses and took leave of each other. Sir James returned, and his intent was to go to his own company the same way that he came, and Sir Matthew Redman to Newcastle.

But Nemesis was quickly on the track of the valorous Scottish knight. He had ridden scarcely half-a-mile through the darkness and mist which had fallen since his encounter with Redman, when he ran into the very arms of the Bishop of Durham and five hundred of his men. Sir James might have escaped from his predicament had he not unhappily mistaken the enemy for his own company, and "when he was among them," Froissart says, "one demanded of him who he was." "I am," quoth he, "Sir James Lindsay." The Bishop heard these words, and stepped to him and said, "Lindsay, ye are taken; yield ye to me." And thus the proud victor of a few minutes earlier found himself a prisoner, and on his way to Newcastle in the wake of his own captive. The later meeting of the two knights, under circumstances so unexpected and humorous is thus quaintly described by Froissart —

After that Sir Matthew Redman was returned to Newcastle, and shewed to divers how he had been taken prisoner by Sir James

Lindsay, then it was shewed to him how the Bishop of Durham had taken the said Sir James Lindsay, and how that he was there in the town as his prisoner.

As soon as the Bishop was departed Sir Matthew Redman went to the Bishop's lodging to see his master, and there he found him in a study of thought, lying in a window, and said :—" What, Sir James Lindsay, what make you here ? " Then Sir James left his study and came forth to him and gave him good-morrow, and said, " By my faith, Sir Matthew, fortune hath brought me hither ; for as soon as I was departed from you, I met by chance the Bishop of Durham, to whom I am prisoner as ye be to me. I believe ye shall not need come to Edinburgh to me to make your finance ; I think rather we shall make an exchange one for another if the Bishop be so content."

"Well, sir," quoth Redman, "we shall accord right well together; ye shall dine this day with me; the Bishop and our men be gone forth to fight with your men ; I cannot tell what shall fall ; we shall know at their return."

" I am content to dine with you," quoth Lindsay. Thus these two knights dined together at Newcastle.

Sir James, by the way, appears to have been unkindly treated by fate, for, instead of recovering his freedom like Sir Matthew Redman, he was still a prisoner on the 25th of September when King Richard issued an order at Cambridge " with the advice of his great Council, to the Earl of Northumberland, not to dismiss Lindsay either for pledge or ransom until further orders."

The story of Sir Matthew's prowess at Otterbourne is told in many of the ballads and chronicles which have brought the picture of this battle so graphically down to us through the centuries. In *The Batayl of Otterbourne*, from *The Chronicle of John Hardyng*, we read

> He sent the lorde syr Thomas Vmfreuyle,
> His brother Robert and also sir Thomas Grey,
> And sir Mawe Redmayn beyond ye Scottes that whyle,

> To holde them in yᵗ they fled not awaye:—
>
> * * * *
>
> The felde was his all yf yᵗ he were take,
> The Vmfreuyle, Grey, Ogle and Redmayne
> Helde the felde hole, yᵗ myght so for his sake,
> And knewe nothyng whetherwarde he was gayn.

And in *De Orygynale Cronykil of Scotland*, by Androw of Wyntown:—"Schyr Mawe of the Redmane" figures conspicuously among the gallant knights to whom Androw pays tribute.

It must have been a very sad home-coming for Sir Matthew, for in addition to the story of a lost battle, a routed army and his own misadventure, he had to break the news to his wife that her brother, a gallant young knight who had probably fought under his own banner, had fallen on the field.

> Ther was slayne upon the Ynglysshe syde,
>   For soth and sertenlye,
> A gentell knyght, Sir John Fitz-hughe,
>   Yt was the more petye.

In the year following the battle of Otterbourne Sir Matthew was peacefully engaged in his magisterial work in Northumberland, varied by an enquiry, with Thomas, Earl Marshal, and others, "as to places in Northumberland burnt by the King's enemies of Scotland"; and by a survey with Sir Thomas Umfraville and others, of certain vessels called "kiles," used for measuring sea-coal at Newcastle-on-Tyne and neighbourhood (Pat. Rolls, Ric. II., 1388-92)—useful and honourable occupations enough, but contrasting strangely with the flash of steel and the clang of armour which had for so many years been to him the breath of life.

But we have been led away by the fascination of Sir Matthew's career as a fighter from the domestic and other peaceful phases of his life. One of his earliest appearances in the records was as a witness in 1364 to a release by "Agnes, relict of Ralph," of her right in certain lands (Hist. MSS. Commission—Rep. 10, part 4—Major Bagot's Levens Hall Papers); and six years later, in 1370, Matthew and Lucy, his (first) wife, are defendants in a suit brought by Thomas de Yealand and Elena, his wife, to recover possession of three messuages, eighty acres of land, &c., in Levens (*Abbr. Rot. Orig.*, vol. ii., p. 310). In 1376 it was found after the death of Joan de Coupland that Matthew de Redman, of Over Levens, held of the said Joan a moiety of the vill of Quinfell, and divers tenements in Selside.

Sir Matthew was twice married, (1) to "Lucy," whose identity has so far defied elucidation, and (2) to Joan, daughter of Henry, Lord Fitzhugh, who, before wedding Sir Matthew, had already been twice a wife, first of William, fourth Lord Greystoke, and secondly of Anthony, third Lord de Lucy, who died in 1368, and by whom she had an infant daughter who died in the following year.

As widow of the wealthy Lord Lucy, Joan was a well-dowered bride, and, among other large possessions, brought to Sir Matthew the castle and manor of Langele, in Northumberland, a third part of the Barony of Egremund, with the advowson of Ulvedale and the manors of Aspatrik and Braythwayt.

In 1378 the Patent Rolls disclose "a licence for Ralph, Baron de Greystock (Joan's son), Matthew de Redemane Kt and Joan, his wife, to grant the town and lordship of Angerton, Co. Northumberland, held in chief, to William de Greystock Esqre., the said Ralph's brother, for life";

68 REDMANS OF LEVENS AND HAREWOOD.

and five years later, in 1383, there was a licence to transfer to Henry, first Earl of Northumberland, and Matilda, his wife, "the castle and manor of Langeley, Co. Northumberland, a moiety of the manor of Aspatrik, and a third part of the Barony of Egermond, Co. Northumberland, with the advowson of Ulvedale, after the death of Joan, wife of Matthew de Redmayne knight."

Henry, the first Earl of Northumberland, had married Matilda, only sister of Anthony de Lucy, Joan's second husband; and on the death of Joan, her dower-lands reverted to Matilda and her husband, on condition that he, the Earl of Northumberland, should bear the arms of Percy,—*or*, with a lion rampant *azure*, quartered with those of Lucy, viz.: *gules*, with three lucies, *argent*.

The following pedigree will perhaps make this transaction clear :—

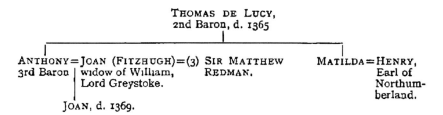

Sir Matthew appears to have had two sons and one daughter. O his elder son, Matthew, the records disclose little beyond the fact that on April 1, 1369, he had a pass to Ireland with William de Windsor; and it seems certain that he died in the lifetime of his father, leaving his younger brother, Richard, to assume the headship of the family, and by his marriage with Elizabeth, daughter and co-heiress of the first Lord Aldeburgh, to transfer the chief activities of the family from Levens, which had been its headquarters for more than two centuries, to Harewood in Yorkshire.

Sir Matthew's daughter, Felicia, the only one traceable, married Sir John, son of Ralph, Lord Lumley, who fell at the battle of Baugy, in Anjou, in 1421. From this union the present Earl of Scarborough and many of our nobles of to-day derive their origin. Her great-grandson, Thomas, wed Elizabeth Plantagenet, the daughter of King Edward IV. by the Lady Elizabeth Lucy.

Sir Matthew Redman was one of the witnesses in the historical dispute between Lord Scrope and Sir Robert Grosvenor as to the right to bear "*azure* a bend *or*"; in which he gave important evidence as to Scrope's second marriage with the lady of Pulford. Sir Matthew died circa 1390, and was succeeded by his son Richard, who was destined to shed still more lustre on the name of Redman.

It is interesting to note that in his will, dated 1407, Richard Burgh, who married Margaret, daughter of Thomas Roos, of Kendal, bequeathed the sum of thirteen marks to two chantry priests for the celebration for one year, of masses for the souls of Richard, King of England, the Duke of Norfolk, Thomas, Lord Clifford, and Sir Matthew Redman. (*Test. Ebor. Sur. Soc.*, 1., 348).

CHAPTER IX.

LEVENS.—MANOR AND HALL.

OF the very early history of Levens, before it came into Redman hands, comparatively little is known. At the time of the Norman conquest it seems to have formed part of the vast possessions of Tosti, Earl of Northumberland, son of Godwin, and brother of Harold, "the Englishman." Tosti was driven by his rebellious Northumbrians to Flanders, and Harold acknowledged Morcar as successor to his earldom and lands.

Such a rich possession as the Honour of Lancaster, which included Levens, was not likely to remain long out of the clutch of the Norman, and we find William bestowing it on Roger, of Poictou, third son of Roger of Montgomery, as a reward for loyal services rendered by his family. Roger, however, proved unworthy of such lavish generosity, for he took a prominent part in the rebellion against William, which followed swiftly on the first distribution of the English spoil.

Among the lands of Roger of Poictou the Domesday Survey includes *Lefuenes* (Levens) with two carucates, a carucate being as much land as could be ploughed by one plough or team in a season; long varying in extent, but determined in 1194 to be one hundred acres (Stubbs's *Select Charters*, p. 536). In later years the barony of Kendal was held of the honour of Westmorland by the De Lancasters, who derived their title from Roger de

Mowbray in the reign of King Stephen, and he from his father Nigel de Albini (Ferguson's *History of Westmorland*, p. 116); and as we have seen (p. 2) Levens was granted by William de Lancaster II. to Norman de Hieland (later "de Redman") sometime about 1170. From this time it descended from father to son down the long Redman line until the latter half of the sixteenth century, when, as we shall see later, it passed to the Bellinghams of Burneside.

It is doubtful whether the head of the Redmans in these early centuries made his home at Levens. It seems to me more probable that the head-quarters of the family were at Yealand, where, as we have seen, the first Matthew appears to have been living when he was burnt out of "house and home" by the raiding Scots and robbed even of his Coroner's Rolls. However this may be, it is probable that by the end of the thirteenth century, the Redmans had built themselves a stout dwelling-place at Levens, the parent of the beautiful pile known to-day throughout England as Levens Hall.

At the time when this parent hall of Levens was built, there was little place for the graces of architecture or the refinements of domestic life. They were years of raids and rapine, when a man must perforce sleep with his sword by his side, and surround himself with strong walls as a protection against a ruthless enemy, who might any day come within sight bringing massacre and ruin with him.

These early homes of our English knights were thus of necessity fortresses,—on a smaller scale, it is true, than the great castles of the Barons,—but stoutly built, able to resist onslaught, and proof against the firebrand. These minor fortresses were scattered thickly over the northern counties, like so many grim, watchful sentinels. Levens has for neighbouring strongholds, more or less near, Sizergh, Burneside, Kentmere, Arnside, Hazelslack, and many another Pele tower, all equally sturdy, and each guarding its own district and offering a refuge to which tenants and labourers, with their wives and children, might flock whenever danger threatened.

In his most interesting book on Levens Hall, Mr. Curwen says —

Regarding the position of the Pele, Canon Weston inclined to the belief that it stood at the north-east corner of the present building, and was built up of plain rubble, without plinth, set off or string-course, over the existing barrel vaulted cellars and their low benchings of stonework. If this were so, it must have measured externally 46 feet by 25 feet, with the end walls 3 feet, and the flank walls 4½ feet thick. By way of comparison we may mention that the Pele of Sizergh measures 60 by 40 feet, with its walls 7 feet thick; Arnside, 48 by 32 feet; Burneside, 45 by 30 feet; Kentmere, 32 by 23 feet; and Hazelslack, 30 by 24 feet

From the plan it will be seen that there are two projecting bays, leading out from the cellars at the north-east and south-east corners, the former of which has a blocked up doorway, which may have been built for protection, as an outer entrance to the Pele, whilst the latter has probably been the basement to a garderobe tower. The three doorways marked C, D, and E are Carnarvon-arched, which clearly indicates 13th or 14th century construction.

From this description it is not difficult to picture the strong, square grey tower, from whose battlements these fierce Redman knights could hold their lands and tenants in survey, or scan the horizon in search of the enemy; and it is of great interest to know that from internal evidence, such as the roughness of the flooring which shows the marks of the adze, and the worn upper flight of the stair, the tower, as we see it to-day, is, in Mr Curwen's opinion, "but little altered since the date of its first erection."

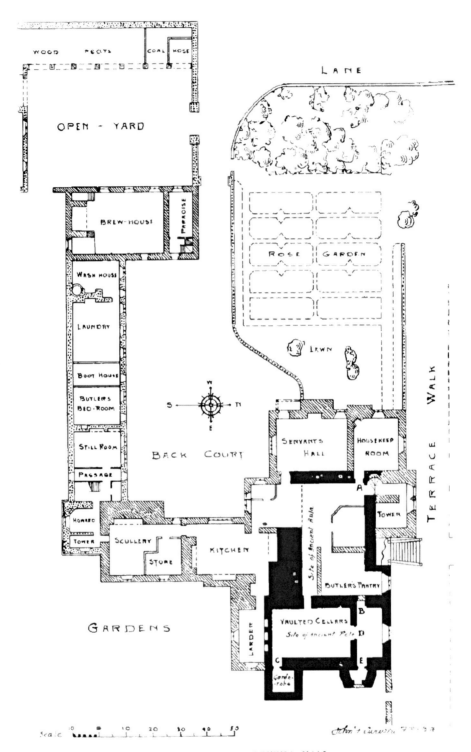

GROUND-PLAN OF LEVENS HALL.

On the west side of this tower of refuge and defence there was an *aula* or great hall, open to its lofty and massive roof of oak—a chamber forty feet long and twenty-two feet wide,—in which the lord would entertain his guests, receive the suit and service of his vassals, conduct the business of his estates, and administer justice. It does not require any great effort of imagination to picture the scenes of festivity of which this hall must often have been the setting—the lord with his family and his principal guests feasting on the raised dais at one end of the chamber; the guests of inferior rank seated below at tables ranged along each side; and, opposite to the dais, the minstrels singing their ballads and playing stirring martial music in the raised gallery. Behind the screen crowned by this gallery would be the kitchen, buttery and the domestic offices.

No doubt, later generations of Redmans made substantial additions to this earliest structure,—and indeed there are still traces of these additions to be found; for "walls of outbuildings have been discovered in the garden with indications of having been destroyed by fire."

There are still to be seen at Levens Hall survivals of these ancient days of Redman occupation, in addition to the Pele tower. There is tapestry, which once draped the walls of the aula, and which was probably worked by the hands of Redman chatelaines; and there are many old charters, the ink of which was dry long before the Great Charter itself was formulated, and which Norman and Henry de Redman must have held in their hands seven hundred years ago as we might do to-day. There is also an interesting relic of Redman times in a cushion on a chair "which," Colonel Bagot informs me, "has some dilapidated arms on it (the three cushions evidently forming part of them) which have always been said to be old Redman arms. They are in old embroidery put on to comparatively modern material (probably 1780 to 1810)."

Levens Hall remained the principal home of the Redmans until the end of the fourteenth century, when the first Sir Richard's marriage to Elizabeth Aldeburgh provided a rival home in Harewood Castle. For the next century and a half the head of the family appears to have made his home alternately at Harewood and Levens, until in the time of the last Matthew of Harewood, the latter manor, with many other ancestral estates, was sold to Alan Bellingham. The date of this alienation of Levens was probably 1568.

Burn, in his *History of Westmorland*, (vol. i., p. 204) is largely responsible for the perpetuation, if not the actual origination, of a strange blunder in connection with this transfer of Levens to the Bellinghams. He says that Sir Edward Redman

> was the last of the name of Redman that we have met with at Levens, and the estate appears to have been sold about this time (1489) . . . . At this time there was a flourishing family of the name of Bellingham at Burneshead, of a younger branch of which family one Alan Bellingham, Esquire, purchased Levens of one Redman by name, who then lived at Thornton, nigh Egleston (? Ingleton), Yorkshire.

How misleading this statement is, is proved by the fact that in 1548, nearly sixty years after this alleged sale, Matthew Redman, of Harewood, in the account of his estates given to the escheator, includes Levens, as well as lands in Malynghall, Hind Castle, Birthwaite and Kirkby-in-Kendal (Harleian MSS. 4630, p. 484)—thus proving conclusively that Burn must in this instance have substituted imagination for fact.

The later history of Levens, which is out of our immediate province, can be disposed of very briefly.

Alan Bellingham, the new owner of Levens, was a younger son of Sir Robert Bellingham, a member of an old Northumberland family. He was a rollicking squire, who prided himself on being a loyal friend and a dangerous enemy :—

> Amicus Amico Alanus
> Belliger Belligero Bellinghamus

was the alliterative couplet in which his dominant characteristics were aptly hit off. He was a man of considerable wealth which he spent lavishly on extending and embellishing his new home. For one hundred and twenty-one years Levens remained in the possession of Alan and his successors of the name, the last of whom, another Alan, is said to have gambled away his patrimony piecemeal to the courtly and crafty Colonel James Grahme, a younger brother of Sir Richard Grahme, of Netherby, and Privy Purse and trusted friend of the second James.

Colonel Bagot, in his story of Colonel James Grahme's romantic career, says that Levens was purchased by him. However this may be,—and Colonel Bagot's word is stronger than mere tradition,—the fact remains that Colonel Grahme, man of fashion, courtier and intriguer, inaugurated the third epoch in the story of Levens. He outlived his three sons, and when he died, after eighty years of a life which in its romance eclipses fiction, his estates, including Levens, passed to his eldest daughter, Catherine, who was wife to her first cousin, Henry Howard, Earl of Berkshire and deputy marshal of England. Colonel Grahme left behind him a beautiful and lasting memorial of his occupation of Levens in the lovely gardens which are in the "style called 'topiary,' a term applied to trees and shrubs clipped into various fantastic shapes, either alone or in groups, or extending in long lines, which form the chief feature of this kind of gardening." "At present, throughout the whole of England," Stanhope writes, in his *History of England*, vol. v., p. 500, "there remains perhaps scarcely more than one private garden presenting in all its parts an entire and true sample of the old designs; this is at the fine old seat of Levens, near Kendal."

It is scarcely necessary to add that these gardens, which were laid out by "Mr. Beaumont, gardener to King James II. and Col. James Grahme," who also laid out the gardens at Hampton Court, and which cover seven acres, are famed for their beauty almost the whole world over.

In 1757, Henry, fifth Earl of Berkshire, grandson of Catherine Grahme, succeeded to Levens on the death of his father, Viscount Andover, and he bequeathed it to his mother, Lady Andover, and on her death to his sister, Frances. Frances married Richard Bagot, fourth son of Sir Walter Bagot, fifth baronet, from whom it has descended to its present owner, Colonel Josceline Fitzroy Bagot, M.P. for South Westmorland.

Whatever changes time and successive tenants have wrought in the Hall, the park of Levens still remains as beautiful and romantic as when, five centuries and more ago, the Redmans hunted the deer in it. It was enclosed by licence in 1360, the year of the fourth Sir Matthew's succession; and in Redman times was a little more extensive than now, including the two fields on the south of the oak avenue.

Mr. Curwen, if I may further add to my obligation to

him, conjures up a vivid panoramic vision of the three epochs of Levens Hall ownership.

And from the realms of fancy we conjure up the warrior Redmans, stern and fierce, marshalling their forces by the riverside; we catch glimpses of the courtly Bellinghams, in velvet and ruffles, walking and talking in their pleasaunce, or drinking to the health of the Virgin Queen in the noble Hall of Banquet; whilst, yet again, our cheeks are scorched by the fierce breath of treason and unrest that swept over Levens in the time of the wily Grahme.

THE REDMANS OF HAREWOOD CASTLE.

CHAPTER X.

Sir Richard (I.), of Harewood,
Speaker of the House of Commons.

SIR Richard Redman, who now assumed the headship of his family and who was destined to become its most distinguished member, must have been born not later than 1360; for in 1381-2 we find him a full-blown knight and drawing revenue from his lands. This fact disposes absolutely of the suggestion that he was the son of Joan Fitzhugh, who did not lose her second husband, Anthony, Lord Lucy, until Richard was at least eight years old. He was thus almost certainly the son of Sir Matthew and his first wife, Lucy, whose identity, as stated before, it still remains to establish.

Under the tutorship of his warlike father, Richard doubtless had an excellent training in arms; and it is not improbable that he was with Sir Matthew at Roxburgh and Berwick, that he took his part in border-guarding and fighting, and that he may have wielded a sword in that "scuffle and scurry" at Otterbourne.

His ability and promise seem to have brought him specially under the King's favour and protection before he had reached the thirties, for in May of 1388, a few months before the affray at Otterbourne, there appears (Patent Rolls 11, Richard II.) a "grant for life to the

King's knight, Richard Redman, of all the lands and tenements which the King has in the town of Blencogo" (in Cumberland). Two years later he was entrusted with the responsible duty of "the survey and the control of the castle, the gate and the towers of Carlisle," under Henry de Percy, the famous "Hotspur," and of estimating the cost of their repair. This was in October, 1390, and in the following month King Richard gave the young Westmorland knight a still further evidence of his approval and favour in the form of a retaining salary for his services.

1390, Nov. 5. Grant for life until further order, with the assent of the Council, to Richard Redman, knight, retained for life to stay with the King, of forty marks a year, in support of his estate, from the issues of Cumberland (Pat. Rolls, 13, Ric. II.). These royal grants of the lands of Blencogo and of the yearly retainer were confirmed by Richard's successor, the fourth Henry, in the year of his accession, 1399. (Oct. 31). It is a little difficult to understand the necessity of the royal allowance for the support of Richard's estates, since at this time he must have succeeded to his rich patrimony, as is evidenced by the fact that in this year he is described in a confirmation of a grant by Sir Matthew as his son and heir:—

"Ric'us Redman, miles, *filius et heres* d'ni Mathei Redman mil, confirmat cartam Mathei de Redman supradict, *quondam antecessoris sui.* Test. D'no Will 'o de Thirkekeld mil'; &c. Dat' apud Kirkeby Kendall, in festo S'c'i Thoma Appl'i, anno d'ni 1390." In the same year, too, we find him confirming an ancient grant of lands to the monks of Byland, made by Henry de Redman and his son Matthew (Hist. MSS. Com., Rep. 10, Pt. 4).

In this year Richard assumes a greater prominence and

finds ampler scope for his exceptional gifts. Within the next twenty-three years he filled the office of sheriff of Cumberland no fewer than six times (in 1390-4-7-9, 1402 and 1413); and in 1390 he was further enriched by the following grant of lands in Heversham and Hutton Roof :—

Johannes, filius Radulphi Arneys, dedit Ric'o de Redemane, militi, omn' terras et tenement' sua in villis de Heversham et Hoton Rofe in Kendale. Test. Waltero de Strickland, milite, &c. (MS. Dods. 159, fol. 195^b).

Two years later we have interesting evidence of Sir Richard's love of knightly exercises, for we find him asking and obtaining the King's permission to engage, together with three companions-in-arms, in a friendly joust with William Haliburton and three others at Carlisle, from the first to the twenty-seventh of June, in the presence of Hotspur, to whom the spectacle of these eight knights engaging in daily tilts would no doubt prove highly entertaining.

This long festival of jousting must have been one of Sir Richard's farewells to bachelor days and licence; for it could not have been long after that he wooed and won a daughter of the first Lord Aldeburgh, and thus brought about a most important revolution in the family history.

Sir Richard's wife was Elizabeth, one of the two daughters of William, first Lord Aldeburgh, and sister of the second Lord who died in 1390, without offspring, leaving his sisters co-heirs to the barony and to large estates, including the castle and manor of Harewood. Of the sisters and co-heiresses, Elizabeth had first married Sir Bryan Stapleton, while Sybil found a husband in Sir William Ryther, of Ryther Castle.

The following pedigree will make this descent clear :—

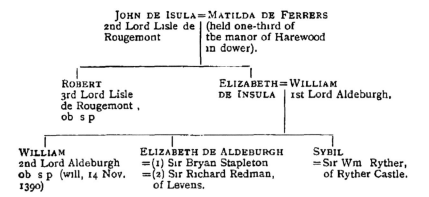

It was after Sir Bryan Stapleton's death that this Redman knight must have gone to woo the fair widow, fresh from his jousting at Carlisle. As a gallant cavalier of long lineage, the son of an old friend of her family, and with a reputation for skill in the arts of chivalry, he probably had no great difficulty in winning Elizabeth's hand and heart, richly-dowered though she was. At what precise time Richard married Elizabeth it is not possible to say. That it was not before 1393 is clear from a fine levied in that year

by Elizabeth, *late wife of Sir Brian Stapleton*, Junior, and Sir William de Ryther and Sybil his wife, daughters and co-heiresses of Sir William de Aldeburgh, knight, deceased, of the manors of Harewood, Lofthouse, Stockhouse, Huby, Weeton, Rigton in the Forest, East Keswick, Dunkeswick, Healthwaite, Horsforth, Yeadon, Weardley, Stockton and Carlton, which were parcel of the manor of Harewood.

In saying that the marriage took place circa 1393-4 we shall probably not be very far from the truth.

Thus, early in the nineties of the fourteenth century we find Sir Richard, at the age of thirty-three or four, wedded to the wealthy widow of Sir Bryan Stapleton, the mother of a son and two daughters, and lady of half Harewood and more than a dozen other fat manors and townships; the other moieties being in the ownership of Sir William Ryther and Sybil his wife. From this period the Redmans and Rythers appear to have occupied the castle of Harewood alternately, under an amicable arrangement which worked smoothly for many generations. When not in residence at Harewood, the Redmans would no doubt make their home at Levens, thus dividing their interests and activities between the two counties of Yorkshire and Westmorland. Sir Richard's wife appears among the legatees in the will of Sir Thomas Roos, of Ingmanthorp, an old family friend, dated 16th July, 1399:—" Item lego dominæ Elizabethæ Redman, meam legendam Sanctorum"; and again, fourteen years later, Sir Henry Vavasour, of Haslewood, remembers her to the extent of leaving her a gold ring:—" Item lego dominæ Elizabethæ de Redman unum annulum de auro." (*Test. Ebor.* I., pp. 351-361. Surtees Society—and *Duchetiana*).

In 1399 Sir Richard found time to indulge again in the knightly exercise of jousting, for he obtained permission to hold a tournament at Carlisle; and in the same year he went with John, 3rd Lord Cobham, to Ireland, a journey for which he had letters of protection. In the following May (1400) he was engaged in the delicate mission of treating for peace with the Scots; and in 1403 he added to his duties those of sheriff of Yorkshire, an office which had, as we have seen, been held by his ancestor, Henry de Redman, two centuries earlier.

In 1401 the *Patent Rolls* disclose a

licence for Richard Redman, chivaler, and Elizabeth, his wife, to enfeoff John de Ingelby and William Curthorpe, parson of the Church of Dyghton, of a moiety of the Manor of Harewood held in chief, and for the latter to regrant the same to them for life with successive remainders to Matthew their son and the heirs male of his body, Richard, his brother, and the heirs male of his body, the heirs male of the bodies of Richard and Elizabeth (by her former husband) and the heirs of his body and the right heirs of Elizabeth.

In the same year (April 14th) there was a grant to the King's knight, Richard Redman, in lieu of a like grant to him by letters patent dated 23rd April, 22 Richard II., which are invalid on account of the ommission of divers words which should be therein, of the custody of all lands late of Richard de Kirkebrid, Kt., deceased, tenant-in-chief, during the minority of Richard de Kirkebrid, his son and heir, with issues to the value of twenty marks yearly and the marriage of the heir without disparagement, provided he find a competent sustenance for the heir, maintain the horses, woods, enclosures and gardens without waste, support all charges and answer for any surplus. (Cal. Pat. Rolls, 2 Hen. IV.)

In 1404 Sir Richard found military employment in arraying all the men-at-arms, bowmen, &c., in the districts of Kendal and Lonsdale:—" Rex dilecto et fideli suo Ricardo Redeman, Chivaler, Salutem. Sciatis quod assignavimus vos ad arraiandum omnes homines ad arma et sagittarios ac alios homines defensabiles in partibus de Kendale et Lonsdale in com. Westmerlandiae. Teste Rege apud Pomfreyt, vij die Julii." (5 Hen. IV.)

In the following year he was empowered to exact fines from those implicated in the ill-fated Percy rising, in which the gallant, if too impulsive, Hotspur lost his life, at Shrewsbury. This year, too, Sir Richard was not only again sheriff for Yorkshire, but he was elected to represent that county in Parliament. In this new sphere of activity he must have exhibited considerable talents as well as zeal, for within eleven years of entering Parliament he reached, as we shall see, the highest office it has to bestow on its members.

In 1407 we find (Fines Term. Pasche, 8 Henry IV.) the following fine:—

Finis inter.——petentem et Ric'um Redman, Chivaler, et Elizabetham uxorem, deforciantes, de medietate manerii de Harwood (the estate was evidently settled on them for their lives, with remainder in tail male to their sons, Matthew and Richard). Si nullus haeres masculus fit inter eos, remaneat heredibus Briani Stapleton, filii predicte Elizabethe, si Brianus obierit sine prole remaneat rectis heredibus predicte Elizabethe." (Dods. MS. 159, fo. 196b.)

In the following year (1408) Sir Richard was appointed to receive submissions from the rebels who had flocked to the Earl of Northumberland's standard when he tried to raise the northern counties against Henry IV., and were defeated on Bramham Moor by Sir Thomas Rokesby, sheriff of Yorkshire; and in 1409 he was appointed, with Richard Holme, canon of York, to arrange terms of peace with the Scottish Commissioners.

Rex dilectis et fidelibus suis Ricardo Redeman, Chivaler, et magistro Ricardo Holme, Canonico Ebor. Salutem. Sciatis quod nos Constituimus et assignamus vos deputatos nostros et nuncios speciales. Given at Westminster, 20th Nov., 1409. (Rot. Scot. ii., 192).

Thus we find Sir Richard, like so many of his forefathers, constantly occupied in responsible and useful work, as sheriff of two counties, as Member of Parliament, arrayer of troops, and as the conductor of negotiations for his Sovereign; and in all this wide range of activities exhibiting conspicuous ability. In 1415 he reached the climax of his career. It was in this year that Henry V., taking advantage of the misfortunes of France, with her

REDMAN QUARTERING ALDEBURGH.
Formerly in the Great Chamber of Harewood Castle.

insane sovereign, Charles VI., and the bitter struggle for the Regency between his brother, the Duke of Orleans, and his cousin, the Duke of Burgundy, a struggle which resulted in civil warfare, determined to carry violent war into that distracted country.

Sir Richard was busily engaged during several months of this year in mobilising the forces with which Edward sailed for France, and which in October inflicted such a crushing defeat on the French army at Agincourt. He does not appear to have taken part in this victorious campaign; for on the 5th of the following month (Nov., 1415) he was elected Speaker of the Parliament which sat at Northampton. In the office of Speaker he succeeded Thomas Chaucer, son of the great poet, and was followed in 1416 by Sir Walter Beauchamp.

Sir Richard's arms (without crest or motto) are to be seen in a window of the Speaker's House at Westminster: but as they were only put there in the first half of last century they are of no antiquarian interest. Richard seems to have reaped none of the substantial fruits which so often fall to Speakers of the House of Commons; and in this respect might have been excused for feeling a little envious of the good fortune of Sir Walter Hungerford, one of the Speakers of the preceding year, who was made a Baron, Knight of the Garter, Admiral of the Fleet, and Treasurer of the Exchequer. His election as Speaker was evidently during the King's absence in France, for we find that he was "presented to the Regent for the confirmation of his election." *(Rolls of Parliament*, 1415, iv., p. 63[a].)

Sir Richard's active life appears practically to have closed with his Speakership; for although he lived eleven years longer, the Records contain but few evidences of his

86 REDMANS OF LEVENS AND HAREWOOD.

doings. From the Patent Rolls, Henry VI., we glean the following further references to him.

1422, 15 Decr. Inspeximus and confirmation of letters patent, dated 14 June, 1 Hy. V., inspecting and confirming the patents dated 31 Octr., 1 Hy. IV., inspecting and confirming letters patent dated 5 Nov., 14 Rd. II., in favour of Rd. Redman, Kt.

1423, 23 Apl. Inspeximus and confirmation of letters patent, etc.

(1) Letters patent dated 1 May, 11 Rd. II., in favour of Rd. Redman, Kt.

(2) Letters patent, dated 5 Nov., 14 Rd. II.

(3) Letters patent, dated at Chester, 2 Oct., 21 Rd. II., in favour of same.

In 1418 his first wife, Elizabeth Aldeburgh, died; and it is probable that before Sir Richard re-emerged from his retirement he had mourned one Elizabeth and wedded another—Elizabeth, daughter of Sir William Gascoigne, Chief Justice of the King's bench. Sir William, whose home was at Gawthorpe, in the parish of Harewood, was a near neighbour and old friend of Sir Richard, whose senior he was by about ten years; and no doubt the two families of the Castle and Hall were on intimate terms. It was Sir William Gascoigne, it will be remembered, who refused to obey the King's command to sentence to death Archbishop Scrope and Mowbray, the Earl Marshal, after the northern insurrection, in 1405; and who is said, although the story lacks historical support, to have committed the dissolute "Prince Hal" to prison for insolence in Court.

This fearless and famous judge, of whom Lord Campbell says, "never was the seat of judgment filled by a more upright or independent magistrate," died in 1419, the year after Sir Richard lost his first wife; and it may have been the mutual sympathy induced by a common bereavement that led to a more tender sentiment between the widowed knight and the late judge's daughter. However this may have been, Sir Richard and Elizabeth Gascoigne became man and wife, probably about the year 1420.

A few years later we get the last glimpse of Sir Richard's prominent activities. In 1424 he was commissioned, in company with Sir Ralph Greystoke, Sir William Ryther, and Sir Robert Roos, "to make inquisition in the county of Yorkshire as to lands, tenements, meadows, pastures, services, wardships, marriages, and escheats alleged to have been concealed from the King within the said county." In 1423-4 he was engaged in magisterial work in the West Riding of Yorkshire; and on Nov. 17, 1426, six months before his death, we find his younger son, Richard, "paying 10 marks for acquiring from Richard Redman, Kt., without licence, the Manor of Blencogo, Co. Cumberland (of which King Richard III. had given him a grant for life nearly forty years earlier), by the name of all the lands and tenements of the said Rd. Redeman,, Kt., in Blencogo, held in chief." Pat. Rolls, 5 Hen. VI.)

Sir Richard died on the 22nd May, in the following year, 1426, and by his will, which is given in full in the Appendix, left the Manor of Levens and certain Harewood estates to Richard, his younger son, in trust for his grandson and successor, Richard, then a boy of eight; on the death of this grandson without heirs, to his own surviving son Richard, and failing heirs of the latter, to John Redman, son of Elene Grene, &c. The manors of Kereby and Kirkby (Kirkby Overblow) he devised to Brian de Stapleton, son of Sir Brian Stapleton, by his (Sir Richard's) first wife, Elizabeth Aldeburgh, under certain conditions as to forfeiture.

Sir Richard's second wife, Elizabeth Gascoigne, survived her husband more than eight years, dying on the 21st December, 1434. On the 1st of March of this year the following inquisition was taken at Selby, co. York, on her predecessor, Elizabeth Aldeburgh :—

The jury say she held for life the manor of Rughford, of the gift of Sir Brian de Stapilton, knight, her son; reversion at her death to the said Sir Brian; held of the heirs of Peter de Brus. The site of the manor is a waste place, with a little wood. There are four tofts, 100 acres of demesne lands, etc., and a 40ˢ rent issuing from 10 messuages in Rughford. Brian de Stapilton, son of the aforesaid Sir Brian, is her heir, æt 21, on Friday after St. Leonard's day last. The said Sir Richard Redeman occupied the manor from his death till he died, viz 22 May, 1426. (Chy. Inq. p m., 12 Hen. VI, No. 18).

It is commonly believed that Richard and his two wives were buried in Harewood Church, where their memory is perpetuated by two magnificent altar-tombs of which I give illustrations. This is evidently a mistake; for in the list of burials in the church of the Friar Preachers, or the Black Friars, of York (written by John Wrythe, Garter King-at-Arms) the following entries appear :—

    It' Messᵉ Richard Redman ch'l'r
    It' Elizabeth de Aldeburgh jadiz dame de Harwode.

Thus there appears to be little doubt that Richard and his first wife found their last resting-place not at Harewood but at York, in spite of the altar-tomb in Harewood church, on which they lie sculptured side by side. This church of the Friars Preachers, at York, was the Aldeburghs' favourite place of sepulture. The second Lord (Elizabeth's brother) and his wife were buried there. Sir Richard had two sons (both by Elizabeth Aldeburgh) :—

(1) *Matthew*, who died during his father's lifetime, and
(2) *Richard*, who survived him, and is probably Richard of Bossall (of whom later),

and one daughter:—

Joan. She married Sir Thomas Wentworth, who fought bravely for Henry VI., at the Battle of Hexham. Joan's grandson was that Sir Thomas Wentworth who won his knighthood by his gallantry in the Battle of the Spurs; who, from his great wealth, was nicknamed *Golden Thomas*; and who, in his later years obtained permission from Henry VIII. to "wear his bonnet" in the Royal presence. But Joan's most famous descendant was the great and ill-fated Earl of Strafford, who died so bravely on the scaffold on Tower Hill, in May, 1641, the victim of a weak and capricious Sovereign whom he had served too well. From Joan, too, came the Marquis of Rockingham, George III.'s Prime Minister, and many another great noble who wrote his name largely on the scroll of his generation.

Sir George Duckett says that Sir Richard had another daughter, whose name he does not give, who became the wife of Richard Duket, "Lord of Grayrigg, Heversham, and Morland." He omits, however, to produce any evidence in support of this alliance. (*Duchetiana*, p. 16.)

CHAPTER XI.

SIR MATTHEW V.

OF Sir Richard's elder son, the fifth of the knightly Matthews of the line of Levens, there is practically nothing to record beyond the facts that he lived, married, and died before his father. For his wife the youthful heir of Harewood went a-wooing to Thurland Castle, on the Lancashire border, where Sir Thomas Tunstall had a bevy of fair daughters for whom he was no doubt prepared to welcome eligible suitors.

Johanna was the daughter who found favour in Matthew's eyes, and he made her his wife, somewhere about 1416. Of Johanna's sisters, it is interesting to note, Mary became the wife of Sir John Radcliffe; Alice, wife of Sir Thomas Parr, was to become the great-grandmother of a Queen in Katherine Parr. Elizabeth found a husband in Sir Robert Bellingham, and from her sprang the Bellinghams of Levens; while Catherine married Sir John Pennington. This was the first of five alliances between the families of Redman and Tunstall.

When Sir Matthew died, in 1419, he left behind him an infant son who, seven years later, was to succeed his grandfather and to become the second Sir Richard, of Harewood.

NOTE. Just thirty years after Matthew's death, another knightly Matthew of Redman name, for whose discovery I am indebted to Mr. Oswald Barron, F.S.A., the learned editor of the *Ancestor*, perished gallantly on the banks of the Sark, on the Scottish border. This Matthew, who is described by Boecé as "Maheus rubente juba (Matthew of the Red Mane) eques auratus," and by a French historian (*Brit. Mus. Vesp.*, c. xvi., p 41) as "Barberouse le Grand," led the van of the English army of 6000 men under Percy, eldest son of the Duke of Northumberland, which gave battle to the Scottish forces under the Earl of Ormond, on Oct. 23, 1449.

The Scots reeled before the deluge of arrows poured into them by the English bowmen, and the battle promised to end in their ignominious flight, when Wallace, of Craigie, commander of Ormond's right column, rallied them with such eloquent scorn that they were "so inraiged and ruschit sa furieouslie upon the Inglisch wangaird with exis (axes), speiris, and halbertes," that Maheus Redmane's men broke and fled. Maheus himself, "a redoubtable leader," was slain; and of the Englishmen 2000 perished, many of them being drowned in the estuary of the Sark, in which the tide was at full. The identity of this valiant Redman knight I have been unable to discover; but it is not improbable that he may have been a cadet of Harewood.

SIR RICHARD (II.), KNIGHT OF THE SHIRE FOR WESTMORLAND.

When the first Richard, of Harewood, died in 1426, his successor of the same name was a boy of eight years, with a long minority before him, under the guardianship of his distant cousin, Thomas Redman, of Thornton-in-Lonsdale, and Sir Richard Duket, of Grayrigg, who according to Sir George Duckett (*Duchetiana*, p. 16) had married one of his aunts. This youthful Richard was destined to hold the headship of his family for half-a-century, a longer tenure than any of his predecessors or successors enjoyed.

His tenure, however, was marked by little of the energy and prominent services which, as we have seen, had characterised those of his forefathers. In 1442, three years after he had attained his majority, he was elected Knight of the Shire for his ancestral county of Westmorland; and in the same county, and probably about the same time he found a wife in Margaret, daughter of Thomas Middleton, of Middleton Hall.

Whatever Richard's Westmorland bride may have brought to him by way of dower, she was at least a lady of distinguished birth, with more than one strain of Royal blood in her veins. Her mother was a Musgrave, a member of a family whose founder, according to Banks, won for his bride by his dexterity with the spear, the daughter of one of the old Emperors of Germany; while through a long line of De Ferrers, Earls of Derby, she could claim a clear descent from King Henry I., of England, and a distant cousinship with John de Baliol and Robert the Bruce.

In 1450 Richard was enriched by a grant from his uncle, Richard, of lands at Hincaster, near Levens:—"Grant by Richard Redmane, son of Richard Redmane Kt, to Richard Redmane, son of Matthew Redmane Kt, of the land of Hincaster, which he had of the gift of John Marshall." (Levens Hall Papers, Hist. MSS., Com. Report 10, part 4). In 1465 he found himself in the very human predicament of being sued by his tailor for a debt he had overlooked. Among the pardons of outlawry in that year we find "Richard Redeman, late of Levens, co. Westmorland, Esq: for not appearing before the same Justices to answer Roger Dawson, Citizen and Tailor of London, touching a debt of £55,"—a sum which must have represented much fine raiment in those far-off days. (Patent Rolls, Ed. IV.)

In the Patent Rolls of two years later, and again in 1469 and 1477, he is referred to as a knight; on 17th

January, 1471, he was in the Commission of the Peace for Westmorland; and in 1474 the Patent Rolls disclose a grant to Thomas Twysday of the lands which the King has or ought to have in Blencogo, co. Cumberland, and which Richard Redman, Kt., lately had of the grant of Henry IV. Thus his placid life ran its uneventful course, making no greater demand on his energies than was necessary for a jaunt to Westminster or occasional hours spent in administering the laws he helped to make; until in 1476 he, too, joined the Redmans who had had their day.

Whatever else may have been his shortcomings, Richard made more than his due contribution to the population. On the evidence of the Vincent and Philpot Pedigrees in the Heralds' College, he had no fewer than thirteen children.

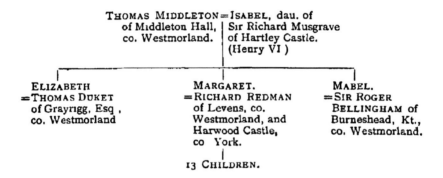

If this Pedigree is reliable it is quite clear that of their thirteen children no fewer than eight must have died young. At any rate the Records do not appear to disclose any trace of them. Sir Richard, however, was undoubtedly the father of

(1) Sir William, his immediate successor.
(2) Sir Edward, who succeeded his brother, William.
(3) Walter, } mentioned in Sir William's Will.
(4) Richard,}

(5) Elizabeth, also mentioned in her brother William's will as his sister. She married John Preston, of Preston Hall and Lower Levens, a Westmorland neighbour of the Redmans His father, Thomas, had married a daughter of a Twisleton Redman; and, it may be interesting to add, from these two alliances no fewer than eight of our present Dukes—Norfolk, Richmond, Devonshire, Westminster, Leeds, Sutherland, Argyll, and Leinster—and many another great noble of to-day, derive a double, if attenuated strain of Redman blood.

Sir Richard's inquisition was taken at Harewood in 1476 He died on the 21st of March in that year.

Sir William, Knight-Banneret.

William, Sir Richard's eldest (surviving) son, had probably advanced some way into the thirties when he succeeded to the family estates which he was destined to enjoy for only seven years. Like his father he sought a bride in Westmorland and found her at the Castle of Sizergh, neighbour to Levens, in Margaret, daughter of Walter Strickland, Esquire, and granddaughter of the doughty Sir Thomas, who so gallantly and proudly carried the banner of St. George on the battlefield of Agincourt. This old warrior had died four years before his granddaughter, Margaret, became the wife of young William Redman, of Harewood As the bride and bridegroom were within the fourth degree of relationship, a Papal dispensation was necessary for a legal union, and this was granted on July 22nd, 1458, by Vincent Clement, the Pope's nuncio. (MSS. of W. C. Strickland, Esq., of Sizergh.)

The Records are tantalizingly reticent about the doings of Sir William. His name appears, in conjunction with

those of his neighbour, Sir William Gascoigne, and Sir Richard Wentworth, in the list of " Knightes made at the mariage of Richard, Duke of Yorke, to Lady Anne, daughter and heir of John, Duke of Norff, 17 vel 18 Januarii, Anno 17 Edward IV., Anno D'ni 1477. The mariage was solemnized on the XVth day of January. These Knights were elected on the 17 day, and dubbed on the 18 day of the same month." (Cotton MS., Claudius, ciii.)

In 1482 Sir William won the coveted title of knight-banneret. His name appears twelfth on the list of " Bannerettes made in Scotland the 24 day of July Anno D'ni, 1482, Anno 22 Edward IV., by the Duke of Gloucester." Other bannerets created at the same time were Sir William Gascoigne, who thus ran neck and neck with his neighbour, Redman, in the race for honours, Sir Bryan Stapleton, Sir Stephen Hammerton, Sir Herbert Greystoke, and Sir Henry Percy. (Cotton MS., as above.)

In 1480 he found useful employment as Commissioner of Array for the West Riding of Yorkshire. This was at the time when Edward IV. was preparing an invasion of France to revenge the indignity of Louis' breach of the treaty of Pecquigni. And two years later we find him defendant in a suit brought by Sir William Thorneburgh for an illegal distress in " Selshede and Whynsell." (De Banco. Trinity, 22 Ed. IV., m. 314.)

Sir William appears to have died somewhat suddenly. He had time, however, to dispose verbally of a few small legacies to his relatives and dependants. By his nuncupative will, on 11th September, 1482, he gives his body to be buried in the church at Heversham, and bequeaths—

Waltero, fratri suo xx^{li}.
Johanni Redeman, servienti suo, iiij marks.
Roberto Tunstall, ,, ,, xxxiij marks.
Georgio Redeman, ,, c^s.

Voluit quod Georgius Redeman sit ballivus de Harwood cum feodo et vadiis, ad quod Edwardus frater meus concessit.

Richardo, fratri suo, xiij marks
Willelmo Redeman, xx^s

Elizabeth Preston, sorori suae, white horse and 5 marks He named as exors., Margaret, his wife, Edwardum Redeman, his brother, Dame (Douce) de Strykland, Thos. Strykland, and John Preston.

It will be seen that the only relatives mentioned in this will are his brothers Edward (executor), Walter and Richard, and his sister, Elizabeth, and it is fair to assume that if he ever had a dozen brothers and sisters, the remaining eight must have ceased to be at this date. His inquisition, taken at Kirkby Kendal on the 14th October, 1483, sets forth that Sir Richard Redmayn was seized of Levens. The said Richard had issue Matthew, which Matthew had issue Richard, and died in the lifetime of Richard his father, the which Richard the father died of such estate so seized, and the inheritance descended to Richard, as son and heir of Matthew. This last-named Richard had issue, William Redman, in the writ named, and also a son, Edward, and gave parcel of the said manor to William, his son, and Margaret, his wife, and the heirs male, &c., &c., William being under the age of twenty, after whose death s.p. it descended to Edward Redmayn as brother and heir.

The following deals with the dower of Sir William's widow:—

Inquisitio capta ap^d. Kirkby-in-Kendall, 21 E. IV. Juratores dicunt super sacramentum suum, quod Ric'us Redman, miles, obiit sei'tus de manerio de Levyns, in d'nico suo ut de feodo, et q^d idem Ric'us sic sei'tus dedit Will'o filio suo et heredi, et Margarete ux'i ejus, p' cellam manerii p^r d'ci, et p^r d'cus Will'us obiit de tali statu sei'tus. Et jur' dicunt quod Margareta Redman, nup' uxor Will'i Redman, militis, inventa est dotabilis, etc. Ergo escaetor assignavit eidem Margaret', p' Thoma' Strikland, militem, attornatum suum, quod Edwardus Redman vel suus attornatus p' promoniciones e'is f'cas assign' tertiam partem omnium mess, etc., de Levyns, etc. (Dods' MS. 159, fo. 196.)

Sir William was buried according to his dying wish "in the middle quyer" of the parish church of Heversham, near the old family seat at Levens—the church in which the third Sir Matthew's bones had been laid nearly a century and a quarter earlier. In 1628 part of his epitaph was still decipherable. It ran thus:—

> " Redman erat certe Levens haeres, Harwode aperte,
> " Edwardo iiij° regi meruit famulari
> "   .   .   .   .   .   "
> "   .   .   .   .   .   "
> "   .   .   .   .   .   "
> " Ye rest broken."
>   (MS. Dods. 119 fo. 74.)

Sir William left no son to follow him; but according to Burke, whose testimony should not perhaps be taken too seriously, he had a daughter Aymé, who became the wife of Adam Beckwith, Esquire, of Thurcroft, Yorkshire.

CHAPTER XII.

SIR EDWARD, ESQUIRE TO KING RICHARD III.

EDWARD, who on his brother William's death without male offspring, succeeded to the Redman inheritance, was a man of twenty-six at the time of his accession, as is evidenced by the escheat of 22 Edward IV., No. 49:—

The Jurors say that Sir William Redman, knight, held the Manor of Levens, on the day on which he died, of William Parr as of his Barony of Kendal, and that Edward Redman is brother and heir of the said William and twenty-six years of age (Dods MS. 70, fo. 141[b].)

The new Redman Lord of Harewood appears to have been a man of greater enterprise and energy than his brother, father, or grandfather, and for a brief time rivalled the industry, if not the discretion, of any of his predecessors. Very soon after his accession, in 1483, we find him discharging magisterial duties in three counties—Westmorland, the West Riding of Yorkshire, and Wiltshire; though what took him so far south as the latter county it is impossible to say. In 1483-4 he was engaged as Commissioner in assessing subsidies, &c., in the county of York; and in the same years we find him actively employed with John, Lord Scrope, of Bolton, and others in arresting and imprisoning the rebels in Devon and Cornwall, who had taken part in the insurrection headed by Henry, Duke of Buckingham, against the infamous

Richard III, the failure of which cost the Duke and many of his sympathisers their heads.

In 1484 Edward was busily engaged in the south of England as Commissioner of Array for the county of Dorset; and for all these loyal services to his Sovereign he was rewarded by the grant of a Somersetshire manor and broad acres in Dorset.

"Grant to Edward Redmayne, alias Redemayne, Esquire of the body, and the heirs male of his body, for his good services against the rebels, of the Lordship or Manor of Illubruar, Co. Somerset, late the property of Thomas Arundell, Knight, and the lands of Middleton, &c., Co. Wilts., late of Roger Tocotes, rendering to the King £6 yearly. (Patent Rolls, 2 Ric. III.)

From this grant we see that Edward was one of the trusted officers of Richard III., who executed the orders of that odious King, and on whom his favours were showered. Two months after Richard had been carried from Bosworth field, flung limp and lifeless across a horse's back, and Henry VII. had come to his throne, Edward was fortunate in receiving a pardon for his misguided loyalty to the tyrant. On October 23rd, 1485, there appears a general pardon and release to "Edward Redmayne, of Harwode, Co. York, alias of Levens, Co. Westmoreland, alias of Shideoke or Chideoke, Co. Dorset, for all manner of offences committed before the date hereof."

After this spell of exuberant activity Edward seems to have settled down into the less stimulating, if safer, life of a country gentleman. As a partisan of Richard he was not likely to be in great favour at the Court of the first of the Tudor Kings; and it may be that the exciting times which culminated on Bosworth field had satisfied his thirst for adventure. At any rate he seems to have held no public office of any kind for several years after receiving his pardon.

In 1489 it was found by an inquisition on Thomas Harrington, Esquire, that he held land in Lupton of Edward Redman, Esquire; and in 1494 Edward emerges from his obscurity to assume the duties of sheriff of Cumberland, an office, as we have seen, which had been held half-a-dozen times by his great-grandfather. Nine years later, in 1503, his name appears with those of Sir Roger Bellingham, Walter Strickland, and others in a Commission for an assessment of aid. (Rolls of Parliament, 19 Hen. VII.)

In 1509 he had succeeded in getting himself into hot water again; for we find Henry VIII., in the first year of his reign, granting a pardon to "Edward Redmayn, brother and heir of William Redmayn, knight; otherwise Sir Edward Redmayn, of Isell, in Co. Cumberland, late Sheriff of Cumberland, lately of Levens, in the County of Westmoreland, Esquire; late Sheriff of Somerset and Dorset; brother and heir of William Redmayn, Knight of Harewod in the County of York, Esquire; of London gentleman; late of Chideoke, in the County of Dorset."

From this variegated description we gather that Edward had been sheriff of the two southern counties of Somerset and Dorset, as well as of Cumberland; that he was a knight at Isell, near the ancestral Redman; an esquire at Levens and elsewhere, and a "gentleman at large" in London; in fact he must have been a veritable chameleon among Redmans, and deserved a pardon if only for the embarrassing burden of his qualifications. So far as I have been able to discover, Edward was the last of his line to be prominently identified with any county south of Yorkshire.

ALTAR-TOMBS IN HAREWOOD CHURCH.

TO FACE P. 102.

Edward married (possibly as his second wife) Elizabeth, widow of Sir — Leigh, of Isell, Cumberland, and daughter of Sir John Huddleston, of Millom Castle, by his wife, Joan, daughter of Sir Miles Stapleton. Her brother, Sir John, it may be interesting to note, was uncle by marriage of Jane Seymour, one of Henry VIII.'s Queens. Elizabeth survived her husband nineteen years, dying in 1529, in which year there was a commission to Sir Richard Tempest, Sir William Middleton, and others, to make inquisition p. m. on the lands and heir of Lady Elizabeth Leigh, wife of Edward Redmayn. (Letters and Papers, Hen. VIII., F. & D., vol. iv.)

Edward had at least four children —

(1) Henry, who married Alice Pilkington and died shortly before his father, leaving an infant daughter, Joan, who, when her grandfather's inquisition was taken, was "one year old and more."

(2) Richard, who succeeded his father on the death of Elizabeth Leigh.

(3) Helen.

(4) Magdalen.

Joan, Edward's granddaughter, found a husband in Marmaduke Gascoigne, of Caley, son of Sir William Gascoigne, of Gawthorpe, and probably died without offspring. According to Sir George Duckett, who bases his statement principally on the Vincent Pedigrees, Joan (or Jane, as he calls her) had for first husband William Duckett, of Flintham, in Nottinghamshire, and by him had two sons, the younger of whom was Sir Lionel Duckett, Lord Mayor of London (temp. Eliz.). According to the pedigree given by Sir George (*Duchetiana*, p. 218) the elder son of this alleged marriage made his will in 1545, at a date when Joan, his alleged mother, was but thirty-six years of age, and scarcely likely to be the mother of a son who had reached manhood.

Edward died on September 27th, 1510, nineteen days after making his will, of which this is a full copy:—

In Dei No'ie Amen. The viijth daie of Septemb'r, the yere of o' Lorde, a thousand V hundreth and ten. I, Edward Redeman, in a full and hoole mynd, make my will in this maner. First, I wil my Soule to God Almightie, o' Lady Sant Mary, and all the Company of Hevyn, my body to be buried in a chapell w'in the church of Harwood, called Redeman chapell. Also I bequeth in the name of my mortuary, my best whick goods. Also it is my will that my wiff shall have, receyve and take to her owne use during her liffe all maners, lands and tent's and other the p'mis's and all the p'fetts and issues, except xxli yerly going out of lands and tent's in Harwood p'ish, which shuld grow to Richard Redeman, my sonne, and Elisab'h, his wiffe, and to theires male of his body lawfully begotten. And I will that Thoms Stray, and Hary Diks, make a lawfull joyncto' according to the covenants of the Indentur made betwixt Sr William Gascoing knight and me for the marriage of my said sonne Richard and Elisab'h, doghter to the said Sr William Gascoing. Also I will that the said maners, lands and tent's, w' all of the p'mis's and all the profetts and issues thereof, aft' the decesse of my wiffe, shall remayn to my said sonne, Richard, and to theires male of his body lawfully begotten, and for defaute of such issew, I will that all the p'mis's shall come and grow to Magdalene Redmayn, my doghter, and to theires male of hir body begotten by any of the sonnes of oon William Redeman, of twisleton; and for defaut of such issew I will that all the p'mis's shall come and grow to thuse and possession of Jean Redeman, doghter to my sonne Herry Redeman, and to theirs male of hir body lawfully begotten by any that hight Redeman, and for defaut of such isshew all the p'miss to remayn to my nevew, Thomas Preston, and to theirs male of his body lawfully begotten; and for the defaut of such issew I will that all the p'miss shall remayn and grow to theires of my body; also where that I have resuyd xl li of lands for terme of yeres, lyve or lyves, to be disposed and ordered at my will by indentures of couenants made betwixt Sr William Gascoyng, knyght, and me for the marriage of my son Richard and Elisab'h, doghter of the said Sr William Gascoing, I will that the foresaid xl li of landes so resued be ordord and disposed for the welle of my soule and mariage of my doghter, Magdalene, at the sight of my wiff, Thoms Stray and Herry Diks be recond afor Robt Rede and his felows. Also I will that my doghter, Alice Redeman, have an anuyte of the yerly valew of xx marks of the said xl li of landes so resuyd during hir liff, soe that she delyver or cause to be deliverd the indento^r made betwixt my lord Archbishop Sauage and me of the mariage of my sonne Herry and the said Alice.

Also I will and make my wiff, and my sonne Richard, myn executors and have the hole disposition of my goods for the welle of my soule and the payment of my detts. Also I bequeth to my household s'u^{a}nts a certayn of my moveable goods at the sight of my wiff and my sonne Richard. Also I desir my brod^r Sr John Huddelston to be good brod^r to my wiff, and good maister to my s'u^{a}nts, and desir hym to have the oversight to the p'fo^{r}mance of my will. These witnes, Henry Diks, John Stodelay, preist, Robert Sherman and William Cowper.

This will exhibits Edward's keen, almost pathetic, anxiety that the inheritance which he was about to leave should at least continue to be associated with the name Redman. At the time of making it his elder son, Henry, had died without male offspring. Richard was married to Elizabeth Gascoigne, but no son had been born to them, nor indeed was a son born to Richard until eighteen years later. Thus there seemed to be a strong probability that the next generation would contain none " that hight Redeman." To guard as far as possible against this undesirable contingency, Edward leaves his lands, in default of male issue of his son Richard, to his daughter Magdalen and her heirs begotten by a Redman, of Twisleton, and failing such heirs, to his granddaughter Joan and her heirs male similarly begotten by a Redman. And it was only in case of this third failure to perpetuate the family name that the inheritance was to pass into Preston hands.

The following inquisitions, taken after Edward's death, are interesting as giving a detailed description of the Redman possessions at this time:—

INQUISITION taken at Kirkby, in Kendale, Co Westmoreland, 14 Jany., 2 Hen. VIII., post mortem of Edward Redmayne. Jurors say that Edward was seized of . . . acres of land, 40 acres of meadow, 100 acres of wood, 500 acres of pasture, 2000 acres of furze and heath, and 40 solidates of rent in Leyvens, in county aforesaid; and of 40 messuages, 1,000 acres of land, 100 acres of meadow, 3,000 acres of furze in Lupton; of 2 messuages, 80 acres of land, 40 acres of meadow in Hinton; of 1 messuage, 40 acres of land, and 10 acres of meadow in Hencaster, and 1 messuage, 10 acres of land, 1½ acres of meadow in Henshill; and he enfeoffed John Huddleston, Knight, and others of the same to the use of said Edward and (Lady) Elizabeth Leigh, then widow, for term of their lives And Joan Redmayne, daughter of Henry Redmayne, son of said Edward Redmayne is his heir, and one year old and more, and and said Edward died 27th Sepr. last past. Eschaetors' Inquisitions. (File 116, No. 3).

INQUISITION taken at Wearby, Co. York, 14 Novr., 2 Hen. VIII., post mortem of Edward Redmayn. Jurors say that said Edward was seized of a moiety of the Castle and Manor of Harewood; of 2 messuages, 80 acres of land, 30 acres of meadow, and 6 acres of pasture in Harwood, Otley Pole, and Holynhall; and, by deed 1 Hen. VII., enfeoffed John Huddleston, Knight, and others of the same to the use of said Edward and Elizabeth Lighe, then widow, and afterwards his wife; remainder to Richard, his son, and Elizabeth, his wife, and their heirs male, and in default to Magdalen Redmayn, daughter of said Edward, and heirs male by any son of Wm. Redmayn, of Twysleton. And said Edward died 27th Sepr. last past, and Joan Redmayn is cousin and heir of Edward, to wit, daughter of Henry Redmayn, son and heir of said Edward, and one year old and more. (File 217, No. 18).

REDMANS OF HAREWOOD CASTLE.

INQUISITION taken at Harwood, Co. York, 10th June, 6 Hen. VIII. (1515) p. m. Edward Redmayn, late seized of the Manor of Hollyng Hall, and 2 messuages, 400 acres of land, etc., in Otley Poole, Hollyng Hall; and of 12 messuages, 100 acres of land, etc., in Harwode, and moiety of the Manor of Harwode; and in 1 Hen. VIII. enfeoffed John Huddleston Knt., and others of the same to the use of the said Edward, and of Elizabeth Leigh afterward his wife, etc. (File 218, No. 13.)

Edward's will and inquisitions present certain problems which, on such information as we possess, are exceedingly difficult to solve. In the Yorkshire inquisition (14 Nov., 2 Henry VIII.) there is a reference to a settlement on his marriage with Elizabeth Leigh made in the first year of Henry VII. (1485), with remainder to Richard, his son, and Elizabeth, his wife. It is evident that either the transcript is incorrect or the effect of the limitation in the settlement at the time of the inquisition is given rather than the language of the instrument itself, since it was not possible for Edward to have had a married son in 1485, when he himself had not yet reached his thirtieth year.

Again, how are we to reconcile the fact that in the inquisitions Edward's granddaughter, Joan, is described as his heir, to the exclusion of his son Richard; while in his will his son Richard becomes entitled on the determination of the widow's life estate, and Joan's interest in the inheritance is deferred even to that of her aunt Magdalene?

It is possible that Edward was twice married and that there was a settlement on his first marriage, under which Joan took as heir of her father, Henry; and a further settlement on his marriage with Elizabeth Leigh under which Richard takes on his elder brother's death. Whatever may be the explanation of the mystery (and there are several possible solutions), it is evident that Richard succeeded to the inheritance on the death of his father's widow in 1529.

In the meantime there had evidently been a serious family dispute over the inheritance, for a letter from Lord Darcy to Wolsey, a few years after Edward's death, states that Sir William Gascoigne, Joan's father-in-law, is detaining the feoffment of Harewood Castle from Lady Leigh, and gives a history of the dispute and of the connection between the families of Gascoigne, Redman, and Sir Ralph Ryder. (Letters and Papers, F. & D., Hen. VIII., vol. ii.) It thus seems that the problem of inheritance which we find so puzzling in the 20th century was a cause of family friction nearly four centuries ago.

RUINS OF HAREWOOD CASTLE.
From Drawing by Herbert Railton.   TO FACE P. 10

CHAPTER XIII.

SIR RICHARD (III.) AND THE PILGRIMAGE OF GRACE.

THE earliest evidence of Richard's ownership of the family estates is in 1530, when there was a confirmation to Henry Ryther and Richard Redmayn of the charter of grant of warren, fair and market at Harewood; and in the two following years, and again in 1535, he was doing magisterial work in Westmorland. (Letters and Papers, F. & D., Hen. VIII., vols. iv. and v.)

In 1536 he appears in the list of names of "Knights, esquires and gentlemen, with the numbers of their household servants, who promissd to serve the King, His Grace, in the company and at the leading of Thomas, Lord Darcy, or his deputy, as he appointed upon an hour's warning." Richard Redman's domestic retinue numbered twenty-four.

Lord Darcy's mission, it will be remembered, was to suppress the rising of the rural population in the North of England, known as the "Pilgrimage of Grace," at the head of which was Robert Aske, of Doncaster. Aske had 40,000 men at his back, and for a time carried all before him, capturing in succession Hull and York. Darcy and his followers sought refuge in Pontefract Castle with the Archbishop of York; and when Aske appeared before the Pomfret walls, both prelate and baron not only yielded to him but actually joined the rebels. Whether or not Richard Redman followed the weak example of his leader and shared in the fiasco with which the "Pilgrimage of

Grace" terminated, it is impossible to say. We know, however, that he did not, like Darcy, lose his head as the result of the adventure.

In the following year he was the hero of an unpleasant incident in Westmorland while hunting in the park of his neighbour, young Walter Strickland of Sizergh, who, although he was a youth still in his teens, had been one of Aske's followers and had been compelled to sue for pardon from the Duke of Norfolk for himself and the men of Kendal.

On the 17th March, 1537, Anthony Layton, a relative of Richard's wife, deposed that " Richard Redman shewed him that divers of the parish of Heysam (Heversham) came to his house, 14 Jany., to swear him to the custom of Kendall and he refused; also that on the 15th, John Stanes, with some 200 persons, took Redman while hunting in Sizar Park and caused him to swear."

In this year, and again in 1539, 41 and 42, he appears as " Ric. Redmayn, knight," among the magistrates for the county in which he was the victim of such highhanded proceedings; while in 1537 he was on the grand jury panel for York, and in the list of freeholders in the West Riding. Two years later he figures in the list of " all gentilmen within the schyer of Westmoreland "; in the muster-roll for the West Riding of Yorkshire, we find the household of Ric. Redman, Esq., of Harewood Castle; and, still in this year 1539, he was engaged with Sir Marmaduke Tunstall (son of Sir Brian, of Flodden, and father-in-law of William Redman, of Ireby) in the muster of the Wapentake of Yewcross taken by them on Bentham moor. (Letters and Papers, Hen. VIII., F. & D., vols. xii to xvii.)

Richard was twice married, (1) as we have seen from

his father's will, to Elizabeth, daughter of Sir William Gascoigne, of Gawthorpe, who was probably his playmate as a boy; and (2) to Dorothy, daughter of William Layton, Esq., of Dalmain, in Cumberland. Dorothy was not improbably a sister, certainly a near relative, of the Grace Layton, daughter of Sir William, of Dalmain, who at the same time was wife to Thomas Redman, of Ireby. The Laytons were an old knightly family who had been lords of Dalmain, in the Barony of Greystoke, since the days of Henry III.

This third Richard of Harewood died in 1544, and the following are copies of the inquisitions taken after his death:—

INQUISITION taken at Appleby, Co. Westmoreland, the 14 Augt., 36 Hen. VIII. (1545), p m., Richard Redmayn—Jurors say that said Richard was seized of the Manor of Lewyns in said Co., and of 40 messuages, 1,000 acres of land, 50 acres of meadow, 200 acres of pasture, 100 acres of wood, 40s. rent, 50 acres of moor, 80 acres of moss or turf, 40 acres of furze in Lewyns (Levens), Malynhall, Hyndcastle, Brythwaith, Synderbarow, Brygster, ffostwayts, Lesgyll, Selside, and Kirkby-in-Kendal, and by indenture between him and Richard Layton, clerk, deceased, concerning a marriage between said Richard and Dorothy, daur. of Wm. Layton, Esqr., granted the aforesaid Manor and premises to said Richard Layton, John Tunstall, chaplain, and another to the use of aforesaid Dorothy. And Sir Richard Redmayn was also seized of 6 messuages, 100 acres of land, etc., in Lupton and Hutton Ruff, and granted the same to Richard Fletcher and others to certain uses specified.

Richard Redmayn, of Harwood, grants to Sir Anthony Brown the wardship and marriage of his son, Matthew; and being seized of a capital messuage and lands, etc., in Hutton Ruff, granted the same to Richard Layton and others, to the use of Francis Redmayne, Cuthbert Redmayne and Richard Redmayne for terms of their lives. And Matthew Redmayne is son and heir of said Richard, and 17 years old at his father's death. (File 137, No. 3.)

INQUISITION taken at Snayth, Co. York, 14 Aug., 36 Hen. VIII., p m.—Richard Redman, who died seized of a moiety of the Castle and Manor of Harwood and advowsons of the churches, chantries, etc., belonging to the said castle. (File 241, 29,)

Richard left behind him five sons and four daughters, probably all of them children of Dorothy Layton; the eldest of them being born eighteen years after his grandfather's death, when we know Richard had for wife Elizabeth Gascoigne. The five sons were—

(1) Matthew, of whom next.

(2) William, who is mentioned in conjunction with his elder brother as stated hereafter.

(3) Francis, whose life estate is mentioned in his father's Westmorland inquisition above.

(4) Cuthbert, whose life estate is mentioned in the same inquisition, and of whom more fully later.

(5) Richard, whose life estate is mentioned as above; and the four daughters were :—

(1) Ann, who became the wife of John Lambert, Esq., of Calton in Craven, and whose grandson was John Lambert, the famous parliamentary general, Cromwell's supporter and later rival, and the leading spirit of the cabal which overthrew his son, Richard. Ann's daughter Aveline married William Redman, of Ireby, and thus united in her descendants the lines of Harewood and Thornton-in-Lonsdale.

(2) Grace, who married Richard Travers of Nateby (or Neatby), Lancashire.

(3) Maud, who married Christopher Irton, of Irton, Cumberland. One of her descendants, Thomas Irton, was knighted by the Earl of Surrey on the field of Flodden.

(4) Margaret, who married Thomas Gargrave of Bolton-in-Craven.

Lambert, of Calton.

JOHN LAMBERT of Calton, Esq., J.P for West Riding, vix 1585
- (1) ELIZABETH, dau. of Robert Lambert, of co. Durham.
- (2) ANNE, dau of Richard Redman, Esq, of Harewood Castle.
- (3) AMY, dau of Mr Pigott

Children:

- BENJAMIN = ELIZABETH, dau. of HENRY, Earl of Cumberland.
- JOSIAS, of Calton, Esq., 1554-1632.
  - JOHN LAMBERT, of Calton, Esq., Parliamentary General, temp. Cromwell (1619-83)
- AVELYN. = WILLIAM REDMAN, Esq., of Ireby.
  - SAMUEL = ELLEN, dau of William Redman, Esq, of Ireby, and Isabel Tunstall

Matthew (VI.)

Last Redman Lord of Harewood.

With Richard's eldest son and successor, the sixth Matthew of his line, we reach the last of the half-dozen Redman lords of Harewood; and it was this boy of seventeen who was destined to destroy the splendid fabric which a dozen generations had raised for him. We have seen from the inquisitions of his father and grandfather what a magnificent heritage had been accumulated through nearly four centuries to descend to this prodigal son; but we search the records in vain to find mention of a single rood of all the square miles of Redman lands which he left behind him.

What form his prodigality took we may never know; but just as Alan Bellingham, nearly a century later, squandered his fine patrimony at Levens, so this thirteenth head of the Redman family played "ducks and drakes" with his ancestral lands; and the very time and place of his death are unknown.

As we have seen, Matthew had four years of minority before him under the guardianship of Sir Anthony (? Humphrey) Brown, when his father died in 1544. In 1548, when he had reached his majority, he gave an account of his estate to the escheator of Yorkshire, from which it appears that he owned the manor of Levens, with lands in Malynghall, Hind Castle, Birthwaite, and Kirkby-in-Kendal, in Westmorland, which he held of the King by knight's service; a moiety of the manor of Harewood and the Castle there; and lands in Selside, Layton, Keswick, and Carleton, in Yorkshire, which he held of the King in chief. (Harleian MSS. 4630, p. 484). Thus we see that Levens and Selside still remained in Redman

SECTION OF ALTAR-TOMB OF SIR WM. RYTHER.
By permission of Mr. H. Speight.   TO FACE P. 112.

hands after more than three centuries and a half of ownership; and Harewood after a lapse of over a century and a half.

In 1561 Matthew appears to have disposed of estates in Westmorland to Alan Bellingham, who a few years later (1568) was to gain possession of Levens, Hencaster, Heversham, and many another fine Redman property in that county.

Indenture, 18 June, 3 Elizabeth, between Matthew Readman, of Harwood, Co. York, Esquire, and Alan Bellingham, of Helsington, Co. Westmorland, of a bargain and sale of lands and tenements in Whinfell (Quhinfell), Kendal, which was sometime the estate of Sir Edward Redman, grandfather of the said Matthew.

Five years later Matthew was called upon "to shew by what title he held the Manor of Harewood." (Jones's Index to Originalia). His further dealings with the Redman estates are illustrated by the following fines for the Tudor period:—

1551. Robert Atherton—Wm. Ryther, Esqr., Humphrey Brown Kt. and Agnes, his wife, and Matthew Redman Esqr.—pasture land and the moiety of the site and Castle of Harewood.

1560 Alexr. Rysheworthe and Ed. Bolling, gents.—Matthew Redman Esq. and John Pleysington, messe. with lands, Harewood, Wardeley, etc.

1562. Richard Appleyard and Geo. Bentley—Matthew Redman Esq.—Manor of Harwood and 30 messes with lands in Harwood and Keswyke.

1570. Edward Mawde—Matthew Redman Esq —pasture land in Harewood.

1573. Wm. Redman, gentn.—Matthew Redman Esqr.—messes, cottes and lands in Harwood, Hetherycke, Werdeley, etc., also the moiety of the Manor of Harewood.

1574-5. James Ryther and William Plumpton—Matthew Redman Esqr. and William Redman, gentn.—ditto.

1600. 32 Eliz. Warrant against Rither, etc., and against Matthew Redman and William—Castle, etc., of Harewood.

Easter Term, 32 Eliz., 1600.

>Robert Chamberlin Esq., John Gregory, Esq., and Henry Atkinson Esq., plaintiffs.
>
>Henry, Earl of Kent, John Pigott, Esq , John Leighfield Sac. Theo. Bach., Robert Rither Esq., Edith Rither, Mary Rither.
>
>Helena Rither, Robert Stapleton Kt , Wm. Middleton Esq.
>
>Henry Bellasis Esq., Robt. Oglethorpe Esq., Wm. Oglethorpe, his son and heir apparent, and Ralph Conyston, deforciants.

The castle and manor of Harewood and 30 messes and 30 cottes with lands and the frank pledge in Harwood, Bondgate, Newhall, Stocton, Lofthouse, Hetherwood, Gawthorpe, etc., etc.

A warrant against James Rither, father of Wm. Rither and g'father of Robert, Edith, Mary, and Helena, and against Matthew and William Readman.

The William Redman, whose name appears in these fines, was no doubt Matthew's brother and next in the entail.

Matthew Redman married Bridget, daughter of Sir William Gascoigne—the last of three alliances between the neighbouring families of Harewood Castle and Gawthorpe Hall.

He appears to have clung to his Harewood possessions until the last year of the sixteenth century when he would be seventy-two years of age. What became of him after he had stripped himself and posterity of the last of his estates is, to the best of my knowledge, unknown. Nor is anything known of the careers of his brothers, with the exception of

CUTHBERT.

As we have seen, Cuthbert was one of Sir Richard's three younger sons who enjoyed a life interest in certain lands in Hutton Roof. When the time came for him to seek a wife he wooed and won his fair kinswoman, Elizabeth, one of the daughters of Sir Oswald Wilstrop, by his wife Agnes, daughter of Thomas Redman, of Bossall, who through her mother, Anne Scrope, was descended from the noble families of Scrope of Bolton, Scrope of Masham, and Zouche. (Flower's *Visitation of Yorks.* 1563-4, Harl. Soc., vol. xvi.)

Cuthbert must have been in the early thirties when he was induced to take part in the conspiracy, headed by the Earls of Northumberland and Westmorland, to liberate Mary, Queen of Scots, from durance, and place her on the throne of England. The rising ended ignominiously without a blow being struck for the fair prisoner, and Cuthbert, who is described as "of Oosburne" (probably Little Ouseburn), was among those who were later "indyted of conspiracy." He appears to have settled in the neighbourhood of Whitby, where he owned lands.

In 1577 he levied a fine against Anne Wilstrop, widow, for the manor of Borrowbye and Newton, and lands in Foxholes and Claxton.

In 1581 Ann Wilstrop and Cuthbert and Elizabeth, his wife, suffer fines in respect of lands at Borrowbye, Newton, and Foxholes.

In 1589 Cuthbert and Elizabeth, his wife, suffer a fine in respect of six messuages and lands in Foxholes; and in 1596 Wilstrop Redmayne and Jane, his wife, suffer a fine of the Manor of Borrowby, in Lythe; and again, in 1599, of lands at Nawmger, Acreynges and Newton Moor, parish of Lythe.

(Borrowby and Newton are both in the parish of Lythe, near Whitby. Foxholes is in the wapentake of Pickering-Lythe; and Claxton is near Bossall).

The Wilstrop Redman, mentioned above, was in all probability Cuthbert's son or grandson. He married (1) Jane, 1596-9 and (2) Grace Leadbitter, of the parish of Leeds. In the licence for his second marriage (1608) he is described as "late of Newton, formerly of York Castle." (Paver's Marriage Licences.)

A son of Cuthbert was probably Thomas Redman of Newton, parish of Lythe, and of "Usburne," who married Isabell (a recusant in 1604), and whose will is dated 1593. Isabel's will appears in 1615; and nine years earlier we find in the Yorkshire wills, the will of a William Readman, of Stowbrowe, parish of Fylinge (where Isabel died), who may conceivably have been another son of Cuthbert. Cuthbert had at least one daughter, Ellinor, who became the wife of Edward Wythes, of Westwick. (Pedigree of Wythe, of Westwick.)

THE REDMANS OF BOSSALL.

CHAPTER XIV.

THE BISHOPS OF ELY AND NORWICH.

FROM Harewood there was one important offshoot, the line of Bossall, which although presenting few notable features of interest, was for five generations a family of wealth and position and, in all probability, counted among its members one of the ablest and most prominent of Redmans—Richard, Abbot of Shap and Bishop of three English dioceses.

The founder of this family of Bossall was Richard Redman, whom there is every reason to identify as the younger son of the Speaker by his first wife, Elizabeth Aldeburgh. He has already appeared more than once in these pages—in 1426, when he paid ten marks for acquiring from his father the Cumberland manor of Blencogo, granted to Sir Richard by his Sovereign; and again in 1449-50 when he granted to his nephew, the second Sir Richard, certain lands at Hincaster.

Richard had land at Newton, in Whitby Strand; and he had also an oratory in his Manor of "Boshall and Seton."

His grandson, Thomas, who died in August, 1514, married Anne, daughter and co-heir of Robert Scrope, son of Henry, Lord Scrope of Bolton, and grandson of John, Lord Scrope of Masham and Upsal. Through her great-

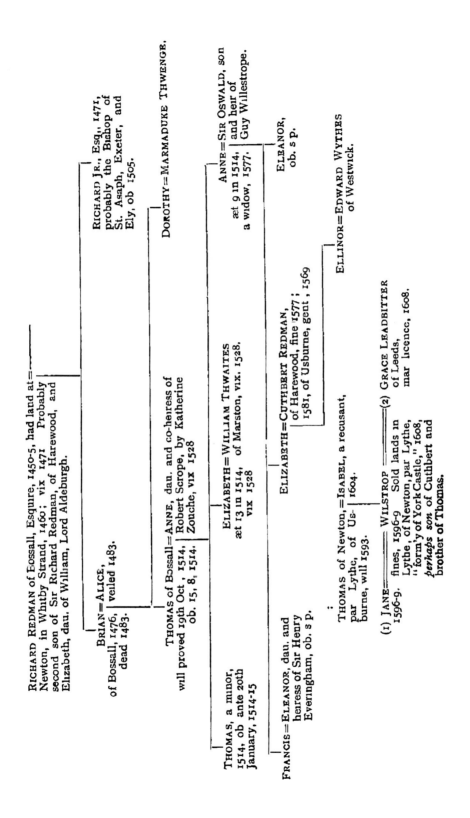

grandmother, Lady Margaret Neville, daughter of Ralph, Earl of Westmorland, Anne could claim a direct descent from the third Henry. It was Thomas's granddaughter, Elizabeth, who became the wife of Cuthbert Redman, of Harewood, whom we have already considered.

Dr. Richard Redman, Bishop of St. Asaph, Exeter, and Ely.

But the Bossall family is chiefly interesting from the strong probability that it produced in Dr. Richard Redman, Bishop of St. Asaph, Exeter, and Ely one of the greatest of all the great churchmen of the fifteenth century. It has been stated, notably by the late Sir George Duckett, in his *Duchetiana*, p. 32, that Richard, the bishop, was the second son of Sir Richard, I., of Harewood, and Elizabeth Aldeburgh; but a very slight consideration of dates should have made this affiliation impossible.

Richard was an Oxford undergraduate in 1449 (Clarke's Register of Oxford University), twenty-three years after the Speaker's death and thirty-one years after that of Elizabeth Aldeburgh. Even assuming that he was as old as twenty-five at this time—a not very probable age for an undergraduate—and thus that he was born in 1424, he would still be half-a-dozen years younger than the second Richard, the Speaker's *grandson* and successor.

More impossible still is the suggestion that he may have been a son of this second Sir Richard. In this event he must have been junior to Edward, Richard's second son, who was born in 1456; and he could not well have come into the world before 1457. And yet the Richard we are considering was appointed Bishop of St. Asaph in 1468, eleven years after the earliest possible date of his birth under this supposition.

It thus appears that he must have belonged to the same generation as the second Richard of Harewood; and the balance of probability is that, as Colonel Parker was, I believe, the first to suggest, Bishop Richard was a grandson of the Speaker and son of Richard of Bossall.

He appears to have been educated at Cambridge as well as at Oxford, and became later a regular Canon of the Premonstratensian Order in the Abbey of Shap, of which, as we have seen, his ancestors were benefactors, being promoted later to the offices of Abbot and Visitor of the Order. His connection with the Abbey of Shap covered thirty-seven of the best years of his life, during which he worked for it and for his Order with a rare devotion.

There is in the British Museum a transcript of a most interesting register of the Premonstratensian Order which contains a large number of the letters, citations, injunctions, etc., of Richard Redman, when abbot of Shap and visitor of the English province. I venture to reproduce a few from Dr. Gasquet's edition of this register. A large number of similar notes will be found in the Rev. Joseph Whiteside's interesting volume, *Shappe in Bygone Days*, pp. 159 et seq.

Sec. 37. Richard Redman appears on the scene as commissary-general of Simon of Prémontré, 11th September, 1458; he warns the Abbot of Welbeck to present subsidies at the approaching visitation, he will visit Welbeck on the 9th of December, and he is to be met and provided for on the 8th at Papplewick, eight miles north of Nottingham.

38. On March 4th, 1458-9, Simon of Prémontré recalls former commissions to the Abbats of Begham and St. Radegund's and confers powers anew on Redman, *de cujus fide, industria, discretione, prudentia et Ordinis zelo, quem et quas, velut aurum in fornace probavimus.*

In 1466 Redman was appointed Visitor for twelve years; and

about five years later he asks for a renewed commission because the last was much spoiled by the wet, the wax of the seal being reduced to a pulp. Although in 1485 Redman informs Hubert of Prémontré that the English houses are in difficulties, three years later he is congratulated by Herbert that the houses are prosperous, and in the same year after assuring Herbert of his good faith and explaining his difficulties, he adds that he has sent a white ambler, *honestum et preciosum*, but unfortunately pirates had captured it. He sends, however, by bearer, by way of substitute, 20 nobles and asks for a new commission.

In 1488 Redman orders the Prior of Sulby to govern the house in place of the dead Abbot and not to allow any of the canons to go wandering forth and chattering, until he can find time to preside at an election. In October he will be at Cockersand for an election there; all canons must attend and not in the meantime gossip with outsiders.

On March 28th, 1493, while lodging in London, he asks the Abbat of Prémontré not to heed the tales of runaway canons, but to send them back to be dealt with.

On October 26th, 1466, Redman has a protection from the King that he may suffer no harm or violence while travelling, from any envious persons or their accomplices.

Redman seems to have exhibited remarkable zeal in the discharge of his duties as abbot and visitor, and by his example and authority to have infused a healthy spirit into the houses under his control. He must have been an exceedingly busy man, since in addition to his manifold and arduous duties in connection with the abbey and his order he had for many years to conduct all the episcopal work of an important diocese. Indeed he is at times compelled to plead the great pressure of his work; as when he writes that he is "*plurimis et arduis negotiis modo in dies prepeditus*, but he will be at Greta Bridge on February 5th, 1492, on his way to St. Agatha's."

Richard was appointed to the bishopric of St. Asaph in

1468, the licence for his consecration being dated October 1471. During this, his first bishopric, he is said to have restored the cathedral of St. Asaph, which had been partly destroyed by fire by Owen Glendower's fanatical followers, nearly three-quarters of a century before; and to have been implicated in the rebellion of the impostor, Simnel, the Pope himself adjudicating on the charge. In 1492 he was engaged as commissioner in treating with the Scots for peace; and in the following year reached the dignity of membership of the Privy Council. On the death of Dr. Oliver King, bishop of Exeter, Richard was appointed his successor; and, four years later, he was transferred to Ely. This was the last of his many promotions; for after a four years' tenure of the Ely bishopric he died at Ely House, Holborn, on August 24th, 1505.

The following is a brief abstract of the bishop's will, which is dated 18th August, 1505, and is in Latin:—

I bequeath my body to be buried in the Cathedral Church of Ely, near the high altar there, where I have appointed and elected my tomb, and I bequeath 100 li. for the expenses of my burial

Item, for the expenses on the eighth day, 20 li.

For the expenses on the thirtieth day, 30 li.

Item, to each of the four orders of friars in Cambridge, 20s.

To the Prior of Ely, 20s., if he happens to perform the office of exequies and mass on the day of my burial.

To each monk of Ely present at my said exequies and mass, 6s. 3d.

Item, I bequeath to the fabric of the Cathedral Church of Ely, 100 marks.

Item, to be distributed among the poor at my burial, 20 li.

To the Abbess and Convent of Chartres, 40s.

To the Prioress and nuns of Sopham, 20s.

To the Prioress and nuns of Ykleton, 20s.

To the Prioress and nuns of Denhay, 20s.

Item, to the monastery of the Blessed Mary Magdalene of Heppa, over which I now rule, all my stock there of oxen and horses, my household utensils, silver and gilt vessels and sums of money remaining there, upon condition that the abbot and convent shall suffer my executors to pay out of such sums of money what they shall think meet to distribute among my kinsfolk and servants, the residue then remaining to the said monastery.

I will that all my domestic or household servants shall receive one year's wages, and meat and drink for six months.

Item, I ordain my executors Master James Hobart, Knight, attorney of our lord the King, John and John, abbots of Wyndham and Terham in the diocese of Norwich, Master William Thornburgh, doctor of laws, Master Leonard Midelton, doctor of decrees, and my nephew, Henry Dukett, my steward and kinsman, and Edward Chambre, my auditor of accounts of the Bishopric of Ely.

Proved 24 October, 1505, by John, Abbot of Wymondham, and Edward Chambre, with power reserved, etc. (P. C. C. Holgrave 38.)

The Bishop was buried in Ely Cathedral, where a magnificent altar-tomb perpetuates his memory. Of this tomb Cole (MS. 41, p. 113) gives the following description:—

On the south side of the altar-tomb are three coats: 1. Gules, two keys endorsed and a sword run through them, all en saltire, or; the original arms of the see of Exeter; 2nd. in a larger shield the arms of Bishop Redman, 1st and 4th, gules, 3 cushions ermine, tassels or, 2nd and 3rd. gules, a lion rampant argent, 3rd, gules, 3 coronets, or, for the see of Ely. At the foot of the altar-tomb, a very small coat of Ely bishopric. On the other side of it half Redman, viz.: 3 cushions and a lion rampant under them, impales Exeter as before; on the other side, half of Redman, as before, impales Ely.

Dr. William Redman, Bishop of Norwich.

Nearly a century after the death of Richard, Bishop of Ely, there died another Redman bishop—who, from his arms, also appears to have sprung from Harewood, although his connection with that branch of the family has not, I believe, yet been traced—to whom the Calendar to the State Papers contains this reference:—

1602, October 15. Dr. Redman, Bishop of Norwich, is dead— "one of the wisest of his coat."

Dr. William Redman, Bishop of Norwich, was the only son of John Redman, of Great Shelford, Cambridge, and Margaret, his wife. He entered Trinity College, Cambridge (of which, by the way, one of his family, Dr. John Redman, was the first Master), in 1558, and took his bachelor's degree five years later. In 1571 he was appointed rector of Ovington, Essex. In 1589 he became Canon of Canterbury, and, after other preferments, was appointed Bishop of Norwich in 1594. He married Isabel Calverley, who survived him eleven years; and died in 1602, leaving four sons and as many daughters. He was one of the executors of Archbishop Grindal, of York and Canterbury. (Corpus Athenæ Cantab., Nat. Dict. Biog., etc.)

Many members of the bishop's family are buried in the church of Great Shelford, and the abundant information given in their epitaphs, which follow, make it easy to construct this pedigree:—

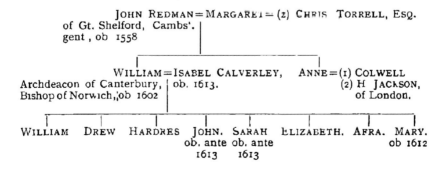

The following epitaphs are in the church of Great Shelford, Cambridge. Against the north wall:—

Of your charyte pray for the sowle of JOHN REDMAN, which decessed the XXVIII day of September, Ao D'ni M⁰V⁰LVIII, and lyeth here buryed under this stone, whose soule God p'do'.

Here lyeth interred expecting a joyfull resurrection, the mortal part of ISABEL REDMAN, widowe, late wife of the reverend father WILLIAM REDMAN, Lord Bishop of Norwich, to whome she brought 4 sonnes, William, Drew, and Hardres surviving, and John deceased; and as many daughters, Sary, Elizabeth, Afra, and Mary, the first and last dying before her. A gentle woman endued in good measure with the blessings of nature, fortune and grace, but especially this last, which enabled her to direct all her actions in piete and patience in this transitory life towards the attaining the aeternall, to which in Christ she was called the VII day of December, in the yeare of grace, 1613. To whose sacred memory her loving sonne, Wm. Redman, Esquire, hath mourninge erected and consecrated this present monument of his sorrow, love and dutye,

---

To the loved memorie of nn deare sister, MARY REDMAN, a young gentealwoman enriched above her age with all maidenly vertues, whom too hasty death in the prime of her yougthe pluckt as a faire flower from the face of the earth to sticke in the bosom of heaven, to which she alwaies aspired, Ao Domini, 1612, and lieth buried in this parish; as also of my brother and sister, JOHN and SARA, who both died infants and are buryed, he in Saint Mary Acte's Church, she in Christ's Church in Canterbury; theyr loving brother, Wm. Redman, Esquire, hath dedicated this testimony of his affection.

Adjoining Arms at the east end of the chancel:—

Az., on a chief erm., a lion rampant. Crest: on a cap of maintenance a lion rampant, issuant.

Monument against the S.E. wall:—

Crest defaced; gules, a cross sable, between four cushions sable, tasseled or.

1615. Beati sunt mortui qui moriuntur in Domino.

To the revered memory of Master JOHN REDMAN, of this Parish, gentleman, and Margaret his wife, after his decease maryed to Christopher Torrell, Esquire, both buryed in this Church, their loving grandchild, William Redman, Esquire, hath dedicated and inscribed this small witness of his greater dutie They had issue one sonne, William, sometime Archdeacon of Canterbury, and after lord bishop of Norwich, married to Isabel Calverly, hereunder intered; one daughter Anne, first married to Collwell, and after to H. Jackson, of London.

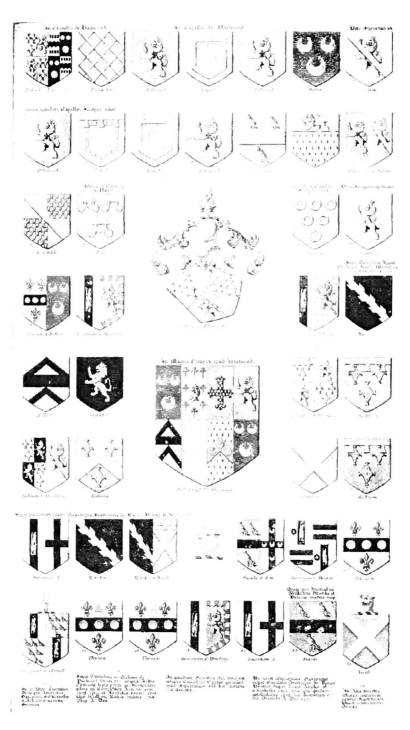

ARMS FORMERLY IN HARWOOD CASTLE AND CHURCH

HAREWOOD MANOR, CASTLE AND CHURCH.

CHAPTER XV.

THE MANOR.

THERE are probably few manors in England which can boast such a long sequence of illustrious lords as that of Harewood, from the Norman Romelli, who must have known the Conqueror, down to the son of the ill-fated Earl of Strafford, who had Redman blood in his veins and who was the last of the line in whom we are immediately concerned.

At the time of Domesday Harewood was as flourishing a parish as any in William's dominions. It had within its boundaries eight townships—Harewood, Alwoodley, East Keswick, Weardley, Wigton, Wike, Dunkeswick, and Weeton,—and it spread itself over 12,180 acres, or more than nineteen square miles of fertile lands. So well cultivated were the Harewood acres in those far-away days that more than two out of every three of them were bearing crops, and of these 1,800 were in the manor of Harewood alone.

When William won his English Throne and began to lavish rewards on his followers it was not likely that so rich a prize as the Harewood lands would long be overlooked. They fell, together with the larger, if less fertile neighbouring fee of Skipton-in-Craven, to the share of

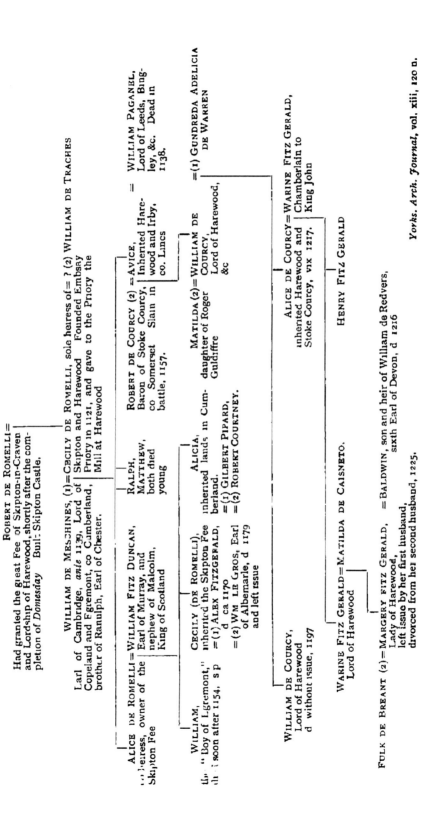

Robert de Romelli, one of William's soldiers. Thus, long before the close of the eleventh century we find the old Saxon lords of Harewood displaced and a Norman warrior reigning in their stead, lord of more splendid possessions than were ever theirs.

Romelli's daughter and heiress, Cecily, married William de Meschines, brother of Ranulph, Earl of Chester, and great-great-nephew of the Conqueror, to whom Henry I. had granted the large Cumberland barony of Copeland, which comprised all the land lying between the rivers Duddon and Derwent and between the lakes Bassenthwaite and Derwentwater. The second generation of Harewood lords thus added to their already vast possessions in Yorkshire a substantial slice of the county of Cumberland.

William and Cecily were not sparing of their wealth, part of which they devoted to the founding and rich endowment of a priory at Embsay; and when William was gathered to his fathers, his widow endowed the priory with more fat lands in honour of her lord's memory. Two sons appear to have been born to Cecily—Ralph and Matthew,—but they must have died young, for she was succeeded in her possessions by her two daughters and co-heiresses, Avice and Alice, each of whom, as was natural to such well-dowered brides, made a splendid alliance.

Alice, who on her mother's death became Lady of the Skipton fee, found a husband in William Fitz Duncan, Earl of Murray, owner of the large Cumberland barony of Allerdale-below-Derwent, and near kinsman to the Scottish King. It was the son of this union, the "Boy of Egremond," who was so tragically drowned in the waters of the Strid in Bolton Woods, and whose untimely end has found such a sympathetic describer in Wordsworth:—

S

> He sprang in glee,—for what cared he
> That the river was strong and the rocks were steep?
> But the greyhound in the leash hung back,
> And checked him in his leap.
> The boy is in the arms of Wharfe
> And strangled by a merciless force;
> For never more was Romelli seen
> Till he rose a lifeless corse

Thus perished Fitz Duncan's only son, the child of great hopes and brilliant expectations, who was not only heir to a small kingdom in lands, but, as second cousin to Malcolm, King of Scotland, and in the same nearness of kinship to Henry II. of England, might even have aspired to a throne. Of his heartbroken mother Wordsworth says:—

> Long, long in darkness did she sit
> And her first words, Let there be
> In Bolton, on the Field of Wharfe
> A stately Priory.

But to return from this digression which has proved irresistible, to the strict line of Harewood lords. It was to Alice's sister, Avice, that Harewood fell with other rich lands; and she took them as dower to Robert de Courcy, Baron of Stoke Courcy, in Somersetshire, who fell in battle at Coleshill, Wales, in 1157. The next Lord of Harewood was William de Courcy, son of Robert and Avice, who married Matilda, a daughter of Roger Guldiffre; and who, after twenty-eight years' tenure of his inheritance, was followed by his son, also William de Courcy, who died without issue a dozen years later, in 1197.

Once more we encounter a lady of Harewood in William's sister, Alice de Courcy, who became the wife of

RUINS OF BOLTON PRIORY
From Drawing by Herbert Railton. TO FACE P. 130

Warine Fitzgerald, chamberlain to King John. Another Warine Fitzgerald followed, son of Alice de Courcy; and in 1208 we find a grant from King John of "free warren in Harewood, and a fair there every year for three days in July. and also a market to be held every Monday for agricultural produce." This second Warine Fitzgerald was succeeded by his only daughter, Margery, who had for husband Baldwin, son and heir of William de Redvers, sixth Earl of Devon, and was left a widow in 1216. According to Matthew Paris the unhappy young widow was forced by King John to marry "that impious, ignoble and base-conditioned man, Falk de Breant," which marriage inspired the following lines by a contemporary poet —

> Lex connectit eos amor et concordia Lecti.
> Sed Lex qualis? Amor qualis? Concordia qualis?
> Lex exlex; amor exosus; concordia discors

During her widowhood Margery granted the mill of Harewood to the church of St. Mary of Bolton, "for the health of my soul, and Warinus, son of Geroldus, my father, and Alice de Curci, my mother"; and to the convent of Arthington she gave a moiety of her lands of Healthwaite, etc. (Harleian MSS.)

Baldwin de Redvers, Margery's son, became, on his grandfather's death, seventh Earl of Devon and Lord of Harewood; and on the death of his son and heir he was succeeded in his enormous estates by his daughter Isabel, wife of William de Fortibus, Earl of Albemarle, who was lord of the Skipton fee, the manor of Harewood and the Craven fee thus being reunited after several generations of severance. Isabel had three sons who died young, and a daughter, Aveline, who, on the death of her parents, succeeded to the earldoms of Albemarle and Devon, to the barony of Skipton, the sovereignty of the Isle of Wight, and the lordship of Harewood. An heiress so richly dowered as Aveline was a prize well worth the winning of a King's son; and thus it came to pass that as a young girl of eighteen, as remarkable for her beauty as for her immense possessions, she was mated with Edmund Plantagenet, afterwards Duke of Lancaster, Henry III's son, the King and Queen and almost all the nobility being present at the wedding. Thus for a few years there was a Royal lord of Harewood; but Aveline's tenure of her vast estates was short, and dying without issue, they passed into other hands.

Harewood found its next lord in Robert, Lord de Lisle, of Rougemont, a lineal descendant of Alice de Courcy and Warine Fitzgerald, who was also lord of many another manor in Cambridgeshire, Oxfordshire and other counties. Robert was father of a valiant son in John de Lisle, his successor in the barony, and to him he gave the manor of Harewood " to enable him the better to serve the King in his wars." Sir John seems to have been a very doughty knight; he fought right gallantly against the French at Vironfosse, was a commander at the seige of Nantes, and saw a great deal of fighting in Gascony and elsewhere.

Sir John was made a banneret, and "for his good services done to King, he granted him a pension of £200 a year for life," to support his new dignity; he was created a baron for valour in battle—some say on the field of Crecy; was made sheriff for life of the counties of Cambridge and Huntingdon, and governor of Cambridge Castle, and all these dignities were crowned by his inclusion in the first batch of Knights of the Garter at the institution of that Order.

On his death, in 1356, from a too well-aimed Gascon arrow, he was succeeded at Harewood and elsewhere by his son, Robert de Lisle, third baron, who after a brief tenure of his dignities and estates died without offspring, leaving a sister and heiress, Elizabeth, whose hand and lands were won by William de Aldeburgh, a gallant knight and trusted friend of Edward Baliol, King of Scotland.

ALDEBURGH.

The family of Aldeburgh, into whose hands the castle and manor of Harewood now came, counted but three generations of any real interest to posterity, but they were generations distinguished by valour and high position. The father of the new lord of Harewood was Ivo de Aldeburgh, a great fighter in his day, with a brilliant record of doughty deeds in the wars waged against the Scots. We find that in 1298 Ivo lost a dark bay horse in a sally made, upon the day of Magdalen, on Nesbit Moor, after the siege of Roxburgh was raised. (Stevenson's Docts., illustrative of Scotland.) He lost another horse valued at 100^s., in a sally at Penyerhocke; and a third charger, this time a dark grey, when supplies were thrown into the Castle of Stirling. In fact, to have Ivo on his back seems to have been almost equivalent to a death certificate to the 13th and 14th century horse.

In Dods. MS. 35 f. 126-135, we find references to the payment of Ivo and his two squires when fighting under Edmund, Earl of Kent; his name figures in the roll of King Edward's followers at Dunfermline and elsewhere in Scotland in 1304—(the list is endorsed " Nomina magnatum qui morabuntur cum domino Rege apud Dumfermelyn in guerra Scoc'"), and again among the "magnates" who served under the King at the siege of Stirling (1304). In the following year he was appointed sheriff of the shires of Edinburgh, Haddington, and Linlithgow; he was a commissioner of array in Tyndale in 1311; in 1321 he was sheriff of Rutland county and custos of the castle of Oakham; and six years later he was treating for peace with Robert Bruce, King of Scotland.

Such was Ivo, father of William de Aldeburgh, who won a well-dowered bride in Elizabeth de Lisle, Lady of Harewood.

William was less conspicuous than his father as a warrior, and is chiefly interesting to his descendants as the friend of Edward Baliol, from whom, as we shall see later, he received large grants of Scottish lands. In 1368 he was sent on a diplomatic mission to Rome, "to treat with Pope Urban V.," and he was summoned to Parliament as a Baron from 8th January, 1371, to 8th August, 1386.

William and Elizabeth de Lisle had three children; a son William, the second Baron Aldeburgh, who, in 1388, was engaged with the fourth Matthew Redman in arraying men-at-arms "for the defence of the realm against the Scots." He married Margery, daughter of Thomas Sutton, of Sutton in Holderness, from whose will I quote later, and died without issue in 1391, his barony falling into abeyance, and his estates going to his two sisters and co-heiresses:—(1) *Elizabeth*, who married (1) Sir Brian Stapleton, and (2) Sir Richard Redman (I.); and (2) *Sybil* who became the wife of Sir W. Ryther, of Ryther Castle.

The following pedigree may be useful in making these descents more clear :—

HAREWOOD MANOR, CASTLE & CHURCH

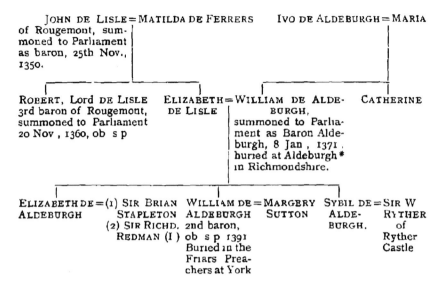

RYTHER.

The family of Ryther which, through Sir William's marriage to the Aldeburgh co-heiress, Sybil, was for so many generations to share the ownership of the castle and manor of Harewood with the Redmans, had for at least two centuries and a half been lords of Ryther on the Wharfe (about two miles from Cawood). As early as 1150 the name of Walter de Rithie appears as witness to the foundation charter of the neighbouring nunnery of Appleton; and Walter was followed by a long succession of Rythers, eminent for their services on the battlefield, in Parliament and in the Church.

One of the greatest of them all was Sir William de Ryther, who was present at the famous siege of Carlaverock (1299).

---

* On the wall of the north aisle of Aldeburgh church there is still to be seen a brass bearing the effigy of an Aldeburgh knight. The only part of the inscription remaining is WILL'S D. ALDEBURGH. From the mixture of plate- and chain-armour on the knight's figure it has been conjectured that the brass must date to a period anterior to 1391 (namely to the date of the first William de Aldeburgh's death)—*Duchetiana*, p. 220

> William de Ridre was there,
> Who in a blue banner did bear
> The crescent of gold so fair.

He fought in Gascony and took part in many a raid into Scotland and affray on the border during the troublous years that ended the thirteenth and opened the fourteenth centuries. He was dubbed knight banneret for prowess on the battlefield, and was summoned to Parliament in 1279 as baron of the realm.

William's son, John, was, according to Dugdale, governor of Skipton castle in 1309. Robert de Ryther, next on the roster, spent his days in exchanging blows with the Scots. His successor, John, was both soldier and diplomatist. He fought with his King (Edward III.) in Picardy, was present at the sieges of Tournay, Vannes and Morlaix; took a brave part in the battle of Sluys, and was in many of the hottest corners at Crecy; and yet, to his honour be it said, this "hero of a hundred fights" would have nothing to do with titles, and carried his scars to the grave of a modest esquire. It was probably the son of gallant William who won the hand of Sybil Aldeburgh and became ancestor of more than two centuries of Harewood lords. The last of the Harewood line of Ryther was James, who died in 1637, and was possibly the last tenant of the castle.

We have now, however imperfectly, traced the long line of the lords of Harewood from the days of the Conqueror down to the verge of the Civil War which, in all probability, closed the "long, eventful history" of their castle. As we have seen, the Redman ownership of a moiety of the manor ceased about the year 1600, when it followed in the wake of the other family estates squandered by Matthew. When and under what circumstances the

ALTAR-TOMB OF SIR. WM. RYTHER, IN RYTHER CHURCH.
By permission of Mr. H. Speight.   TO FACE P. 136.

other moiety passed out of the Ryther hands is at the best a subject for speculation. All that we know is that in some mysterious way, which may someday be made clear, the two moieties were reunited in the family of Wentworth; and, it is said, were carried into that family by Margaret Gascoigne, daughter and heir of Sir William Gascoigne, of Gawthorpe, on her marriage to Thomas Wentworth, high sheriff of Yorkshire.

On this point Whitaker says:—

how or when the property of the Redmaynes terminated at Harewood is uncertain. Henry Redmayne, however, had a daughter and heir, Johanna, married to Marmaduke, fourth son of Sir William Gascoigne, and if the estate was unentailed, one moiety of the manor of Harewood may have accrued to the Gascoignes by that match (we have already seen that it did not.—W.G.) If otherwise, it may have been sold to them by Matthew Redmayne, who also married a Gascoigne The moiety of the Rythers must have been purchased by Gascoigne.

However this may be, it is beyond doubt that the castle and manor of Harewood were among the possessions of Sir William Wentworth, son of Margaret Gascoigne and Thomas Wentworth, and from him they descended to his son, Sir Thomas Wentworth, the great Earl of Strafford, Knight of the Garter, and Lord Lieutenant of Ireland. It is probable that Lord Strafford never made his home in Harewood Castle; he seems to have preferred the more humble, and possibly more comfortable, hall of Gawthorpe, which had sheltered Chief-Justice Gascoigne, his great ancestor, two centuries earlier. It was to this ancestral home of the Gascoignes, which used to stand a few hundred yards south of the present Harewood House and of which to-day no trace remains, that the greatest of all the Wentworths loved to escape from the stress and rancours of public life, there to forget even his ambitions for a time in his passion for rustic peace.

How sincere was his love of this country home we can see from his letters. Indeed this man whose lot was cast in such a turbulent environment was the most domestic of men, who under other conditions would have made an ideal, home-loving country squire. This is how he writes at Gawthorpe on August 31st, 1624:—

Our harvest is all in, a most fine season to make fishponds; our plums all gone and past; peaches, quinces and grapes almost fully ripe, which will, I know, hold better relish with a Thistleworth palate These only we country men muse of, hoping in such harmless retirements for a just defence from the higher powers, and, possessing ourselves in contentment, play with Dryope in the poet:—

> "Et si qua est Pietas, ab acutæ vulnere falcis
> Et pecoris morsu frondes defendite nostras."

In such a strain of rural contentment might Horace have written from his Sabine farm, or Virgil from his father's farm on the banks of the Mincio, and yet when Strafford penned these lines he was on the brink of that turbulent, if splendid career which, after loading him with honours, ended so tragically, seventeen years later, on Tower Hill. And again, in 1636, fresh from his almost regal rule of Ireland, he wrote to Laud from his Gawthorpe retreat:

I am gotten hither to a poor house I have, having been this last week almost feasted to death at York. Lord! with what quietness in myself could I live here, in comparison of that noise and labour I meet with elsewhere; and, I protest, put more crowns in my purse at the year's end, too.

His last thoughts on the scaffold were of his distant Harewood home, and of the family and servants he had left there to mourn him:—

Next, Lord, was his dying prayer, we commend unto Thee that family, that house which is now ready to be left desolate, that wife which by and by shall want a husband, those children which by and by shall want a father, those servants which by and by shall want a master. O blessed Lord, be Thou a husband to that widow, a father to those orphans, be Thou a master to those servants.

After Lord Strafford's execution, Harewood manor with other large estates descended to his son William, who, on the re-establishment of the monarchy, was restored to all his father's honours. This second Earl Strafford, the last of the long line of Harewood lords connected by ties of blood, sold the manor and castle in 1657 to two London merchants, Sir John Cutler and Sir John Lewis. That it was financial embarrassment which compelled Lord Strafford to part with these ancestral possessions is evidenced by two letters from his lordship to Cutler, asking for an advance of the purchase money, in one case "for the redeeming of some Jewells and towards ye somme y^t. Coll Bright is to have, and this must necesarylie be done to-day."

The advertisement of the sale is so interesting that I am tempted to quote the following passages from it:—

10th Novemb., 1656.

A particular of the castle and mannor of Harwood, conteyneinge the mannor of Gawthorpe and divers lands, tenem^{ts} and hereditam^{ts} hereafter mentioned, in the county of Yorke, belonging unto the Right Hono'ble Will'm Earle of Strafford:

The Castle decaied.

The seigniory noble, of a great extent, though formerly greater before the out parts thereof was cutt of.

The castle of Harwood decaied, yet the stones thereof being much ashler, and the timber that is left fit for building an hansom new house, etc., may save a deal of charges in the stone work, or els (if allowed to tennants of Harwood towne, for repayers and building) would bee very usefull, and necessary and serviceable for that purpose, considering it is a market-towne, . . .

There is a charter for a market to bee held every Munday in this towne of Harwood, wch charter was procured by my late lord of Strafford, about 23 years agoe wth 2 head faires besides a fortnight faier in summer tyme etc. There is a mannor of a great extent, wth court leet and court baron, waives and estrayes and fellon goods, etc., belonging the same, also large comons, the whole Lo^p stored with all kind of wild fowl, the River of Wharfe there affording great store of fishe, as salmon, trout, chevins, oumers and eyles

The Lord of the Mannor being the impropriat^r hath the presentation of the Vicar to the Viccaridge.

In the grounds contained in this particular there is great store of timber, trees and wood, besides the hedge rowes and besides wood to be left for the repayer of houses and mill dames, worth at least 2000£.

The stank or pond att Hollin Hall is well stored with carpes and eyles. The stank or pond at Gawthorpe wth trout, roch, gudgeon and eyles

Then follows a detailed description of Gawthorpe Hall, "the materealls of which house, if sould, would raise 500£ at least," and of the park, garden and orchards.

The court leet and court baron, it is explained, extended over the following townships:—Harewood, East Keswick, Wike, Wigton, Weardley, Weeton-cum-Wescoehill, and Dunkeswick.

The sale was completed on the 16th June, 1657, and the parties to it were, on the first part, the Rt. Hon. William, Earl of Strafford; Thomas Chichiley, of Wimpole, in the county of Cambridge, esquire; John Rushworth, of Lincoln's Inn, esquire; and John Morris, of London, gentleman. On the second part, John Cutler, of London, esquire; on the third part, John Lewis, of London, esquire; and on the fourth part, George Lulls, of the Middle Temple, London, gent., and William Daynes, of London, gent.

The price stipulated was as follows:—

	£	s.	d.
Harwood, Gawthorpe, Loftus or Lofthouse, Weardley, Weeton, Dunkeswick, Huby, Nuby, Wescoe Hill, Swindon, Rigton, Broad Elves, Wigton, Alwoodley, East Keswick, Keirby, including the Rectory of Harewood, the Great Tythes, and the Advowson of the Parish Church.	25,347	18	8
Shadwell and Wike	2,680	3	6

With Sir John Cutler, into whose hands Harewood came and to whom reference is made later, we have little concern. He seems to have made his home at Gawthorpe Hall, where he led a life of miserly seclusion attended by one old servant. Maude in his *Verbeia* says:—

> Thither by whim or thrift was Cutler led
> To scanty viands and his thrice-laid bed,
> Where spidered walls their meagre fate bemoaned
> And Misery, the child of Avarice, groaned.

He died in 1693, devising his estates to his daughter, Elizabeth, wife of the Earl of Radnor, with remainder to his relative, John Boulter, esquire, who succeeded to the estates on the death of the countess, three years later, without issue.

The new owner of Harewood, who also lived at Gawthorpe Hall, proved, according to Thoresby, to be "a most worthy gentleman," and charitable withal. After his death the manor with its appurtenances was sold, in 1738, by his son's trustees, to Henry Lascelles, Esquire, whose son and successor in the ownership was created Baron Harewood, in 1790; and on his death, without issue, five years later, it passed to his cousin, Edward

Lascelles, Esquire, who was created in succession Baron Harewood, Viscount Lascelles, and Earl of Harewood. To-day the lands and ruined castle, whose history and varied fortunes we have traced through more than eight centuries, form part of the large possessions of his descendant, Henry Ulick Lascelles, fifth and present Earl of Harewood.

The Castle.

The famous Yorkshire castle, which was the home of six generations of Redmans, has for more than two centuries been a dismantled ruin—which, however noble in its decay and however picturesque, is but a pathetic reminder of long-gone days when it so proudly dominated the broad lands of which its lords were masters.

There seems to be some probability that there was a castle on the same site at a period not very long after the Conquest. Camden speaks of one, of which the "Curcies" were lords in the days of Stephen, when stout baronial castles rose in hundreds in every part of England; and, as some evidence of the existence of this earlier structure, King, in his *History of British Castles*, gives drawings of two windows, which once formed part of the present building and the design of which clearly indicates Norman architecture. Of the nature of this alleged parent castle we can only speculate. If it existed, it no doubt had its day of pride and strength, and ultimately yielded its place to the castle which William of Aldeburgh, according to the accepted opinion, built about the middle of the fourteenth century as a fitting home for himself and Elizabeth de Insula, his richly-dowered bride.

On this point Mr. Speight says, in his fascinating volume, *Lower Wharfedale* :—

Neither in charter, fine nor inquisition can I find any distinct mention of a *castrum* at Harewood before the acquisition of the manor through the marriage of Sir William de Aldeburgh with the heiress of the de Lisles, or Insula, in 1365. In a charter of the Prior of Bolton, dated 1352, respecting a chantry of six chaplains in the church of Harewood, John de Insula, to whom the grant is made, is described as "Lord of Rougemonte," and there can be little doubt that the ancient moated manor-hall of Rougemont, on the north bank of the river, remained the seat of the lords of Harewood down to the change of ownership in 1365. Moreover in the year following, 1366, Sir William de Aldeburgh obtained licence to crenelate his manor of Harewood, and this is the first distinct information of a castellated building within the manor

Whatever may be the truth of this matter, our immediate concern is with the castle which probably came into existence five and a half centuries ago, and with which the Redmans were so long identified. Few of our English castles occupy a more picturesque or dominating position. Built on a long declivity sloping down to the southern banks of the Wharfe, it commands a prospect of almost unrivalled beauty. Beneath it spreads the beautiful valley of the Wharfe, far away to the north-west the horizon is bounded by the hills of Craven, to the east the lovely country stretches towards York, while immediately to the south is the picturesque village of Harewood, six miles removed from the smoke and bustle of Leeds.

The castle, as built by William of Aldeburgh, consisted of a large, square tower, with massive walls ranging in thickness from 6 feet in the less exposed parts to $9\frac{1}{4}$ feet on the east and more vulnerable side. The dimensions of the tower are:—on the north, 54 feet; south, 67 feet; east, 111 feet; and on the west, 123 feet. "The north face, which is plain and without projecting towers, contains three storeys, of which the two lower are lighted only by narrow loopholes, while the uppermost had large, square windows, divided by a mullion and transom. The south front, which is also the loftiest, has a tower at each corner which projects half its breadth from the main wall." Such briefly is the external aspect of this castle of Harewood, which seems to have relied for its security chiefly on the height and strength of its massive walls of freestone. It is probable, however, that this tower by no means represents the whole of the castle in its prime, and that a large portion of the original structure has disappeared.

On this point Jewell says :—

The extent of the castle when entire must have been very considerable, for we now observe a great quantity of ground around the remaining building covered with half-buried walls and fragments of ruins. Dr. Story was at Harewood in 1790; he made mention of this castle, not doubting that it had been a place of great note, aud pointed out many places which had been adjoining, but now in ruins and buried in the grass.

The principal entrance to the castle was beneath a square turret on the east side. Over the portcullised gateway, lofty enough to admit a knight on horseback, may still be seen the predestinarian motto of the founder of the castle, VAT SAL BE SAL, flanked on the right by the Aldeburgh arms of the rampant lion charged with a fleur de lys on the shoulder, and on the left by the arms of Edward Baliol, King of Scotland,—an orle. There has been much speculation as to the relations between Baliol and the Aldeburghs, the intimate character of which is so abundantly attested. Not only do his arms appear thus prominently displayed over the main entrance to the castle, but they were to be seen on three shields within its walls, and even on the tapestry in its chambers. The

widow of the second Lord Aldeburgh mentions in her will (as we shall see later) "one red tapestry with crimson border, with the arms of Baliol and Aldeburgh"; and she also bequeaths "one best bassinett with head, also one cuirass which was Ed. Baliol's"; all of which is eloquent evidence of the prized friendship which must have existed between the Scottish King and the family of Aldeburgh.

Indeed there is abundant evidence in the Records of this intimacy. William de Aldeburgh, the first, was an esquire of the body and confidential friend of Baliol. He is described by Edward III. on several occasions as "Valettus of our beloved and faithful cousin, Edward Baliol, King of Scotland," (Rot. Scot. 24 Ed. III., m. 1)—"Valettus" being equivalent to what afterwards was designated 'gentleman of the privy chamber' or 'esquire of the body' about the person of the King." (*Dutchetiana*, p. 223). He acted as Baliol's trusted ambassador to the English King, and received from him large grants of lands, including "divers castles and manors in Galloway."

When Edward Baliol, after his brief tenure of the Scottish throne, retired to Wheatley, near Doncaster, to end his days there, it is more than probable that frequent visits were interchanged between the exiled King and Sir William Aldeburgh—indeed we find the latter at Wheatley witnessing the charter by which Baliol ceded to Edward his castle and town of Helicourt in Veymont; and it is quite conceivable that Baliol was among the first to see his arms, fresh from the chisel, displayed over the gateway of Harewood Castle.

But to return to the castle. Immediately over the gateway was the chapel in which may still be seen faint traces of the sculptured arms of Sutton, Aldeburgh,

Baliol, Vipont and many another ancient family with which in its prime it was richly embellished. Passing through the principal entrance we find ourselves in the great hall—nearly 55 feet long and 29 feet wide—in which for three centuries the lords of Harewood entertained their guests, held their courts, and administered justice. This hall is chiefly notable for a canopied recess which was for long mistaken for a tomb, until Whitaker proved that it was really nothing more gruesome than a sideboard which must have done excellent service during centuries of banqueting. "If it is a tomb, whose is it?" Dr. Whitaker pertinently asks. "Certainly not the supposed founder of the castle, for he was buried in the Parish Church. Besides, who ever dreamt in those days of being interred in unconsecrated ground? or what heir would have permitted so incongruous a circumstance in a scene of conviviality?"

This recess is in the west wall. "The beautifully crocketted canopy," Mr. Speight says, "is enclosed in a rectangular frame of carved stone. The foils of the arch are cusped, plain, with leaf ornaments in the spandrils, and there is an excellently wrought vignette of foliage at the base, terminated in mask-heads. One must lament the decay of so beautiful and unique an example of fourteenth century sculpture, now a prey to the elements."

But fascinating as the subject is, there is no space to describe further in detail the architecture of this ancient castle, with its many chambers, its winding staircases, and passages, its dark dungeons, its mysterious vaults, its parapets and sally-ports; and we can only afford a hasty and fearful glance at the neighbouring Gallows Hill, on which the lords of Harewood strung up the victims of their summary justice in days when they had the power of life and death within their small kingdom.

SIDEBOARD IN THE GREAT HALL OF
HAREWOOD CASTLE.   TO FACE P. 146.

HAREWOOD MANOR, CASTLE & CHURCH.

The castle appears to have been rich in heraldic embellishment. The following is a list of the arms "in stained glass and graven in stone on the walls of the castle and chapell," as seen and thus recorded by Glover, in 1584, during the occupation of the last of the Harewood Redmans:—

(1) *Redman*—gules, 3 cushions ermine, buttons and tassels, or; and *Daincourt*—arg. a fess dancetté, between 8 billets, or.
  This shield appears really to have been Redman, quartering Aldeburgh, impaling Daincourt, quartering Strickland.

(2) *Huddleston*—gules, a fret or.
(3) *Aldeburgh*—gules, a lion rampant, charged with a fleur de lys.
(4) *Baliol*—gules, an orle, arg.
  Nos. 3 and 4 were in the Chapel.
(6) *Ryther*—az. 3 crescents, or.
(7) *Sutton*—az. a lion rampant, or, under a bend gobony, arg and gules.
(8) *Aldeburgh*—see No. 3.
(9 & 10) *Baliol*—see No. 4.
(12) *Thwenge*—arg. a fess gules, between 3 popinjays vert, collared, or.
(13) *Bordesley* (or *Grauncester*)—ermine, on a chief, a lion passant, guardant.
(14) *Aldeburgh* and *Sutton*—see Nos. 3 & 7.
  The last four shields were, according to Glover, "graven in stone on the walls in the Chappel"
(15) *Constable*—quarterly, gules and vair, over all a bend or.
(16) *Ross*—gules, 3 water bougets, argent.
(17) *Vipont*—gules, six annulets, or, 3, 2 and 1.
(18) *Galloway*—arg. a lion rampant, az. crowned or.
(19) *Redman* quartering *Aldeburgh*, with the Redman crest—"in the great chamber of Harwood Castle." (Glover).
(20) *Ryther*, with his quarterings, surmounted by the Ryther crest, a crescent This shield, Glover says, "was made in a scucheon in metall sett up in the great chamber at Harwoode." (Harl. MSS. 1394, fo. 329).

Such, then, is a brief and inadequate presentment of Harewood Castle in the days of its prime, when mailed feet trod its corridors and parapets, and gallant knights sallied forth from its gate with their retinue in all the splendid trappings of the age of chivalry. "It is not difficult," Mr. Fletcher says, in his beautifully-produced *History of Yorkshire*, "to imagine the scenes which must have centred round it in the days when knights and squires and men-at-arms rode up the steep road from the valley to enter through the portcullised gateway." But it is not so easy to conjure up a vision of the domestic life of this grim castle,—of the fair ladies in cowl and wimple, butterfly or steeple head-dress, in cloaks gay with armorial bearings, and richly-trimmed petticoats, and all the successive vagaries of the female fashion of three centuries; and of the furnishings of the rooms in which they lived and moved.

If I yield to the temptation of quoting liberally from the will of Margery, widow of the second Lord Aldeburgh (made in 1391), it is with the object of supplying some material from which it may be possible to construct a fairly reliable picture of the internal equipment of the castle at the time when the great Sir Richard Redman went there to woo his Aldeburgh bride. The picture suggested is one of rich colouring, refinement and luxury, such as one is scarcely prepared to associate with the grim environment of a medieval fortress.

> I give and bequeath to Peter Mauley, my son, one cup of silver, with a lid bearing the arms of Mauley and my father. Item, one silver gilt *fatte* with a gilt lid, also one gold ring with a fair diamond; also two beds, one of crimson and black with white and red roses, with three coverlets, two blankets and two linen sheets, the other bed of Northfolk work with foxes, with four coverlets, two blankets

and two sheets. Also to the same, one red tapestry with crimson border, with the arms of Baliol and Aldburgh. Also to the same, seven cushions of scarlet. Also to the same, one doublet with breastplate. Also to the same, one *jak* of defence closed with black velvet.

Also I give and bequeath to John Mauley, my son, £40, one bed of scarlet embroidered with a tree and unicorn, with *(cellatura)* and tester, three curtains, three scarlet coverlets, two blankets and two sheets. Also another bed of crimson and grey with vine leaves, two blankets and two sheets; also another bed of green and grey, with birds and rabbits; also one white dotted pillow; and one cup of silver with a lid, with the arms of Sutton and Aldburgh on the knob of the lid.

Also I give and bequeath to Constance, my daughter, £40; also one pair *(lacqueorum)* and one fillett of pearl of one suit, also one fillett of pearl with one treyl of roses, also one other fillett of pearl with 5 leaves, also 200 pearls of which any one is worth 6d., and 100 of which any one is worth 1d. Also one scarlet gown trimmed with ermine, with a hood of the same suit, also a red cloak with hood, one cloak of scarlet trimmed with mynevor, one red tunic with scarlet sleeves, one red bed embroidered with a tree and lion lying down, and the arms of Aldburgh and Tillsolf, with four coverlets, cradle, etc etc

Also I give and bequeath to Elizabeth de Mauley, my daughter, 200 pearls of one suit, one green bed with red fret work six coverlets etc, also one coverlet of green and gold with lions. Also I give and bequeath to Peter de Mauley, my son, one precious red pillow, with the arms of Scotland, etc. Also I give and bequeath to Elisot, my housekeeper, £40; to Maria, my husband's nurse, one scarlet gown furred with gris, to the Friars Preachers at York, to build a tower, one mantle furred with mynevor, also one green cloak similarly furred, with two furred hoods of the same work.

Also I bequeath to Constance, my daughter, a red chest with the arms of Mauley and Sutton painted upon it. Also I bequeath to Peter Mauley, my son, one best bassinett with head, also one cuirass which was Ed. Baliol's, also armour for the arms, legs and feet, also gauntlets for the hands; also I bequeath to Constance, my daughter, two new napkins of Parisian work, and one pair of gloves of the same work. Also I bequeath to Elizabeth de Stapylton one gold ring inscribed, "Jesu be my help,"

There is little doubt that Harewood Castle had tenants for some years after it ceased to shelter a Redman; and it is established that in 1657 when it was sold by the second Earl of Strafford to the two London merchants, Sir John Lewis and Sir John Cutler, it had fallen into such a condition of decay and ruin that, as we have seen, it was actually advertised for sale as so much building material. By what evil chance it had thus been reduced within a few years from a noble and stalwart castle with the prospect of centuries of useful existence, to a pile of stone and timber fit for nothing but "saving a deale of charges in the stonework" of the builder of a "hansom house &c." can only be conjectured.

It may, in Camden's opinion, have suffered, as so many brave castles did, during the war between King and Parliament which was waged so fiercely at Tadcaster and elsewhere, almost within sight of its walls; or it may have shared the fate of the Yorkshire castles which were dismantled and left ruined in the spring months of 1646. However this may be, we can point the finger to one vandal who continued, and with still less justification, this work of destruction; and that was the ex-London apprentice, Cutler, who, instead of preserving the historic building it had been his privilege to purchase, robbed it of stone and timber to build his farmhouses and cottages. Even to-day they will show you in Harewood village a cottage which bears unmistakeable evidence of having been built from castle stone, and which flaunts over its doorway the initials J. C. with the date 1678.

It was this old rascal on whom Pope emptied the vials of his satire in the following lines:—

> Cutler saw tenants break and houses fall
> For very want; he could not build a wall.
> His only daughter in a stranger's power,
> For very want; he could not pay a dower.
> A few gray hairs his rev'rend temples crown'd
> 'Twas very want that sold them for a pound.
> What ev'n deny'd a cordial at his end,
> Banished the doctor and expelled the friend?
> What but a want, which you perhaps think mad,
> Yet numbers feel, the want of what he had!
> Cutler and Brutus, dying, both exclaim
> 'Virtue and wealth! what are ye but a name?'

Later attempts, it is said, were made to use the castle material for building and repairing, but it was found that the walls were so firmly welded by the cement that it was really cheaper to quarry the stone. Nature has been kinder than man to this grand old fabric, for she has thrown round it a mantle of ivy and has thus invested it in its decay with an external beauty which it never boasted in its sturdy prime.

The Church.

About half-a-mile westward from Harewood village is the ancient church in which several generations of Redmans are sleeping their last sleep within their own "Redman chapel." There seems to be a strong probability that the original church was venerable before the walls of the neighbouring castle began to rise; indeed the date of its foundation has been suggested as 1116, while Robert de Romelli was probably the living lord of Harewood manor.

Jewell, in his History of Harewood, says:—

In the year 1793 (he was living at Harewood at the time and speaks of what he probably saw) when the church was new-roofed, was found on an old beam the following inscription cut in ancient characters, which was made away with by the workmen. The English of it was thus.—" We adore and praise thee, thou holy Jesus, because thou hast redeemed us by thy Holy Cross."—Dated 1116.

As Mr. Speight, however, points out, in these early centuries dates were recorded in the year of the reigning monarch, and one must not attach too much importance to the figures carved on this old beam. It has been inferred, too, from this old inscription, that the church was originally dedicated to the Holy Cross, an assumption which may perhaps be accepted as correct.

But without attempting to assign any precise date to the founding of this church, there is no doubt that there was a church at Harewood in the early years of Henry II's reign (*circa* 1160) when Avicia de Romelli, after the death of her husband, Robert de Courcy, gave the church of Harewood towards the support of the chapel of St. Mary and Holy Angels, in York cathedral.

Dodsworth refers to this gift in the following passage from his MSS. (vol. 129, fo. 59) relating to the

advowson of the Church of Harwode, which Warynus, son of Geroldus and Alice de Curci, his wife, claimed against the monks and chaplains of St. Mary and St. Sepulchre. And the monks come and say that Avicia de Romelli gave that church to the Church of St. Mary, St. Michael, and All Angels, to the sustenance of the monks, and therefore produce the charter of the said Avicia, which testifieth the same, and the confirmation of Roger, Archbishop.

Warine appears to have established his claim; for we find that " Warinus, son of Geroldus, recovered his presentation to the church of Harwode, against the monks and chaplains of St. Mary and St. Sepulchre, at York." (Harl. MSS., vol. 802). For several generations the lords of Harewood dispensed the patronage of the church, until in the days of John de Lisle, of Rougemont (1353), the church was appropriated to the Priory of Bolton-in-Craven on condition that a rent-charge of £100 a year should be granted to him and his heirs out of lands at Rawden, Wigton, and elsewhere, and that a chantry of six priests should be founded at Harewood to sing masses daily for the souls of his parents and brothers and sisters; in addition to a special collect for himself and his children.

At this time the church was evidently of a good age, for provision is made for its repair and the rebuilding of the chancel which had fallen into decay.

It is probable that but little of the original building of Norman days survives in the present church. Dr. Whitaker indeed says:—

The Church of Harewood bears no marks of the original structure. It was probably renewed by the Lords of the Manor about the time of Ed. III., and the figure of John, Lord Lisle, one of the first Knights of the Garter, was remaining entire in the east window of the north chapel, distinguished by the arms of the family, a fess between two chevronels, on his tabard, till the church was repaired, A.D 1793. This nobleman, however, from the style of the building, appears to have been the restorer of the church.

But a detailed history of this old church, however agreeable it might be to attempt it, is beyond the scope of this little book of Redman history. Having established its antiquity and its association with the early lords of Harewood it only remains to refer to the memorials of immediate interest which still survive within its walls.

They were very ruthless hands which were responsible for the repair of the church in 1793, for they seem to have stripped it of many of its most cherished treasures. The stained-glass windows, rich with the armorial achievements of successive lords of Harewood, were wantonly removed to give place to ordinary windows of glass. Dr. Whitaker declares that these heraldic treasures were "deposited in a lumber-room in Harewood House"; but according to Jones, whose evidence on this point, if not on others, may perhaps be accepted,

> old people can recollect its removal. It was indiscriminately taken away, some was secretly sold, the children of the village played with other portions. I have been informed on good authority that some portion of this stained glass found its way into Cheshire, where it adorns (at the present time) the windows of a private chapel, belonging to a gentleman of property.

Even the altar-tombs of Redman and Ryther seem to have been robbed of their canopies; and the altar-rails of carved oak, bearing Lord Strafford's initials, were consigned to some ignominious fate.

The following is a list of the arms in Harewood Church in the days of Elizabeth, as recorded by Glover, Somerset Herald.

(1) *Thwayts*—arg. three torteaux in a fess sable, between 3 fleur de lys; and *Ryther*, az. three crescents, or.

(2) *Gascoigne*—arg on a pale sable a lucy's head, hauriant, or; and *Mowbray*—gules, a lion rampant, arg., within a border gobony, or and sa.

(3) *Gascoigne*, as above; and *Pickering*—ermine, a lion rampant, az, crowned, or.

> These are the arms of Chief Justice Gascoigne, who married (1) Elizabeth Mowbray, and (2) Joan Pickering.

(4) *Manston*—sable, a bend ragulée, arg.

(5) *Lisle*, of Rougemont—or, a fess between 2 chevronels, sable.

(6) *Stapleton*—arg. a lion rampant sable, langued and armed, gules.

(7) *Redman* and *Aldeburgh*.

(8) *Redman*.

(9) *Redman* and *Stapleton*—see No. 6.

> These arms are really Redman, quartering Stapleton and impaling Sutton. Of them Glover says, "a man kneeling in his coat

armour, with Redman's coate on him, and on the woman, this." The "woman" was, no doubt, Elizabeth Aldeburgh, who married (1) Sir Bryan Stapleton, (2) Sir Richard Redman (I.) and whose sister-in-law was Margery Sutton, wife of the second Lord Aldeburgh.

(10) *Redman.*

(11) *Rylstone*—sable, a saltire, arg.

(12) *Gascoigne* and . . . . .

(13) *Manston*—see No. 4; and *Neville,* gules, a saltire, arg.

(14) *Franke*—gules, a fess sable, between 3 martlets, arg; and *Ellis*—on a plain cross, sable, five crescents arg.

(15) *Gascoigne*—see No. 2; and *Heaton*—arg. two bars sable.

(16) *Thwayts*—see No 1.

(17) *Gascoigne*—see No. 2; and *Clarell*—gules, six martlets, arg, 3, 2, & 1.

(18) *Franke,* of Alwoodley Hall. See No. 14.

(19) *Nevill*—sec No. 13

The church of Harewood is singularly rich in the number and magnificence of its altar-tombs, which have come down to us through four or five centuries in a remarkable state of preservation, in spite of the sacrilegious hands which have tried to mutilate them and have carved names and initials on them as memorials of their vandalism.

Of the six altar-tombs three are of peculiar interest to students of Redman history.

Under the arch on the north side of the chancel is a magnificent tomb, a photograph of which I reproduce, to the memory of Sir Richard Redman (I.), the Speaker, and his first wife, Elizabeth Aldeburgh, on which are cumbent figures of the knight in his armour, with crested helmet, sword and dagger; and of his lady in pleated gown with loose sleeves, with arched head-dress, necklace and ringed fingers, and angels at her cushioned head. Of this tomb Glover, who saw it in 1585, wrote:—

In Harewood Church, north aisle, belonging to Harewood Castle, an altar-tomb, effigies of a knight and lady cumbent, his head on helmet, and crest, a horse's head, which denotes it to have been a Redman; feet on lion, on which sits a monk with beads, against which sole of the right foot rests.

Under the arch in the south wall of the chancel is a tomb to the memory of the same Sir Richard, who here lies side by side with his second wife, Elizabeth Gascoigne. On this tomb, which is also reproduced, Sir Richard appears in armour, but shorn of the sweeping moustache which adorns him on the former tomb, with flowing hair and with hands upraised in an attitude of prayer; while his lady, with hands similarly raised, wears a wimple and carries a rosary. The tomb exhibits a remarkably fine series of sculptured saints, which Gough, in his "Sepulchral Monuments," declares to be the finest he has seen.

Adjoining this latter tomb is that of Sir William Gascoigne, the famous Chief Justice, and his wife Elizabeth, daughter of Sir Alexander Mowbray, of Kirklington, co. York; so that Elizabeth Gascoigne "lies in sculptured calm" between her husband and her father. Around the tomb, which is not less splendid than its companions, there was once, according to Dodsworth, a Latin inscription which may be translated thus:—

Here lies William Gascoigne, late Chief Justice of the Bench of Henry IV, late King of England, and Elizabeth, his wife. Which William died on the 17th day of December, A.D. 1419.

> Gascoigne, thy tomb a fitting altar is
> Whereon to swear the patriot Englishman,
> When he devotes him to his country's cause.
> Reverently kneeling by this hallowed marble,
> He shall recall thy resolute worth and draw
> New virtue from the holy recollection.

ALTAR-TOMB OF CHIEF-JUSTICE SIR WM. GASCOIGNE,
IN HAREWOOD CHURCH.

By permission of Mr. H. Speight.

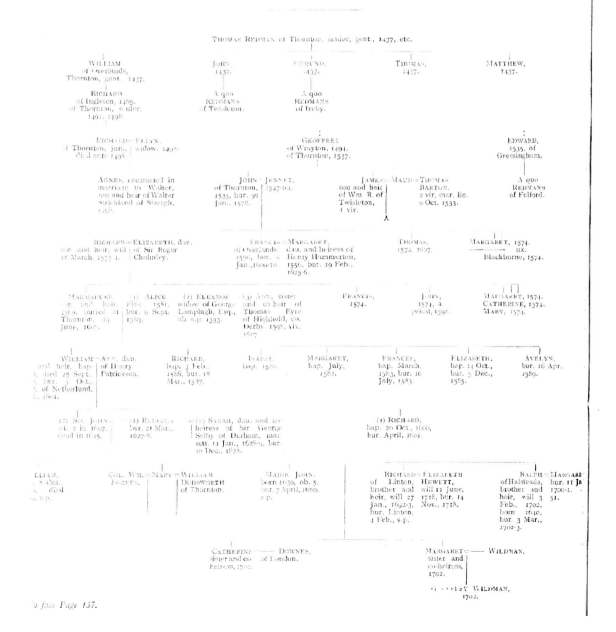

REDMANS OF THORNTON-IN-LONSDALE

CHAPTER XVI

IN leaving Harewood and Levens for Thornton-in-Lonsdale we turn our backs on the stirring epoch of Redman history, when each generation produced its soldiers, its politicians, its diplomatists, or its churchmen who played their respective parts in the national drama of their time, and enter on a period of placid, uneventful days when the Redmans, with a few notable exceptions, were content to lead the simple lives of country squires and to leave behind them records marked principally by births, marriages and deaths, and the conduct of their estates

Such chronicles naturally possess little general interest, even for those more directly concerned with the story of the family they but serve as material for fashioning pedigrees, and for this reason a detailed account of all the individual members of the different branches in this district would make rather dreary and profitless reading The accompanying pedigrees, which have been most carefully compiled from the original records and for which I am indebted to the kindness of Colonel Parker, are exceedingly valuable They contain all the information that is at all necessary about most of the Redmans of this colony, and I propose simply to supplement them by notes of more particular interest on the prominent names they include.

It still remains to discover with certainty the origin of the colony of Redmans which settled near the Lancashire border of Yorkshire in the fourteenth century, and which flourished there for more than three hundred years. As has been shewn earlier, in 1359 the third Sir Matthew Redman, and Margaret, his wife, gave twenty marks for the custody of the manor of Twisleton, in this district, which had belonged to John, of Twisleton, and for the marriage of his daughters.

It is conceivable and even probable that this transaction led to marriage between one or more of Matthew's sons and one or more of the Twisleton heiresses, and that thus the family of Redman got its first footing in this part of Lonsdale. There appears to be no evidence in actual support of this view; but it is precisely what one might expect to happen, and is the most plausible explanation of the planting of this colony.

It is in 1379 that we find the first recorded evidence of a Redman living in this neighbourhood. In the list of those who paid the poll-tax levied on the accession of Richard II., in the wapentake of Ewecross, we find the following entry under Ingleton—"Johannes de Redmane, Armatus, vjs viijd,"—this being the sum at which an esquire was commonly rated. It is possible that this John Redmane was a son of Matthew (III) of Levens, and husband of one of the daughters of John Twisleton, whose manor was close to Ingleton. He was not, however the only member of his family in the district at this time, for there was a Richard Redman just over the border, who figures in the Lancashire Poll-tax of the same date, under Lonsdale; and as early as 1332 there was a John Redman at Farleton, and Norman at Broghton.

Between 1379 and 1416 the history of the Thornton Redmans is dark; but in the latter year we emerge into the light, and for three centuries the story of the family is told by abundant evidences.

In 1416 THOMAS Redman, of Thornton, witnessed the deed of assignment by William Tunstall, of his castle of Thurland in Lancashire, and other lands in Yorkshire and Westmorland. (Dods. MS. 62, fo. 2). It was to him, in conjunction with Sir Richard Duket, of Grayrigg, that (in 1427) was granted the custody of the moiety of the manor of Harewood during the minority of his young kinsman, Richard, grandson of the Speaker. Ten years later "Thomas Redman, senior, of Thornton, gentleman," William, Thomas Jr, John, Edmund and Matthew Redman, together with Christopher Middleton, of Ingleton, were parties to a bond (dated 15th March, 20 Hen. VI.) by which they were bound in 200 marks each to stand the award of William, Lord Fitz Hugh and Henry Bromflete, concerning all actions, disputes, &c., between the said Thomas and others on the one part and the said Henry on the other part.

This was probably some family dispute respecting Tunstall property; it is not improbable that the wife of Thomas Redman was a Tunstall. Sir Henry Bromflete, afterwards Lord Vescy (1449) had married Eleanor, daughter of Henry, Lord Fitz Hugh, after the death of her first husband, Sir Thomas Tunstall, whose sister, Johanna, was wife to Sir Matthew Redman, of Harewood.

The relation of these Redmans (Colonel Parker says) is not definitely proved, except that William was son of Thomas, senior. I believe, however, they were related as placed in the pedigree, and that Christopher Middleton married a daughter of Thomas, senior, and in this way was mixed up in the family feud. In later disputes Matthew is described as "of Lancaster", and in 1472 he appears as administrator of the goods of Elizabeth Curwen (late wife of John Curwen) who died intestate.

There was also about this time a Giles Redman, who was probably either son or brother of Thomas, senior. He was instituted rector of Bentham, 10th May, 1443, on the presentation of Margaret Pickering, and was inducted by John Grene, rector of Thornton. Thomas Redman, of Thornton, junior, may have been the Thomas Redman who was appointed Vicar of Whittington, 30th March, 1440.

WILLIAM Redman, who is described as "of Overlandes in Thornton, gentleman," in 1437, and as "of Lund," twelve years later, probably figures with his son Richard in the following romantic incident, the story of which is told in the Lancashire Plea Rolls (No. 31. Lent 7 Ed. IV., m. 5 d.):—

Nicholas Gardener and Katherine, his wife, who was wife of Carburie (?), armiger, by attorney came and offered themselves against William Redman, of Thornton-in-Lonsdale, Co. York, armiger, and Richard Redman, of Ingleton, in the Co. York, son of William Redman, armiger, in a plea of wherefore they by violence and arms seized and carried off John, son and heir of the aforesaid Catherine, to his loss and damage and against the King's peace. The assault took place at Pulton-in-Lonsdale. As these Redmaynes did not appear, order was given that they should be attached; but as the sheriff did not issue the writ, they are to be attached on the day next the Assumption of the Blessed Mary.

William, evidently the ringleader in this high-handed proceeding, which we learn was conducted with swords, bows and arrows, was duly attached later. (No. 33, m. 18).

William's successor, RICHARD, is described in 1465 as son of Wm. Redman, of Ingleton, Esq.; and in 1499 as "of Thornton, senior," when he was engaged in a dispute with John Preston, of Preston Hall. He had two sons, of whom the elder, Richard, died during his father's lifetime sometime before 1498, in which year Ellen Redman, described as his widow, covenanted (in company with John Preston, probably a near kinsman) with Walter Strickland for her daughter Agnes's marriage According to Lady Edeline Strickland ("Sizergh Castle, &c." Genl. Notes) it was Sir Walter Strickland, whose birth year she gives as 1497, who married Agnes, daughter of Richard Redman, at a time when, if her dates are correct, he must still have been playing with his toys. It seems more probable that the contemplated bridegroom of the 1498 covenant was the father of this Walter, who was born in 1460, and died forty years later. It will be remembered, perhaps, that Sir William Redman, of Harewood, married Margaret, daughter of a still earlier Sir Walter Strickland, in 1458. Lady Edeline gives 1503 as the date of Agnes's death, and there was no issue of the marriage.

Richard had another son, GEOFFREY, who was "of Wrayton," in 1494. He was possibly the "Geoffrey Redman, nuper de Thornton, gentilman," who in 1494-5 was charged with Thomas Gibbonson, Cansfield of Cansfield and others, with breaking houses and taking goods and chattels to the value of fifty pounds. In this feat of mediæval housebreaking, in which let us hope it was really some other Geoffrey who was concerned, bows, arrows and swords were used. In 1533 the supervisors of the will of Thomas Proctor, of Horton, were "The Abbot of Furnace, Mr. Geffray Redman and Mr. John, his son."

Geoffrey, who was still living in 1537, had a son John,

who succeeded him, and a daughter Maud or Matilda, who married, for her first husband, her kinsman, James Redman, of Twisleton; and secondly, Thomas Barton, Esquire, for which marriage a dispensation was granted in 1533. (Letters and Papers, F & D, vol. vi.) "In Broughton church on the chapel screen on the north side is a boar's head and the arms of Thomas Barton and Matilda, his wife, daughter of Geoff. Redman of Thornton, Esq." (Whitaker's *Richmondshire*, vol. ii., p. 423).

JOHN Redman, Geoffrey's successor, appears in 1536 in company with his son and heir, Thomas, on the list of "liberi tenentes" of the honour and manor of Hornby Castle. Among other tenants on the same list are the Abbot of Croxton, the Prior of Hornby, Sir Marmaduke Tunstall, and Francis Morley, Esquire. And in the previous year he was, together with Thomas, son and heir of Sir Thomas Wharton, and John, son and heir of Sir Geoffrey Middleton, one of the trustees of the marriage settlement of Henry, heir of Sir Stephen Hamerton and Joan Stapleton, of Wighill. (Harleian MSS. 804—8 May, 27 Hen. VIII.) He also purchased the manor of Austwick for £230. 14. 11. (Whitaker's *Richmondshire*). John, who married Jennet ——, and who died in 1578, had at least three sons and two daughters.

(1) THOMAS, "the son and heir" in the list of liberi tenentes above-mentioned. It was probably this Thomas who, with his brother Richard, appears in the following extract from the will of Thomas Andrewe, vicar of Melling, dated Oct. 17, 1563:—

Also I put ye boye yt. I have brought upp to Thames (sic) Redman and to Margrett, his wyfe, desyring them to bringe him upp . . . . . he be liable to put to an occupation, and I will that Thames Redman and Margret his wyfe shall gyfe him, when he cometh to ye age of XX yeares, XL^s . . . and I desyre Maister Rycharde Redmayn to be a supervisor of this my will . . . and I gyfe to Maister Redmayn for his paynestakynge X^t.

Thomas appears to have died during his father's lifetime.

(2) RICHARD, who also died before his father, married Elizabeth, daughter of Sir Roger Cholmley, of Roxby, by Katherine, daughter of Sir Robert Constable, who fought at Flodden, was attainted, and was executed at Hull. Through her Constable ancestors Elizabeth Cholmley was descended from the Wentworths, Gascoignes, Fitz Hughs, the Counts of Brittany and the Dukes of Normandy. Her brother was Sir Richard Cholmley, known to fame as the "Black Knight of the North," of whom it is recorded that he "loved pomp, and generally had 50 or 60 servants about his house, nor would he ever go up to London without a retinue of 30 or 40 men." (Foster's *County Families*). He, too, fought gallantly at Flodden; and as captain of Norham Castle defended it against the Scots until the last cannon-ball was fired and the last crust eaten.

Richard's will, of which the following is a summary, is rich in genealogical information. He directs that his body shall be buried in Thornton Church amongst his "ensetors," and that certain debts owing to George Clapame, William Redman, of London Stone, Thomas Reder, parson, of Thornton, and to Sir Richard Cholmelaie, his brother-in-law, shall be paid. He refers to his younger children, Francis, John, Margaret, Catherine, and Marie Redman; directs his son Marmaduke to renew a lease, and leaves him all such land as he is in possession of, to pay his mother her dower and to help his brothers and sisters; refers to his sister, Blackburn, and to his brother, Thomas Redman. "My sonne Marmaduke Redman, Thomas Redman and Francis Redman, my

brethren," he makes executors of his will. Supervisors—
"Mr. John Redman, of Thornton, Esquire, my father, and
Richard Redman of Gressington."

(3) FRANCIS, "of Overlands, 1556," married Margaret,
daughter of Henry Hamerton Esqre, by his wife Joan,
daughter of Christopher Stapleton, of Wighill, Esquire;
and grand-daughter of Sir Stephen Hamerton, Lord of
the manors of Hamerton, Knolsmere, Wigglesworth, Hellifield, Langfield, &c. Sir Stephen was among the Yorkshire knights and squires who flocked to the standard of
Aske and took part in his disastrous Pilgrimage of Grace.
For this act of treason he was hanged, drawn and quartered at Tyburn and his large possessions were forfeited
to the Crown.

His manor of Hellifield came into the hands of Sir
Arthur Darcy, who in the second and third Philip and
Mary, had a licence to alienate it to John Redman, Esq.,
father, as we have seen, of Francis, who had married the
granddaughter of the attainted Sir Stephen; and by fine
levied at Westminster, 3 Elizabeth (1561) the said John
and Francis, and Margaret, wife of Francis, in conjunction
with Anthony Watson, Thomas Watson, and Alice, his
wife, passed the manor to John Hamerton, Esq., son of
Richard, younger brother of Sir Stephen. (Speight's
Craven, p. 362, and Whitaker's *Craven*).

The two daughters of John Redman were Margaret, and
another, married to a Blackburne. On the death of John,
in 1578, he was succeeded by his grandson, MARMADUKE,
son of Richard Redman and Elizabeth Cholmley, who, in
1569, is described as "son and heir" to his father Richard.

In a dispute concerning tenant-right, in 1580, "Marmaduke Readmanne, of Thornton, in the County of York,
Esquire," says that "upon information given unto him

REDMAN ARMS IN WINDOW OF THORNTON CHURCH.

TO FACE P. 164.

immediately after the death of *John Readmanne, his grandfather*, great variance, stryfe, suit, contention and contrariness hath been stirred, moved and had between the said Marmaduke and Rowland Hardye, of Manserghe, Westmorland, his tenant, within his lordship of Manserghe, concerning tenant-right upon a certain ground called Tyrrebanke, part of the inheritance, &c."

Marmaduke had three wives:—

(1) ALICE, who appears in a fine of 1581, and who was buried on the 9th of September, 1589.

(2) ELEANOR, widow of George Lamplugh, Esq. She died without offspring in 1593.

(3) ANN, sister and co-heiress of Thomas Eyre, of Highfield, co. Derby, 1598. She was living in 1607.

Marmaduke figures in the following Chancery proceedings relating to the dower of two of his wives:—

Eyre v. Eyre and Marmaduke Redmayne and Anne, his wife—re manors, &c., in Derbyshire; and Marmaduke Redman v. Patrickson, Fletcher and Lamplough, Cumberland.

" The plaintiff being upon a treaty of marriage with Elinor Lamplough, widow, (since his wife), proposed to settle his own lands and tenements, and she also proposed to make a settlement of her property, but which she was prevented doing by the interference of defendants. (Chancery proceedings. Queen Eliz[th]. Rolls Series, vols. i. and ii.

I think (Colonel Parker writes) that Alice, first wife of Marmaduke, was a Protestant, the other two wives being Roman Catholics; for I find both Marmaduke and his third wife, Anne, in the list of Papists, in 1604, which does not include William, his son by Alice. Marmaduke was a Justice of the Peace in 1585. John, his brother, was a priest (West Riding Sessions Roll, 1598); and Francis and Thomas, his uncles, were both of the old faith. This is probably the reason why the family does not appear in the Visitations.

Marmaduke died in June, 1607, and his burial is thus mysteriously recorded in the Thornton Register :—

June 24 Aº 1607. Marmaduke Readmayne, ar. was Buried upon the nighte by unknown p'sons.

Marmaduke had quite a "quiverful" of children, of whom two sons and five daughters will be found in the annexed pedigree. Four of them appear to have died in infancy. His successor, WILLIAM, was twenty-nine years old on his accession; and he probably married Ann, daughter of Henry Patrickson. A settlement was made for this marriage, but whether it took place or not is not proved. In 1598 she is styled Anna Redman, alias Patrickson, spinster. "Anne, wief of William Readman," appears in the list of Roman Catholics at Thornton in 1604 (Rawlinson MSS., p. 452, Bodleian Liby.); and William Redman, gent, and Ann, his wife, appear in a fine of 1602.

William died on 25th September, 1607, having survived his father only three months, and was buried eight days later. He had two sons—

(1) John, his successor, an infant two years old at his father's death;

(2) Richard, who died in infancy.

The following is a copy of the inquisition taken after his death :—

17 Nov., 1607. Inquisition taken at York Castle, 17 Nov. 5 Jas I. (1607) before John Tayler, Esq , Escheator. after the death of William Readman of Thornton, co York, Esquire

The said William Readman was seized in fee of a Capital Messuage, four other Messuages, eight cottages, another Capital Messuage called Overlandes, 120 acres of arable land, meadow and pasture in Thornton, a water-mill in Thornton; also the Manor of

Wrayton, co. Lancaster, six messuages and 50 acres of land, meadow and pasture in Wrayton; a Capital Messuage called Netherlandes, within the lordship of Burton, co. York.

The Capital Messuage and other the Messuages, etc. in Overlandes and Thornton are held of the King as of his Manor of Thornton, parcel of his honour of Richmond, by Knight's service and 10s. 2½d. rent, and they are worth per annum (clear) £3 11s. The premises in Wrayton are held of William, Lord Monteagle, as of his Manor of Hornby by Knight's service, and by yearly rent of 24s. 4d. and they are worth per annum (clear) 18 shillings. The premises in Netherlandes worth per annum (clear) 10s. are held of William, Earl of Derby, as of his Manor of Burton by Knight's service and by 3s. 4d yearly rent.

William Readman died 25 Sept. last (1607) and John Readman, his son and heir, at the time of his father's death was aged two years and more.

SIR JOHN REDMAYNE.

Of the career of John Redmayne, who was thus left fatherless while still an infant, the Records tell us little, although he was a man of importance in his time. We know that he was dubbed a knight, that he espoused the cause of his Sovereign in the Civil War, that the reward of his loyalty was the sequestration of his estates and that he died (he was probably killed) during the war. His life, the close of which was cast in such stirring times, must have been full of interest; and it is a misfortune that so little of it is revealed to us.

As a matter of fact we know more of the doings of his eldest son and of his son-in-law in the Civil War than of the part Sir John played in it. It was in all probability his heir, William, who was the first to fall among the defenders of Pontefract Castle during its second siege in the spring of 1645.

In Nathan Drake's quaint diary, in which he so faithfully kept a chronicle of the siege, he wrote on "Fridday, the 21th March (1645), about 2 of the clock in the afternoone the Enemy Came in again and took the upp' towne, killd Captin Redma' about the bridge and a souldyer upon the toppe of the Round Tower, and tooke 3 of our men prisoners." The tragedy which robbed this young royalist of life was heightened by the fact that the second siege did not really commence till the following day. He seems to have wandered away from the protection of the castle to the exposed bridge, a quarter-of-a-mile distant, and to have been killed by a random shot.

By a curious irony of fate one of the principal leaders of the besieging army—he appears to have been second in command to Lord Fairfax—was young Redman's own brother-in-law, Colonel William Forbes, the husband of Mary Redman, who played a conspicuous part in the siege. It was he who on the 16th January, 1645, took to the governor of Pontefract castle Fairfax's letter demanding its surrender "without the effusion of blood"; and four days later, having received no anwer, Colonel Forbes wrote the following letter:—

> Sr, I desire to have a positive answer of the Summons sent in upon Thursday last, that I may give an account to my Lord (who is now heare) of your resolutions. likewise I desire to know whether Mr. (Ogales) exchanged for Leiutenant Browne or for money, and if (for money) for what summe.
> Sr. I shall remaine your
> friend, WILL. FORBES.

Not many days earlier he had been slightly wounded: "the 9th being Thursday," Drake writes, "the besieged plaid one cannon again Newhall wheare it broke a hoale into the wall and one of the stones hitt Generall Forbus on the face, but was but a little hurt."

During part of the siege he seems to have been in command of the Parliamentary forces:—" The enemy basely stayd all wine from coming to the Castle for serving of the Communion on Eastre day allthough Forbus (their Governor) had graunted p'tecktion for the same—"; and in the following August we find him so far wavering towards a return to loyalty that he was accused of conspiring with Colonel Fairfax and Major Morris to seize the Castle for the King after its surrender.

Colonel Forbes lived, however, to die in the service of Parliament; while his father-in-law, Sir John, lost his estates, and probably his life, in the opposite cause.

The story of the different attempts of Sir John's widow and children to recover the forfeited lands is told in the following Royalist Composition Papers.

Sir John Redmaine, of Thornton.

No. 482.

G. 203, p. 159. 14 Sept., 1647. PETITION of Mary Forbes, widow of Col. Wm. Forbes, daughter of Sir John Redmain, Knt. that the estate of her father being sequestered for his delinquency, the sequestration not being taken off in his lifetime nor in that of his eldest son, her brother german, the last of them dying above 2 years since, prays to compound for an estate in Lancashire called Wreatoune worth 20 li. per annum descended to her; her husband hath done many good things to the Parliament and lost his life in its service.

Fined 12 Oct., 1647, 40 li

G. 203, p. 160. 13 June, 1649. PETITION to compound for lands in Thornton. Referred to Mr. Reading.

G. 203, p. 157. 26 June, 1649. REPORT.—Sir John Redman was sequestered 1645, his son William died 1645.

Fine at a tenth 140 li. Total fine 180 li.

G. 113, p. 564. 4 June, 1652. PETITION of Dame Sarah Redmaine widow, relict of Sir John Redmaine, that her husband, before his intermarriage with her settled several manors in the Counties of York and Lancaster upon John Brackenbury, Esq. and Thomas Birkbeck, gent. in trust for her jointure, which are now sequestered for his delinquency and the Committee refuse to discharge the same without your order. She prays witnesses be examined and reference to Counsell for her title and in the meantime to receive the profits upon security.

Ordered to certify and refer to Mr. Brereton.

G. 113, p. 562. 23 July, 1652 Further petition that she hath not received any fifth part of the estate towards the maintenance of herself and children, for Francis Dodsworth who is tenant of the Commonwealth refuses to pay it although the same is deducted out of his rent. She prays to receive her fifths.

Ordered to have the fifth.

G 113, p. 557. 20 July, 1653. Further petition that Sir John Redmaine being dead and his name inserted in the last Act for Sale she put in her claim at the Committee of Obstructions for the allowance of the premises which was allowed by the Committee, 31 Mar., 1653. She prays they may be discharged from sequestration and she may receive the rents till her title shall be allowed.

Referred to Mr. Brereton.

G 113, p 555. 26 July, 1653. PETITION of John Redmaine, Esq, eldest son and heir of Sir John to compound for the reversion of his mother's jointure and for the rest of the estate.

Referred to Mr Brereton

G. 113, p. 577. 31 Aug, 1653. The Drury House Committee write to the Commissioners for compounding at Haberdashers' Hall. We find that John Redman hath compounded with you for lands in Thornton formerly the possession of Sir John Redmaine Knt. we give you notice that we proceeded to the sale of the lands 15 July last to William Dodsworth, gent, (no composition being entered here within the 30 days limited in the Act); we further inform you that we are told that the party whom you have admitted to compound is neither heir nor assignee of his father, and that the said Dodsworth's wife is heir to William Redman, who was eldest son and heir to Sir John. We conceive you will stop all proceedings as to the composition.

G. 113, p 574. 12 Oct., 1653. PETITION of Dame Sarah Redmaine for discharge and allowance of her arrears for 24 Dec., 1649.

G. 19, p. 1130. 12 Oct., 1653. Claim allowed.

G. 18, p. 904. 7 and 9 Dec. 1653. Thomas Wharton and William Dodsworth * having bought from the Treason Trustees lands in Burton and Thornton Hall in Thornton formerly belonging to Sir John Redmaine Knt. they are to receive the rents.

G. 81, p. 9. 7 July, 1653. PETITION of William Dodsworth of Thornton that his wife as heir of lands in Thornton as daughter of Sir John Redmaine whose estate it was being now surveyed may compound for them.

Referred to Mr Brereton to Report.

Sir John was twice married:—

(1) To REBECCA, whose identity has never, to the best of my knowledge, been established, but who was not improbably a Middleton. She died in March, 1627-8, surviving her marriage a very brief period, but sufficiently long to leave two children:

> *(1)* WILLIAM, who was baptised in Thornton church on the 8th October, 1626, when his father had barely reached his majority, and who, as we have seen, died a youth of nineteen, in 1645.
>
> *(2)* MARY, who was first married to Colonel Forbes. Her second husband was William Dodsworth, Esquire, member of an old Yorkshire family, allied by marriage with the families of Stapleton, Tunstall and Hutton. John Dodsworth married Henrietta, sister of Dr. Hutton, Archbishop of Canterbury, and an earlier John had for wife Frances, daughter of Sir Timothy Hutton and granddaughter of Matthew, Archbishop of York.

---

* William Dodsworth, who, with Thomas Wharton purchased Thornton Hall and the lands in Burton, was the second husband of Mary Redman, Sir John's daughter and Colonel Forbes's widow

In the Act of 1652, relating to the estates of delinquents, Sir John's name appears twice, (1) as "Sir John Redman, of Writon (Wrayton), in the Co of Lancaster", and (2) as Sir John Redman, late of Newcastle, in the Co. of York (*sic*) (Scobell's Acts and Ordinances of the Commonwealth).

Rebecca had not long been dead when Sir John, who was but twenty-two years old when he was left a widower, sought and found a second wife in

(2) SARAH, one of the daughters and co-heirs of Sir George Selby, a well-to-do knight of Durham and a member of the ancient family of Selby of Earle and Biddleston. The first notable member of this Northumbrian stock was a Sir Walter who flourished when Henry III. was King, and who received large grants of lands from his successor, Edward I. Another Sir Walter was governor of Liddell Castle (16 Ed. III.), which he held for a time against all the strength of the Scottish King David; and a later Selby, Ralph, was a Baron of Exchequer and Privy Councillor of Henry IV. and V. He lies buried in Westminster Abbey, and was described in his epitaph as "one exceedingly beloved and favoured by Kings Henry IV. and V."

Sarah Selby had more than her long descent to boast of when she gave her hand to the young Thornton widower; for, as will appear later, she brought him a substantial dower "of the value of £7000 and upwards"; and doubtless her sister and co-heiress, Isabella, was similarly dowered when she became the wife of Sir Patricius Curwen, Bart., whose arms may be seen to-day impaling those of Selby over the front door of Workington Hall; while within is his portrait in all the seventeenth century splendour of slashed crimson doublet, and trunk hose, scarlet stockings, collars and cuffs of white point lace, and gold-embroidered sword belt. (Curwen's *Workington Hall*, p. 7).

Lady Sarah's wedded life was by no means a bed of roses. After about thirteen years of placid living, during which she bore six children, the Civil War brought to the

Thornton household, as to many another English family, years of constant alarms and anxiety, and the loss of husband, fortune, and home. When Sir John died, in 1645, his widow and her six young children were turned out of their home with nothing left to preserve them from perishing, as her son, Hugh, in 1660, states in a petition to the Crown.

Lady Sarah, however, lived long enough to see Cromwell underground, and the Civil War and the Commonwealth but an unpleasant memory. She saw eighteen years of the second Charles's reign and died in December, 1678, leaving four sons, all in comfortable circumstances, and two daughters suitably married.

She appears to have been living in Thornton in 1668, as is evidenced by a letter written in that year by the Rev. B. Oley, a former curate of the neighbouring parish of Burton-in-Lonsdale, to a Mr. Foxcroft. The letter begins thus:—

"Mr. Foxcroft—I salute you in Xt. and pray you to give my humble service to my Lady Redmayne and her family, also to Mr. Akerigg, Mr. Hodgson, and John Redman, and all that know me. . . ." And on December 10th, 1678, she was buried "in her own Quire" in Thornton church. Her tombstone, the Rev. A. J. Warwick, M.A., vicar of Thornton, who has rendered me much courteous assistance, tells me, was removed from the church at its restoration in 1868, and is now in the churchyard exposed to the weather and to the destructive feet of careless passers-by. Much of the lettering is now undecipherable, but the following is probably an accurate rendering of the original inscription. The letters in brackets have been obliterated.

HERE LYES
THE LADY SARAH [R]EDM[AYNE]
WHO DYED THE VII OF D[ECEMBER]
MDCLXXVIII [IN THE LXX YEAR]
OF HER AGE.
SHE WILL AWA[KE R]ESUM[E HER BREATH]
THEN SING THE TRIUMPH [OVER DEATH]
O DEATH
WHERE IS THY STING
O GRAVE
WHERE IS THY VICTORY?

Beneath the inscription are the Redman arms, impaling those of Selby-barry of eight.

To Sir John and Sarah Selby were born six children, (1) JOHN, the eldest, who was born in 1630, never married and died just half a century later, in April, 1680, having survived his mother two years. His name appears, in 1665, first on the list of "sworn men" of Thornton; and part of his life seems to have been spent in the neighbourhood of Newcastle-on-Tyne. The inventory of his goods is curiously dated 12 March, 1680—the month before his death.

12 March 1680.
    Inventory of goods &c. of John Redmayne Esq;
Total £50. 7. 6.
        Ral Redmayne
        George Greenbanke
        John Dixon.
Bond, Richard Redmayne Esq. of Thornton Hall and Leonard Burton of Dent. Above Richard, administrator of the estate

John's virtues are thus quaintly commemorated on a brass in the vestry of Thornton church. Above the inscription are the Redman arms, with the Thornton crest, a hand (dexter) couped at the wrist.

TOMBSTONE OF THE LADY SARAH REDMAYNE,
AT THORNTON

To face p. 174.

REDMANS OF THORNTON-IN-LONSDALE.

> Here Lieth the Body of Major JOHN
> REDMAYNE, Eldest son to Sr John
> Redmayne, who Departed this life ye Fifth
> Of April, Anno Dom, 1680, in ye 50th Year of's age.
> Here Lieth a Mirror matchless in his Time
> For human Learning and a great Divine.
> Firme in his faith and Valiant for his King,
> Stout as an AJAX, Just in everything,
> Well arm'd for Death he did for Mercy call;
> To be with Christ he knew was best of all.
> By his example therefore spend your hours,
> His bitter cup is past, the next turne's yours.

(2) RICHARD, the second son, who on his brother's death succeeded to the remnant of the family estates, lived at Linton-in-Craven during the latter years of his life. He was at Linton in March, 1688, when he was one of the trustees of the marriage settlement of Edward Parker, Esq., of Browsholme; and he was buried there on the 4th February, 1692-3. His wife Elizabeth (probably either a Hewitt or a Benson) survived him twenty-six years, dying at Linton in 1718, at the age of seventy-seven, and being buried in the church, where her memory is preserved by a brass in the vestry. Her will is dated 11 June, 1718.

By his will, dated 27 Jan., 1692 (York Probate Registry), Richard bequeathed to his brother Ralph £20, a bond of £14 owing to him, and "all the household goods which he hath already received and had out of my house at Thornton Hall; but all the other household goods I give to my loving wife, Elizabeth Redmaine, now remaineing and being in the said hall." To Ralph, too, he gives "one iron chest (called the Lead), with all intering therein which concerns my lands at Thorneton or elsewhere in Lancashire, now in my possession at Linton, to be delivered to him or his heires after the death of my wife; but my wife to have and enjoy the same for life without diminishing the same."

To his nephew, John Downes " (if living and come to receive the same)," he bequeaths £15 "in full of all demands from his grandmother, the Lady Sarah Redmayne deceased, and if he do not acquit her and her executors, then 20/- only. Also to his sister, late Sara Downes, £20 if she be living at my death and come to receive the same herself and acquit her grandmother, the said Lady Sara Redmayne and her executors, and, if not, 20/- only."

Among other legacies are :—To " Jeffray " Wildman (a nephew) 10/-; Mistress Catherine Downe (a sister) 10/; the executors of George Selby, late of Newcastle (probably his mother's brother) £10, which was borrowed of him by Lady Redmayne. His "cousin," Mr. Thomas Redmaine, of Water Fowford (Fulford, near York), receives £10; and small legacies go to his clerk, to two men- and two maid-servants, the late and present "parsons of Linton," &c. The residue of his goods he leaves to his "loveing and dear wife, Elizabeth Redmaine, executrix."

(3) RALPH, the third of Sir John's surviving sons, appears to have been exceedingly badly treated by the widow of his dead brother, Richard, who not only concealed her husband's death from him, but retained possession of the lands which ought to have come to Ralph as Richard's heir.

I am tempted to quote here portions of Ralph's petition to the Court of Chancery in 1693, which is interesting not only from the family information it supplies but as shewing how essentially human these ancestors of ours were in their little jealousies and deceptions, their greed and spitefulness. It is quite clear that Ralph had no reason whatever to love his sister-in-law, Elizabeth, of Linton, and he does not hesitate to express his opinion of her in terms of amusing candour.

REDMAN v. REDMAN Widow and others.
25th November, 1693.

The humble suppliant, RALPH REDMAYNE, of Thornton in Lonsdale, co. Ebor. Esq. That whereas Sir John Redmayne, late of Thornton-in-Lonsdale, Knight, your Orator's late father was in his lifetime, that is about sixty years ago, seized of a capital messuage called Thornton Hall, together with various other messuages and lands, tenements, etc. situate in Thornton-in-Lonsdale, Westhouse, Masongill and Burton-in-Lonsdale in said Co. of York, of the yearly value of £150, and being so seized intermarried with Dame Sara Redman being before her marriage of equal quality with him and bringing to him a fortune or marriage-portion of the value of £7000 and upwards, in consideration of which marriage and portion the said Sir John Redmayne did by his indenture or some other writings duly executed, settle all the said capital messuage etc. to the use of him and his said wife, your Orator's said father and mother, for their lives and for that of the longer liver of them, and from and immediately after the decease of the longer liver, then to the use of first, second, third etc. and every other son and sons of their two bodies lawfully begotten or to be begotten and the heirs male of their bodies, as they should be in seniority of age and priority of birth, with divers remainders over etc.

After the said Sir John Redmaine lived divers years and died, and your Orator's mother, the Lady Redmaine, survived and enjoyed all the said messuage (capital) and premises during her life and died about sixteen years ago; after whose death the same came to and descended to John Redmaine, Esq. your Orator's late eldest brother, who entered and died unmarried and without issue; after whose death, by virtue of such settlement the premises came to Richard Redmayne, Esq. next brother to the said John Redmaine, and elder brother to your Orator, who entered thereto and being seized in fee tayle was persuaded by one Elizabeth Hewett, now named Elizabeth Redmayne, a defendant hereinafter named, to intermarrie with her (she) being a person far inferior and very unsuitable to the degree and quality of the said Richard Redmaine; and after their marriage after very great promises and hopes of having a very great fortune by her was persuaded, by her or her friends, to settle the said capital messuage so as the same should come to and be enjoyed by her, the said Elizabeth Redmaine, for her life as a jointure, with divers remainders to divers of the said Elizabeth's relations and friends or other persons unknown to your Orator, without making any provision at all for your Orator, although he, the said Richard Redmaine, had no power so to do being only tenant in taile and therefore could only settle the said premises, etc. no longer than for his own life. That the said Richard Redmaine, your Orator's brother, on or about the 27th day of January, 1692, made his last will and testament, as your Orator is informed by another and has no reason to disbelieve, devised to your Orator among other things one bond, &c.

Ralph then goes on to say that Richard died without issue and that after his death the estates ought to come to him as next in the entail. Elizabeth, however, not only concealed from him the news of his brother's death for a considerable time, but entered into possession of the estates and refused to show Ralph the settlement, fines, recoveries, etc., under which she professed to be entitled.

To add to her iniquities she also got possession of the settlement made by Sir John and "all the ancient deeds, writings and evidences touching the said estates," and "divers other records, charts and antiquities touching the petitioner's family, and hath since cancelled, defaced, and dispersed the same so that he is quite unable to make out his title."

Elizabeth has further conspired with one Anthony Wile, of Belfast, and Rebecca, his wife (probably a daughter of Ralph's step-sister, Mary, daughter of Sir John, by his first wife, Rebecca) who have formerly professed some title to the estates, to assist her in her nefarious schemes, "all of which doings are contrary to right and equity, and tend to the utter ruin of the Orator and his family having been of great antiquity." He finally prays that a subpœna may be served on Elizabeth Redmaine, Anthony Wile and Rebecca, his wife, commanding them to appear personally before his Lordship.

Ralph appears to have made his home at Thornton, and it seems probable that he found his wife in the district in a daughter of the old house of Tatham; which had at least one common descent with the Redmans from Waldieve, Lord of Ulverston, whose granddaughter Henry de Redman had married five centuries earlier. He seems to have spent at least the latter part of his life at Halsteads, a delightful sixteenth century house which sheltered some generations of Tathams; and to have led the placid life of a country gentleman, no doubt nursing his grievances against his sister-in-law who had so wickedly deprived him of his birthright. Margaret, Ralph's wife, died childless in 1701, and the following epitaph on a brass in the vestry of Thornton church perpetuates the memory of her amiable qualities.—

> Here Lieth the Body of MARGAR
> ET REDMAYNE, wife to RALPH
> REDMAYNE, Esq. who Departed this Life
> ye eleventh of JANUARY, Anno Dōni,
> 1701, in the 51st year of her Age.
> She was a woman of a generous dis-
> position, Courteous to all and kind to ye poore.

Ralph survived his wife a little over two years, dying on the 3rd March, 1703, at the age of sixty-two. He too has his brass memorial, near to that of his wife in the church of Thornton; and his epitaph is an eloquent tribute to his piety and his generosity.

> Here lyeth the Body of RALPH REDMAYNE,
> Esq. who Departed this life the third Day of March,
> Anno Doni, 1703, in the 63rd yeare of his age.
> Speak Tomb, can Brass and Marble die?
> > They may my sweaty fears reply
> What then indures? Goodnesse alone
> > Survives the Brass, the marble Tomb
> That warmes his ashes here enshrined,
> > And beames the Lustre of his mind.
> By this his name, his coat doth stand
> > More famed than by the bloody hand.
> Let his last generosity
> > To Altar, School and Poverty
> For ever witness this; and dead
> > With deathlesse Laurels crowne His head
> Thus will the actions of the just
> > Smell sweet and blossome in the dust.

His will, a copy of which is treasured among the records of Thornton parish, is, I think, sufficiently interesting to be given in full. It will be seen that such small possessions as he had enjoyed he left principally to the local poor and for the endowing of a grammnr school; while his silver he bequeathed to the church of Thornton for conversion into the handsome altar-plate which is pictured opposite. It will also be noticed that he left to the church two damask napkins, one of which has the figure of the Temple of Jerusalem woven therein, and which may not improbably have come down to him from some crusading ancestor.

WILL of RALPH REDMAYNE Esquire, of Halsteads, in the Parish of Thornton, County of York, dated Feb. 3, 1702, proved Mar. 30, 1703.

In the name of God, Amen. I, Ralph Redmayne, of Halsteads, in the Parish of Thornton and County of York, Esquire, being sick of body but of sound mind and perfect memory, praised be Almighty

ALTAR-PLATE OF THORNTON CHURCH,
Made from silver bequeathed by Ralph Redmayne, Esq.

TO FACE P. 181.

God for the same, doe make and ordaine this my last will and testament in manner and forme following (that is to say)—ffirst and principally I commend my soul into the hands of Almighty God hopeing through the merits and death of my Saviour Jesus Christ to have full and free pardon and forgiveness of all my sins and to inherit everlasting life, and my body I commit to the earth to be decently buryed att the discretion of my executors hereafter named. And as touching the disposal of all and temporall estates as it hath pleased Almighty God to bestow upon me I give and dispose thereof as followeth :—

ffirst, I will that my debts, legacies and funerall expenses shall be paid and discharged.

Item. I give and bequeathe to the use of the Church of Thornton one damask napkin having the figure of the Temple of Jerusalem woven therein; one damask napkin, one large silver Tankard haveing my coat-of-arms on it, one little silver Tankard, Two silver Pottingers, two silver salts, six silver spoons, three silver castors, and two silver salvers—all to be made, melted downe or exchanged into a less silver salver, into two silver Flaggons, and a silver Bowl with a cover, both to be double gilt, and to have the image of our Saviour crucified on the top thereof. And I will and order that they shall all be to and for the use of the said Church of Thornton for ever.

Item. I give and bequeathe to the use of the poor people of Thornton for ever, the poor people of Ireby only excepted, the sum of ffifty Pounds of lawfull English money to be paid by my Executors hereafter named at the end of one year after my decease. And my will and mind is that the interest and consideration and yearly profitt and increase of the said ffifty Pounds be given and distributed to the poor people of the said Parish of Thornton yearly and every year for ever, the poor people of Ireby only excepted.

Item. I will give and bequeathe the sum of two hundred pounds of lawfull money of England to be paid at the end of one year next after my decease unto Thomas Topping of Barneywick, Roland Tatham, Thomas Yetts, and John Knowles, in the Parish of Thornton, yeoman, to be bestowed and lett out by them upon land or to be lett out on interest till they can conveniently well bestow and secure the said money upon land to and for the use and interest that the yearly interest rents and profits and revenues which may issue etc by reason of the said two hundred pounds be paid to the schoolmaster of the school at Neither West House Green*, in the Parish of Thornton, yearly for ever for his teaching and educating in the said school, which said school I will, order and appoint shall be free to and for all such children and scholars as shall come to the same, whose parents, guardians and tutors shall dwell and inhabit within the said Parish of Thornton, except those within Ireby I doe not will, order and appoint to be free of the same. And likewise I doe here nominate, ordaine and appoint the said Thomas Topping etc. to be ffeoffees, overseers, trustees and supervisors in the premisses, etc. etc.

Item. I will and bequeathe to Sir William Gerrard, Baronet, one iron chest called the "Lead," standing and being at Lynton, and all deedes, evidences and writings therein or elsewhere belonging or appertaining to any of the premises purchased of me by the said Sir William Gerrard, Baronet.

Item. I will and bequeathe to John Fenwick, Esquire, one case of pistoles and Holsters and one gold ring having my name and death's head engraved on it. * * *

Item. I will and bequeathe to Elizabeth Mayer, my servant, the sume of sixty pounds of lawful English money, and also the interest and consideration which shall be behind at my decease due to me by one Thomas Bateman of Parke, the said John Fenwick, Esquire, stands bound to me.

Then follow legacies of money and furniture to two maid-servants and one man-servant, and of furniture to Ellen Tatham. All the rest of his personal estate Ralph bequeaths to William Tatham, of Halsteads, whom he appoints sole executor.

Memorandum of the silver-plate above-mentioned given and bequeathed to the Church: weight in all 124 ounces; and it is the will and desire of the testator that ye Two fflagons to be made for

---

* In Lewis's *Topographical Dictionary* the following entry appears under "Thornton":—

> "Ralph Redmayne, Esq, in 1702, founded a free school and endowed it with £200, which having been invested in land, produces annually £50"

ye Church as abovesaid contain three pints apiece and the Bowl contains one pint.

                        signed: Ralph Redmayne.

Witnesses: Thomas Talbot.   Administration granted to
           Bryan Nicholson. William Tatham, Esquire,
           Robert Mayer.   the sole executor.
                                   March, the thirtieth, 1703.

(4) HUGH, Sir John's fourth and youngest surviving son, was born circa 1642, and probably died without offspring before 1692. In 1660, when he was but a youth, Hugh, after recounting the misfortunes his family had suffered in the Royalist cause, to which reference has been made earlier, petitions Charles II., who had recently come to his throne, for a commission in the Lifeguards, or, failing that, an appointment at his Court as Page of the Backstairs. The commission he did not get; and whether or not his alternative request was granted I cannot say.

It is possible, although not probable, that he may have been the Hugh Redman who appears in the State papers for 1692. In that year a company was formed to fish for pearls in the river Irt and in other Cumberland waters. The leading spirit of this curious enterprise (which, strange to say, resulted in the recovery of £800 worth of pearls) was Mr. Thomas Patrickson, of How Hall, Ennerdale; and among others whose names appear associated with his in the charter are Giles and Hugh Redman.

He was almost certainly dead when his brother Richard made his will in January, 1692, since, although the testator remembers his sisters' children, there is no mention of Hugh; and if this may be accepted as evidence, it is scarcely likely that at this date he would feel any interest in fishing for pearls in Cumberland waters. Sir John had two daughters by Sarah Selby:—

(1) CATHERINE, who became the wife of a London husband of the name of Downe; and

(2) MARGARET, who married Thomas Wildman and had a son, Geoffrey, mentioned in his uncle Richard's will.

Thus, although Sir John had at least eight children by his two wives, not one of his five sons seems to have left any issue; while his daughters made their homes and brought up their families away from the place of their childhood.

THORNTON HALL, which probably sheltered many generations of this branch of the Redman family, and which was a spacious, stoutly-built manor house, with walls two yards thick, has long vanished. A trace of it, it is said, is still to be seen in an adjacent farm-building in the form of an arch, which may once have been part of a fireplace in the Hall, bearing the initials J. B. and T. B. and the date 1659—a striking illustration of the fate that overtakes the homes of once flourishing families as well as the families themselves. In the new Hall, too, are stones and mullions which probably formed part of the earlier building.

The present CHURCH of St. Oswald at THORNTON, in and around which so many generations of Redmans are sleeping, retains little of the structure of the older church, which it largely replaced in 1869-70, with the exception of the fifteenth century tower and three of the original Norman arches at the west end of the north arcade. It has, however, in addition to the brasses mentioned earlier, a most interesting seventeenth or eighteenth century window, containing the Redman arms in stained glass, with the Thornton crest, a hand (in this presentment, the *left* hand) gules.

The Thornton registers are rich in material for students of Redman genealogy. The earliest baptismal entry is that of "Wm. the sonne of Marmaduke Redmayne, Esquire," who was baptized anno 1578; and between that year and August, 1847, no fewer than one hundred and sixty-four little Redmans followed William to the Thornton font. The marriage entries begin three years later, in 1581, when one Robert Commynge led Margaret Redmayne to the altar, to be followed by seventy-five more of the name down to November, 1821; and there are one hundred and forty-one burial entries between that of "Jenett, daughter of Oswalde Redmayne, on Oct. 29, A° 1577," and that of John Redmayne, of Burton, in January, 1847.

THE REDMANS OF IREBY.

CHAPTER XVII.

THE Ireby branch of Redman had for founder EDMUND, younger son of the Thomas Redman of Thornton, from whom the three lines of Thornton, Ireby, and Twisleton equally spring. This Edmund appears in De Banco Roll, Easter 23 Hen VI m 455, as "Edūs Reedmane de Ireby Lathes in parochiâ de Thornton, in Com. Lanc gentilman", and for more than a century and a half his descendants flourished as greatly as their neighbours and kinsmen of the senior or Thornton line

Their chronicles, however, are equally unmarked by features of extraneous interest Their ambition appears to have been bounded by the narrow range of country life They married well, managed their estates, which they handed on undiminished and often augmented to their descendants, and seem to have troubled themselves little with the concerns of the greater world which wagged beyond their quiet manors

The original Edmund had a son and successor THOMAS, of whom the records tell us little. He was probably the Thomas Redmayne of Yreby who, with Bryan Redmayn, of Gressingham, appears in a Jury list dated March 4th, 1513, signed by Sir Edward Stanley, of Hornby Castle, six months before he played his gallant part on Flodden Field The jury consisted of six priests and as many lay-

Redman of Ireby.

EDMUND REDMAN of Ireby Lathes in Thornton, gent., son of Thomas R. of Thornton, Esq., vix 15 March, 1442-3, &c.
|
THOMAS REDMAN of Ireby, son and heir, 11 Edw IV, 9 Hen VII, 17 Hen VII, &c.
|
├── EDMUND REDMAN = JENNET, heiress of Wraton
│   of Ireby, son and heir, of Wraton 9 Hen VII, 17 Hen VII, died 29 Mar 1511, Inq p.m. 3 May, 1511
│ |
│   THOMAS REDMAN = GRACE LAYTON, dau of William Layton of Dalcman
│   of Ireby, son and heir, born 1493, died 1536
│ |
│   WILLIAM REDMAN = ISABEL TUNSTALL, dau of Sir Marmaduke Tunstall of Thurland Castle, and Alice, dau and co heiress of Sir Robert Scargill bur 10 Jan, 1598-9
│   of Ireby, son and heir, born 1524, died 1598, bur 8 June, 1598
│ |
│   ├── JULIAN dau of Nich Leybourne of Cunswark, mar lic 1579, London
│   │   = (2) — BROUGH
│   │ |
│   │   s, dau = CHRISTOPHER CONYERS of Danby 1599
│   │   bp 1599
│   │
│   ├── WILLIAM REDMAN, of Ireby, brother and heir
│   │   = AVELYN LAMBERT, granddaughter of Richard Redman, Esq., of Harewood
│   │ |
│   │   GEORGE, b 1601
│   │
│   ├── MARMADUKE of Clifford (?), gent, d 1594
│   │ |
│   │   JAMES, d 1604
│   │
│   ├── CHRISTOPHER, 1579
│   │ |
│   │   JOSIAS, d 1604
│   │
│   ├── FRANCIS of Burton, gent will 7 August, 1598
│   │   = JENNET [? LULLON, wed 1594] o s p
│   │
│   ├── GABRIEL = MARY dau of James Danby, next in entail to William, wed 1583, wed 1607; widow of Roger Walker; (3) Posthumus Coulton, Esq., 1616
│   │ |
│   │   ├── J(A)SON, b 1594
│   │   └── BRIDGET, d 1613
│   │
│   ├── ELLEN = ROBERT BAINES, of Sellet 1584
│   │   (2) SAMUEL LAMBERT
│   │
│   ├── ANN prob wed Thos Morley, of Weatington, 1583
│   │ |
│   │   MARY = RICHARD CONYERS, of York and Northallerton
│   │
│   └── MARY, 1579
│
├── BRYAN = ELIZABETH, dau and co heiress of Rich Southworth of Gressingham, widow 33 Hen VIII
│   17 Hen VII
│
├── PIERS, 17 Hen VII, 16 Hen VIII
│
└── ROBERT, 17 Hen VII, 16 Hen VIII, of Clapham

To face Page 186

INGLETON CHURCH.
From Drawing by F. C. Tilney.

men, and the dispute related to certain glebe lands in Burton in Kendal. This document, the Rev. W. B. Grenside, M.A., the courteous vicar of Melling, informs me, is in possession of the Roman catholic priest at Hornby.

Thomas had an heir EDMUND, with at least three other sons, of whom Bryan wed Elizabeth, daughter and coheiress of Richard Southworth, of Gressingham, one of whose sisters, Cecily, found a husband in Edward, of Thornton, parent of the lines of Gressingham and Fulford, while a second sister, Mabel, had for guardian Christopher Parker, Esquire, of Radholme. Edmund married an heiress of Wrayton, and died on 29th March, 1511, seized of lands in Ireby, Tatham, Hornby, Wrayton, Claughton, and Tunstall (Duchy of Lancaster, Inq. p.m. 3 Hen. VIII. vol. IV., No. 42), and leaving an heir, Thomas, who was a youth of eighteen at his father's death.

THOMAS, the new head of the Ireby branch, was born in 1493, and wed Grace, daughter of William Layton, of Dalemayn, in Cumberland, whose mother was not improbably a Tunstall, of Thurland. He had no long tenure of his estates, for he died at the early age of forty-three (in 1536); and the inquest after his death (Duchy of Lancs. vol VII., No. 2, 27 Hen. VIII.) shews that he held lands in Ireby, Tunstall, Hornby, Wrayton infra Melling, and Claughton.

His successor was his son WILLIAM, a boy of twelve, with a long minority before him under the guardianship of a kinsman, probably a brother of his mother. In the Letters and Papers, Hen. VIII., vol. xiv (15 May, 1539) we find a "grant to Ed. Layton, clk., Archdeacon of Bucks, of all messuages, lands, &c., in Ireby, Tunstall, Hornby, Wratton, and Clayghton, or elsewhere in the County of Lancashire, which belonged to Thomas Redmayne, deceased, during the minority of William Redmayne, son and heir of the said Thomas, with wardship and marriage of the said William."

Six years later the young heir had licence of entry on his estates—William Redmayne, Esq., son and heir of Thomas Redmayne, Esquire, deceased. Special licence of entry without proof of age and without livery upon all the lands of his inheritance. (Duchy of Lancs. General and Special Liveries. Dep. Keeper's Rept., 39 App., p. 558).

William had not far to go to look for a wife, for he found her half-an-hour's good ride away at Thurland Castle, in Isabel, a daughter of Sir Marmaduke Tunstall and Alice, daughter and co-heiress of Sir Robert Scargill. Isabell was one of three sisters, born a few years after their grandfather, Sir Brian, had fallen at Flodden; great niece of Cuthbert Tunstall, the bishop, and of Mrs. William Redmayne, of Twisleton.

William, no doubt enriched by this Tunstall alliance, was a man of considerable importance in his time; and we are not surprised to find him, in 1588, among the "gentlemen of the best calling in the County of Lancaster." It is no doubt this William whose name appears with that of his brother-in-law, Francis Tunstall, in the list of Lancashire gentlemen who, at this time, were leagued together for the defence of Queen Elizabeth against the evil machinations of Mary, Queen of Scots, and the other enemies of the State. (Baines's *Lancashire* i., p. 183).

William and Isabel were blessed, probably beyond their wishes, with children, of whom seven sons and three daughters are on record. The eldest son, GEORGE, appears to have been anything but the comfort he ought to have been to his father in his old age, as is shown by the following bill of complaint from the Duchy of Lancaster Pleadings, vol. 115, R. 4.

Bill of Complaint of George Redman, of Ireby, Co. Lancs, gentleman—William Redman, of Ireby, Esquire (father of George) was lawfully seized of an estate of inheritance in the Manor and Lordship of Ireby, &c., and by his deed dated in or about the month of March, 25 Elizabeth (1582-3) covenanted with petitioner, being his eldest son, Thomas Morley, Thomas Redman and John Wood, that he (William) and Isabell, his wife, should, before the feast of St. Michael next (29 Sept., 1583) levy a fine of the said Manor &c to the use of said William and Isabell his wife, for life, and then to the use of petitioner, with remainder over &c. By the same deed it was agreed that George Redman should enjoy two chambers on the west side of the said manor-house, with a garden belonging to the same, &c. &c.

The fine was levied, and now both deeds are in the possession of the said William Redman, who will not allow petitioner to have pasture for three kyne and two geldings as arranged under the deed.

The answer of William Redman, the father, states that the matters are put forward by complainant as a most unkind son towards his natural father, aged about seventy years, and dwelling nine score miles from the court, &c. He says that about the feast of Michaelmas last past, George put upon the pastures divers horses or geldings "infected with vile and most horrible diseases," and so he ordered his servant to remove them.

The undutiful heir did not very long survive this legal dispute, for he died five years before his old father, and was buried at Thornton, 20th March, 1592-3. He must have been both husband and father at the time he was living under the paternal roof at Ireby, for in 1579 he wed Julian, daughter of Nicholas Leybourne, of Cunswick, who found solace after his death by becoming Mrs. Brough; and he had a daughter and heiress, Frances (vix 1599), who became wife to Christopher Coniers, of Danby, and who figures in a Chancery suit with William Redman, her uncle.

> Christopher Coniers and Frances, his wife, plts Wm. Redman, Deft } Bill for payment of môy by settlement charged on the Manor of Irebye, and lands in Tunstall, Lecke, Wraton, Hornebye, Todgill, Westhouse, &c.

(*Chancery Proceedings*, Queen Elizth., Rolls Series, vol. 1., p. 155).

(2) WILLIAM, the second son of William Redman and Isabel Tunstall, by his marriage linked the long-severed lines of Harewood and Thornton; for his wife was Aveline Lambert, granddaughter of the third and last Richard, of Harewood, daughter of John Lambert, of Calton, and aunt of the great General Lambert of later years.

William and his wife figure in the following fines:—

1596. Samuel Lambert, gent (Aveline's brother)
—— William Redmayne, gent and Aveline his wife—
messuage and lands in Burton-in-Lonsdale.
1597. Giles Foxcroft—Wm. Redmayne Esq. and Isabel his wife; Wm. Redmayne and Aveline his wife, Francis Redmayne, gent, and Jenetta, his wife—Lands in Netherlands and Thornton.

Evidently William, senior, was tenant in tail in possession and William and Francis, his two sons, were tenants in tail in remainder successively; the wives being joined to bar their dower.

1602. Edward Garnet—William Redmayne, gent, and Aveline, his wife—Lands in Burton in Mewthe (Mewith, near Bentham).

REDMANS OF IREBY.

William also figures in these earlier fines:—

1585. William Redmayne, gent—Rosse, gent—Three messuages and lands in Burton and Burton Moor
1587. William and George Redmayne—Johnson, Lands in Burton.
1592. William Redmayne, gent, and others—Johnson and Eliz, his wife—Lands in Burton.
1594. Robert Cansfield and others—Wm. Redmayne and others—11 messuages with tenements in Thornton, Westhouse, Burton, Over Bentham, and Nether Bentham

To William and Aveline were born two sons and a daughter who died young, and a son, George, born in 1601, of whose future nothing appears to be known. It is not improbable that there were other children whose names do not appear in the local registers.

(3) MARMADUKE, the third son of William Redman and Isabel Tunstall, was probably "Marmaduke, of Clifford, gentleman," who died in 1594, a year or so after his eldest brother, George, and while his father was still alive.

(4) CHRISTOPHER, who appears in 1579.

(5) FRANCIS, "of Burton, gentleman," who married Jennet, and whose will is dated, 7 August, 1598. He left all to his widow, and among the creditors mentioned in his will is "Mrs. Redman, of Ireby, my mother." Francis appears to have died without offspring, and his wife was probably Jennet Lullson who, on the evidence of the Thornton Register, married "ffrancis Redmayne on Aug. 11, Anno 1594."

(6) GABRIEL, who in 1583, is curiously mentioned as next in the entail to William, married (in 1607) Mary, daughter of James Danby, and widow of Roger Walker, who nine years later made a third matrimonial venture, this time with Posthumus Coulton, Esq. Of Gabriel's children, Mary became the wife of Richard Conyers, of

York and Northallerton, and had issue :—James, Richard, Francis, Ann, and Mary, who wed, in 1680, J. Saville, of York. Gabriel's will is dated 1613,

(7) JASON, who died in 1594.

Of the daughters of William Redman and Isabel Tunstall :—

(1) ELLEN was twice married, (a) to Robert Baines, of Sellet House, on 18th April, 1584, and (b) to Samuel Lambert, brother of Aveline Lambert, and grandson of Richard Redman, of Harewood. By Samuel Lambert, Ellen had issue John, born in 1607, and other children.

(2) ANN, who seems to have married Thomas Morley, of Wennington, in 1583 ; and

(3) MARY, living in 1579.

All these children, with the exception of George, appear as legatees for small sums in the will of their grandmother, Dame Marie Tunstall, widow of Sir Marmaduke. The will is dated 31 December, 21 Eliz. (1579), and contains the following bequests :—

To my daughter Isabell Readman £40. To Ellen Redman, her daughter, £40. Item—I do give to William, Marmaduke, Christopher, Francis, Gabriel, Jason, Ann and Marie Readman, children of William Readman, Esquire, my sonne in law, gotten of the bodie of my said daughter Isabell, £130 to be equally divided amongst them.

Supervisors, John Dawney (Sir John Dawnay, of Sessay, co. York, who married Elizabeth, another daughter of Sir Marmaduke and Lady Tunstall), and William Readman, Esquire, my son-in-law.

Witnesses—George Readman and others.

Probate 21 March, 1578-9.

William and Isabel, when they looked on their seven sons, might well have thought that whatever fate befell other branches of their family the perpetuation of the Ireby line was secured against any possibility of failure; but, such is the irony of life, the family of Ireby seems to have come to its close at the very time when its continuance seemed to be most assured. Not one of William's seven sons appears to have left an heir, with the possible exception of William, whose son George appears on the register of births in 1601, only to vanish from all later view.

This William (husband of Avelyn Lambert) seems to have dissipated the family estates; for a generation later —in 1647—we find the manor of Ireby in the possession of a son of James Redman, of Thornton.

The hall of Ireby (now known as Over Hall), which probably sheltered several generations of this branch of the Redman family, is still in existence, although it has been largely rebuilt since their day. Of this ancient house Mr. Speight gives the following interesting account in his *Craven and North West Yorkshire Highlands* (pp. 269-70).

It is a sturdy mansion, with walls in some places six feet thick, and has an antique-looking square tower with open battlements at its north end. On entering the ancient stone-porch we pass by a ponderous oak-door, pegged with wooden nails, which opens into a spacious apartment called the Justice Hall. It was formerly the great dining-hall, and had a low ceiling; but many years ago it was thrown open to the rooms above.

At one time this was used as a Court-room, and some oak benches and the table before which the justices sat, are still preserved. The oldest portions of the house date apparently from the earliest years of the 16th century. The earlier house is said to have been much larger than the present building, and occasionally old foundations are met with. It was approached by a handsome carriage-drive half-a-mile long; and there is a legend to the effect that a subterranean passage used to exist between the old Masongill Hall and

Ireby Hall, but what was its direction or whether it ever really existed we have not had means to discover.

Ireby Hall was restored late in the seventh century by Oliver Tatham, member of an ancient and gentle family with which the Redmans made several matrimonial alliances. The last of the Tathams who made Ireby Hall his home was High Sheriff of Lancashire, and he lies, neighbour to many dead and gone Redmans, under the chancel of Thornton church.

Many of the Redmans of this branch were baptized, married and buried in the parish church of Ingleton, the registers of which contain numerous entries. The earliest baptismal record is that of "Alicia Redmaine, daughter of Roger Redmaine, March 5, 1608," and one hundred and thirty-two little Redmaynes followed Alicia to the font, of which, as of the church, I am able to give a picture. The marriage entries begin in 1607 (May 24th), with the wedding of Margaret Redman to Christopher Houlme; and the burial entries, in the same year, with Agnes Redman, daughter of Marmaduke, who was laid to rest in the church. The Redman entries in the registers of the neighbouring parishes of Bentham, Melling, Kirkby Lonsdale and Giggleswick are very few.

FONT, INGLETON CHURCH.

THE REDMANS OF TWISLETON.

CHAPTER XVIII.

THE Redmans of Twisleton, like their kinsmen of Ireby, owed their existence to a younger son of the pioneer Thomas, of Thornton — to one JOHN Redman, who in 1437 appears as "John Redman of Westhouse, in Thornton, gentleman," as a party to the bond relating, it is surmised, to a dispute as to Tunstall property.

WILLIAM, John's son and successor, found a wife in Cecily, elder daughter of Sir Thomas de Strickland, of Sizergh, and Mabel, daughter of Sir John de Bethom. It was William's father-in-law, Sir Thomas, who carried the banner of St. George in the fight at Agincourt; he distinguished himself in later years at the siege of Harfleur, and at the capture of Rouen, and was one of King Henry VI.'s brilliant escort when he went to Paris to be crowned King of France in the church of Notre Dame. The marriage of his daughter Cecily probably took place early in 1436, a few months before Sir Thomas, then someway advanced in the fifties, set sail for France, taking the precaution to make his will before embarking at Sandwich, although he lived to revise his last testament twenty-four years later. On January 31, 1435-6, William of Twisleton was enfeoffed by his father-in-law in Little Urswick manor. The Redman ownership of this manor was signalised by the change of name of the ancient Hall of Urswick to Redmayne Hall.

Redman of Twisleton.

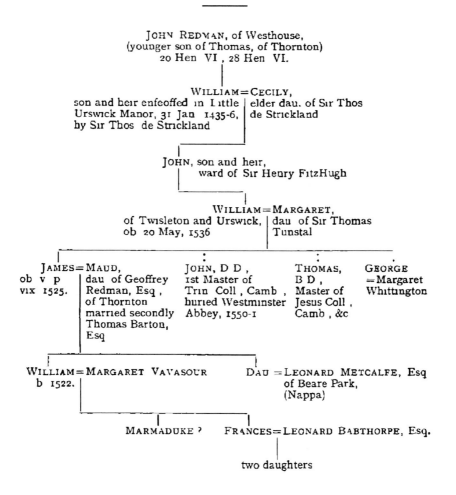

JOHN REDMAN, of Westhouse,
(younger son of Thomas, of Thornton)
20 Hen VI., 28 Hen VI.
|
WILLIAM = CECILY,
son and heir enfeoffed in Little Urswick Manor, 31 Jan 1435-6, by Sir Thos de Strickland | elder dau. of Sir Thos de Strickland
|
JOHN, son and heir, ward of Sir Henry FitzHugh
|
WILLIAM = MARGARET,
of Twisleton and Urswick, ob 20 May, 1536 | dau of Sir Thomas Tunstal

- JAMES = MAUD, dau of Geoffrey Redman, Esq, of Thornton, married secondly Thomas Barton, Esq. ob v p vix 1525.
- JOHN, D D, 1st Master of Trin Coll, Camb, buried Westminster Abbey, 1550-1
- THOMAS, B D, Master of Jesus Coll, Camb, &c
- GEORGE = Margaret Whittington

WILLIAM = MARGARET VAVASOUR, b 1522.
DAU = LEONARD METCALFE, Esq of Beare Park, (Nappa)

MARMADUKE ?
FRANCES = LEONARD BABTHORPE, Esq.
|
two daughters

William and Cecily had a son, JOHN, of whose existence the only evidence seems to be that a wicked uncle ran away with him. In 1467 we find Giles Redman (probably the Giles who was vicar of Bentham in 1445) defendant in a case of abduction of John, son and heir of William Redman, from the custody of Sir Henry Fitz Hugh, Knight. John's guardian, from whose custody he was so unceremoniously taken was probably Henry, fifth Lord Fitz Hugh, who in the following year, actuated by some pious motive, made a pilgrimage to the Holy Sepulchre, and on his return founded a chantry for two priests in his castle at Ravensworth.

Whether or not the abducted John survived his father I cannot say. It is probable, however, that WILLIAM of Twisleton and Urswick, who appears later and with more prominence on the scene, was his son. This William took for wife Margaret, daughter of Sir Thomas Tunstall by Alice, daughter of George Nevill, Archbishop of York, and thus a lineal descendant of John of Gaunt and the third Edward. William makes several appearances in connection with his distinguished brothers-in-law Cuthbert, the bishop, and Brian, the knight.

He was, as we shall see later, one of the executors of the will which Sir Brian made shortly before going to his death at Flodden; and received a small legacy from him "for my syster marryage." Cuthbert Tunstall, in a letter to Cardinal Wolsey, dated 14 Dec. 1520, refers to his brother-in-law, William Redmayn; and again on 29 Jan. 1536, Tunstall, then Bishop of Durham, when sending bulls to Cromwell, says "William Redmayne, the bearer, will deliver them." (Letters and Papers, F. & D. Hen. VIII., vols. iii. and x.) As William, however, died in the following May advanced in years, it is perhaps more probable that the messenger to Cromwell was some unknown namesake. It could scarcely be William's grandson and successor who in 1536 was only a boy of fourteen.

In 4 Hen. VIII. (1512), there was an award between the abbot of Furness and John Flemyng, of Rydale, Esq., made by Brian Tunstall, Sir John Lowther, John Lamplugh and William Redmayne, of Twisleton, relating to the manor of Coniston (Beck's *Furness Annals*, p. 305); seven years later, on 8th July, 1519, William was appointed a commissioner to search for suspected persons, in company with the Chancellor of Lancaster, the Master of the Rolls, and Dr. Throckmorton (Letters & Papers, F. & D., Hen. VIII., vol. iv); and he is probably the William Redmayne who appears in the following fine (Michaelmas Term, 19 Hen. VIII., 1527):—

Plaintiffs: Cuthbert, Bishop of London, John Norton, of Norton, William Redmayne and Richard Redmayne, Esq[rs]., Richard Huddleston and Thomas Redmayne. *Deforciants*: Thomas Wentworth Kt. and Thomas Wentworth, gent , his son and heir apparent.—Manor of Massynggyll, and 30 messuages and a water mill, with lands in Massynggyll, Burton and Thornton.

William died on the 20th May, 1536, and according to his inquisition p.m. (28 Hen. VIII.) was seized of the following estates in Lancashire: Parva Urswyke Manor, Ulverston in Fourness, Claghton, Over Kellet and Gressyngham. He seems to have taken his leave of life in the county of Durham, as is evidenced by a transfer of the lease of certain vaccaries in Wynsdale, in 1542, to John Middleton, Esq., in which it is mentioned that he died at Okeland, co. Durham, having previously made his will there and appointed as his executors Cuthbert, Bishop of Durham, and John Redmayn, S. T. D., who surrender the lease granted to William Redmayn, in favour of a new one to John Middleton. According to the Lancashire Inquisition John Middleton held the lands at Urswick, &c., during the minority of William's grandson and heir.

Of William's sons, the eldest, JAMES, who in 16 Hen. VIII. (1524) is styled "James Redman, nuper de Barwick, in Com. Lanc, gentilman, filius Will. Redmayn," (Lanc. Assize Roll 6), married his kinswoman, Matilda or Maud, daughter of Geoffrey Redman, of Thornton, who later became the wife of Thomas Barton, Esquire. James died eleven years before his father, leaving a son and heir, WILLIAM, born in 1522, who succeeded his grandfather in 1536.

DR. JOHN REDMAN.

A younger son of William and Margaret Tunstall was, in all probability, Dr. JOHN Redman, a cleric of note and one of the finest scholars of his century. He was born in 1499, was a boy of fourteen when his uncle Brian fared forth to find death and glory at Flodden; and, a little later, by the advice, it is said, of his uncle, Cuthbert Tunstall, then probably doing parson's work at Harrow-on-the-Hill, he was sent to Corpus Christi, Oxford. From Oxford he went to see what Paris could teach him, and celebrated his majority by entering his name at St. John's College, Cambridge, where he donned his bachelor's hood at the age of twenty-six. He was M.A. in 1530, a Fellow in the same year, and a full-blown Doctor of Divinity in 1537.

Thus trained under the eye and backed by the influence of his uncle, the bishop, John of Twisleton could scarcely fail to make something of a success of his life; and although he never reached any higher position in the church than that of Archdeacon, he certainly left his mark on the history of his time. He was one of the accommodating clergy whose mission it was to discover some pretext which might justify Henry VIII. in getting rid of the "unattractive Dutch lady," Anne of Cleves, whose misfortune it was to be his Queen; and his signature appears on the decree declaring the marriage invalid. In 1540 he was made Prebendary of Westminster and Wells, and five years later he was Archdeacon of Stafford.

With Parker, later Archbishop of Canterbury, Dr. John was appointed a commissioner to survey the property of colleges; and his name figures on many another commission, including the heresy commission of 1549. He was one of the witnesses at Bishop Gardiner's trial, Master of King's Hall, Cambridge, the first Master of Trinity College, Cambridge, and one of the compilers of the Book of Common Prayer. Consumption carried him off in November, 1551, when he had not long completed his half-century of years. Officious protestants it is said, "crowded round his death-bed to try and get some declaration of his religious opinions." He was buried in Westminster Abbey. The precise date of his death is entered in a copy of the Roman Breviary (1519) in the library of the Dean and Chapter of York, in a list of obits of members and friends of the Vavasour family of Spaldington. The entry, which is in the handwriting of John Vavasour, Esq., who died in 1560, reads thus:—

Nov. 28, 1551. Obitus Jo. Redman, coctoris

Like his uncle, Bishop Tunstall, Dr. John Redmayne left behind him a few Latin treatises, some of which have survived to our day. It was my good fortune, a few months ago, to pick up a small volume printed at Antwerp in 1555, fours years after John's death. This volume contains two Latin treatises—of which the first bears this title :—

IOHANNIS REDMANI sacrae Theologiae professoris de justificatione opus. Huic accessit Hymnus ejusdem argumenti per eundem authorem

The tract is prefaced by an introduction by Cuthbert Constall (*sic*), Bishop of Durham, and contains this interesting personal reference to the author and the work :—

de justificatione tractatum quem Ioannes Redmanus sacrae Theologie professor dum viveret, absolvit, et celeberrimae memoriae Henrico octavo Angliae, Franciae et Hiberniae Regi et fidei defensori, cujus sacellanus erat, obtulit etc. Nam is tractatus integer ad manus nostras pervenit, quem indignum putavimus ut in tenebris delitesceret et quem ille ipse si vixisset omnibus edere decreverat sed non poterat, morte praeventus.

The tract, which is a short one of about 7,500 words, is followed by a hymn containing thirty-eight verses, of which it may perhaps be interesting to quote the following examples :—

> Iesu salus mortalium,
> Spes, vita, lux et gloria,
> Sermo dei factus caro,
> Servator orbis unice.
>
> Tu veritas es et via,
> Tu vita, lux et omnia,
> In te fidelis quisquis est
> Mortis ruinam non timet.

The second treatise of my little volume is headed :—

CONTRA IMPIOS Blasphematores Dei praedestinationis opus Cuthberti Tonstalli Dunelmensis Episcopi.

A third probable son of William was THOMAS Redman, B.D., who was master of Jesus College, Cambridge, and chaplain to Dr. Thomas Thirlby, when Bishop of Ely (1554-9).

And a fourth son was, I think, GEORGE, who may, however, have been of the Ireby branch. On this point Colonel Parker says:—

George Redmayne, who wed Margaret Whittington, was most probably a son of William, of Twisleton, and Margaret Tunstall; but I only gather this from the fact that William purchased the wardship of the Whittington heiress, and one would reasonably expect that his object was to marry his sons well. There, is, however, one thing that makes me believe that George, of Borwick, may have been of Ireby; and that is that his sons bear Ireby names. Now if he was a son of Thomas Redmayne, of Ireby, and Grace Layton, of Dalemayn, we have at once an explanation of his own name, George, which was a Layton favourite, and also of the name of their own son and heir, Thomas.

He may, indeed, have been son of Thomas, and younger brother of William of Ireby.

George Redman, whom perhaps the balance of evidence marks as a son of William of Twisleton, married Margaret Whittington, heiress of Borwick, a Lancashire manor, which, in 1489, was held by the tenth part of a knight's fee by Thomas Whittington (Duc. Lanc., vol. iii., n. 47), and in 1511 had passed to John Whyttyngton of Le Hirst Houses juxta Dokker Warton (Ibid. vol. iv., n. 43). It is described in 9 Hen. VIII. as Berwyk juxta Warton Manor, in the inquisition after the death of Thomas Whittington (Ibid. n. 86) George, who died 1st May, 1565, appears to have had two sons, Thomas and Marmaduke, who in 1567 sold the manor of Borwick together with other lands in Yorkshire and Westmorland, as evidenced by the following proceeding in Chancery:—

Rob Byndelose plt. and Thos. Newton def.—Bill to establish purchase of the Manor of Barwicke, Co. Lancs. and divers other lands in Yorkshire and Westmorland sold to the plaintiff by Thomas and Marmaduke Redmayne, deceased. (Chancery Proceedings. Queen Elizth. Rolls series, vol. i., p. 83).

The new owner of Borwick was probably a son of Sir Christopher Bindloss, a cloth-dealer and alderman of Kendal, in 1579.

On Borwick Hall, which probably was the home of George and his family for some years, Baines (*History of Lancashire*, p. 606) has this note:—

Borwick Hall is a spacious decayed house, *temp.* Charles I., but with a much older peel at the east end. The great hall is still entire. Over the fireplace are the arms of Bindloss, impaling West, and beneath the names, " Byndlos West," the second wife of Sir Francis having been Cecilia, daughter of Thomas West, Lord de la Ware. One of the bedrooms was the ancient chapel, and adjoining is the priest's closet, beneath which still remains a secret place, into which the persecuted ecclesiastics, on pressing part of the floor, suddenly descending, eluded for the time all further search. When Charles II. was at Borwick Hall, in August, 1651, he was little aware in how few days he was to be indebted for his crown and life to a similar contrivance

After George's death his widow appears to have found speedy solace for his loss in a second husband; for in the following year, 1566, we find her the wife of Thomas Atkinson. Margaret and her second husband evidently got into serious trouble with her son Thomas, for we find " Thomas Atkinson and Margaret his wife" plaintiffs and Thomas Redman defendant, in an action for false imprisonment in Lancaster gaol for trespass on Bewick manor, co. Lancs. In the previous year, 1565, we also find Robert Greenbancke claiming as lessee of George

Redman, who was seized in fee in right of his wife, plaintiff, and Margaret Redmayne, widow, Richard Blackhouse, John Browne, Richard Wilson in right of said Margaret Redmayne, defendants, concerning a capital messuage, called Bewick Hall, Lancs.

In fact, after George's death his widow appears to have found herself generally in troubled waters, and no doubt spent part of her seclusion in Lancaster gaol in brooding over the iniquities of sons and the imprudence of second marriages.

The following pedigree will probably help to the understanding of this part of the Twisleton History :—

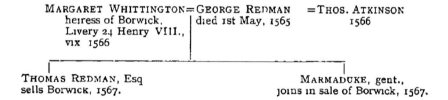

```
MARGARET WHITTINGTON = GEORGE REDMAN    = THOS. ATKINSON
heiress of Borwick,     died 1st May, 1565    1566
Livery 24 Henry VIII.,
vix 1566
        |
  ┌─────┴─────────────────────────────┐
THOMAS REDMAN, Esq            MARMADUKE, gent.,
sells Borwick, 1567.          joins in sale of Borwick, 1567.
```

Thomas and Marmaduke both died before 1587, and evidently without offspring, for in that year we find Thomas Newton claiming as "cousin and heir of Thomas and Marmaduke Redman, now deceased"

Having thus considered the four probable sons of William Redman and Margaret Tunstall—the absolute identity of only one of whom, James, is established—we may return to William's successor in the headship of the Twisleton branch, his grandson William, eldest son of James. When the older William died in 1536, his grandson and successor was barely fourteen years old, and a suitable guardian was found for him in his great-uncle, Cuthbert Tunstall, brother of his grandmother, Margaret Tunstall. On 7th May, 1539, Cuthbert, Bishop of Durham, receives a grant of an annuity of twenty marks issuing from the manor of Twisleton and the messuages, lands, etc., in Bentham, Burton, Westhus, Thornton, Urswicke, Kellote, Gressingham, in Yorkshire and Lancashire, which belonged to William Redmayne, deceased, during the minority of William Redmayne, kinsman and heir of the said William, with the wardship and marriage of the said heir. (Letters and Papers, F. & D., Hen. VIII., vol. xiv.)

On 26th May, 36 Henry VIII. (1544), William Redmayne, gentleman, cousin and heir of William Redmayne, Esquire, deceased, namely the grandson and heir of the said William, deceased, has special licence of entry without proof of age and without livery upon all the lands of his inheritance. (General and Special Liveries).

William, the new Lord of Twisleton, married Margaret, daughter of John Vavasour, Esq., of Hazlewood, Yorks, by Anne, daughter of Henry, seventh Lord Scrope, of Bolton. Through her mother Margaret was descended from the Fitz Hughs, Percies and Nevills, and could if she were so disposed, have boasted a liberal strain of Plantagenet blood.

William and Margaret Redmayne had a daughter Frances who became the wife of Leonard Babthorpe, Esquire; and within three generations all the goodly lands of the Twisleton inheritance seem to have passed from Redman hands. The manor of Redman and Redman (or Redmayne) Hall in Urswick were sold by William in 1565 to Richard Wycliffe, citizen and goldsmith of London (Close Roll—677); and the remaining estates were sold by himself and his immediate descendants, as is evidenced by numerous fines during the latter part of the sixteenth century.

OFF-SHOOTS FROM THE THORNTON COLONY.

CHAPTER XIX.

Kirkby Lonsdale and Ireland.

IN the early years of the seventeenth century a family of Redmans, whose story presents some features of interest, was settled at Kirkby Lonsdale, a few miles distant from the colony of Thornton-in-Lonsdale, of which it was probably an off-shoot. This was the household of "Dominus Jacobus" Redman, who seems to have been vicar of Kirkby Lonsdale, and later, of Halton. The Reverend James married Agnes Otway, of Middleton, bore at least seven children to her husband, and after his death spent the closing years of her life among her own people at Middleton, where she died in 1628.

By her will (3rd September, 1628) in which she is described as "Agnes, widow of James Redman, late parson of Halton," she leaves to her daughters, Isabel and Sarah, portions equal to those which their sisters enjoyed. She bequeaths small legacies to her daughter Rebecca's children, Bryan and James Mansergh; to her sister, "John Otway's wife," and her two daughters; to her "Aunt Bower"; to Dorothy Staveley; and to Mr. Leake, for the care of her children. Her daughter, Margaret, is to have her household goods at a reasonable rate; and the

residue of her property she divides among her seven children.

One of the youngest of these seven surviving children was Daniel, who was born on November 30th, 1617, and thus at the time of his mother's death would be a boy of nearly eleven. He was destined to play a prominent part in the Civil War which broke out a quarter of a century later, and to become the ancestor of some of the Irish nobles of to-day.

When Daniel in his turn sought a wife he found her among his mother's people in Abigail, daughter of Roger Otway, of Middleton, who was probably his first cousin; and by this marriage he became brother-in-law of Sir John Otway, who was three years his junior, and who, at the time of the marriage was probably studying law at one of the Inns of Court in London. In later life Otway played a conspicuous part as a supporter of his king in the Civil War, was appointed vice-chancellor of the Duchy of Lancaster and chancellor of the county palatine of Durham, and died at the good age of 73.

When the Civil War began, Daniel, who had probably been trained as a soldier, threw in his lot with the Parliamentarians, served in Ireland under Henry Cromwell, younger son of the Protector, and rose to the rank of colonel. His brother-in-law, Otway, was just as zealous in the cause of the Royalists; and thus, as in so many other cases, including that of Sir John Redmayne and his son-in-law, Colonel Forbes, we find two members of a family espousing opposite causes and bearing arms against each other.

This unnatural state of things was naturally not pleasing to Otway, and, setting to work to convince his brother-in law of his iniquity, he succeeded so well that he actually converted him into one of Charles's most staunch champions. The records give us at least one interesting glimpse of Colonel Daniel in his martial character :—

"When General Lambert was endeavouring to oppose Monk's march from Scotland, Redman hastened up to Yorkshire from London, and as soon as the soldiers who had served under him in Ireland caught sight of their old commander, they vowed they would be led by no other officer; and accordingly 1500 horsemen followed him without more ado, leaving Lambert in the lurch, and clearing the road for the passage of General Monk." (*Sedbergh, &c.*, by W. Thompson, M.A.).

For his military services Redman was rewarded by a grant of large estates in Ireland; and to the church of Kirkby Lonsdale, the place of his birth, he gave part of an estate which he had received for his exertions in capturing a castle at Ballinabole, near Kilkenny. These acres at one time yielded a rental of about £70 a year; but for the last twenty years, I understand, they have contributed nothing to the Kirkby Lonsdale living. It may be mentioned that among the Lansdowne MSS. are certain letters written by James Redman (probably Daniel's father) to Henry Cromwell, chief governor of Ireland, under whom his son was serving.

When Colonel Redman had no more use for his sword he seems to have settled down peacefully on his Kilkenny estates. He had two daughters, Ellinor and Elizabeth, the former of whom became the wife of Viscount Ikerrin, ancestor of the Earls of Carrick, Clancarty and others of our present-day nobles.

The following are summaries of the wills of Daniel and his wife, Elizabeth, who seems to have survived him a few years :—

By his will, dated 14th December, 1674, "Daniell Redman, esquire, of Ballilinck, in the county of Kilkenny, appoints his wife, Abigail Redman, sole executrix." He refers to his well-beloved sister, Ellinor Jeonar, directs the residue of his personalty after the death of his wife, to be divided between his two daughters, Ellinor and Elizabeth.

He gives to Ellinor Jeonar the castle, town and lands of Inishmay, barony of Killclogher, for her life; and after her death to his daughters or one of them according to his wife's discretion. He appoints as overseers of his will Richard Stephens, and Nathaniel Dunbavant, esquires, of the city of Dublin, counsellors-at-law.

Signed and sealed with the Redman coat-of-arms.

The will of Abigail Redman, widow of Colonel Daniel Redman, is dated 7th May, 1680.

She appoints as executrixes her daughters, Ellinor and Elizabeth, and gives land at Glanmagorn to be equally divided between them. To her sister, Ellinor Jeonar, the lease of her house in Kilkenny for life, remainder to testatrix's daughter, the Viscountess Ikerrin, and her daughter, Elizabeth.

To her grandchild, Pierce Butler, the lease of Loughmarash; to her daughter, Elizabeth, her coach and pair of horses and her little riding-horse. To her kinswoman, Sara Hebblethwaite, six milch cows and other stock. She directs that her funeral shall be private and by torchlight, and appoints her sister, Ellinor Jeonar, and her kinsman, Captain Thomas Mayers, to be overseers of her will.

Colonel Daniel was not however the first member of his family to own large estates in Ireland. Just twenty years before he was cradled at Kirkby Lonsdale, Marmaduke Redmayne, esquire, of Thornton-in-Lonsdale, received the substantial grant of 8,000 of the forfeited acres of Munster, in company with Thomas Fleetwood, esquire, whose slice of the disaffected province ran to 12,000 acres. The following is part of the original grant:—

39th year of Elizabeth.

Grant to Thomas Fleetewood, esq., son and heir of John Fleetewood, of Caldwich, Staffordshire, esq., and Marmaduke Redmayne, of Thorneton, Yorkshire, esq., of the lands of Cloghlych, containing by estimation one ploughland, Glanmore alias Glancure, and Ballenekarigry 1½ pl., Kyllordy, 2 pl. Kariginutan and Muckrony, ½ pl., Ballenhowe, alias Ballenderawyn 1 pl., etc., etc., etc., amounting in all by estimation to 12,667 English acres, as parcels of two seignories, one of 12,000 acres allotted to Fleetewood, and one of 8,000 acres allotted to Redmayne. To hold by the name of Colonye Fleetewood for ever, in fee farm, by fealty, in common socage. Rent £71 2s. 6½d., English, from 1594 (half for three years preceeding). If the lands are found to contain more than the estimated number of acres, grantee shall pay 1⅜d for each additional English acre. Grantees to erect houses for 95 families, of which one to be for themselves, 8 for freeholders, 6 for farmers, and 42 for copyholders. Other conditions usual in grants for planting the undertakers in Munster.

I have been unable to identify the Marmaduke of this grant with certainty, as there were two Marmadukes of position living at the same time in the district of Thornton—one, the son of Richard Redmayne and Elizabeth Cholmeley, who survived to 1607; and the other, Marmaduke, third son of William Redman, of Ireby, by Isabel Tunstall. A third Marmaduke of the district, who, however, appears to have been dead a dozen years before the date of the grant, was the younger son of George Redman (? of Twisleton) by Margaret Whittington, heiress of Borwick.

For some reason or other Marmaduke never took possession of his Munster acres, probably owing to the extremely disturbed condition of the province, which in the following year was invaded and ravaged by Tyrone. It was not, indeed, until Sir George Carew became president of Munster in 1600 that it could be considered at all a possible place to settle in. Marmaduke's 8,000 acres were regranted to others, *temp* James I.

FULFORD.

It was from Thornton-in-Lonsdale that the Redmans of Fulford, near York, derived their origin, the following account of which appears among the Parker manuscripts, at Browsholme, written by Robert Parker, Esq., of Marley, as long ago as 1666:—

"Redman of ffulforth bears for his coate armour, gules, three quishons ermine, buttons and taschelles, or.

EDWARD Redmane, of Gressingham, in the county of Lancaster, discarded out of the family of Thorneton, being a second son, married to Alice, daughter of Mr. Thomas Southworth, (He married Cicile, younger daughter and co-heir to Richard Southworth, of Gressingham) by her had issue John, who purchased lands att ffulforth, near the city of York. (He married Isabel, daughter of . . . . . but had no issue. Inq. p. m. 2 June 1575, will dated 1574. Dec. 13, died 31 Dec. 1574). Richard Readman, brother and heir, aged 60 years and more; but died without issue, having given the said lands unto John, son and heir of Richard, his younger brother.

"Richard Redmane, second son of Edward, maried Margaret, daughter of Mr. Christopher Mayler, by her had issue John Redmane, of ffulforth; Margaret, married to Mr. John Parkinson; Isabell, to Mr. William Robinson, alderman of the city of York; Agnes, to Mr. John Metcalf, and Ellen to Mr. John Tompkin."

According to the following fragmentary pedigree, Edward Redman, of Gressingham, founder of the family of Fulford, was second son of Richard of Thornton,—probably a great-grandson of the original Thomas, and younger brother of Richard, who died v. p. ante 1498 (see Thornton pedigree):—

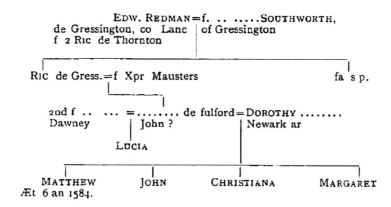

The knightly family of Southworth from which Edward took his wife was of considerable antiquity and standing in Lancashire. A Gilbert de Southworth appears as witness to a deed in Edward I.'s time. A later Gilbert was sheriff of Lancashire in 1320-1; and a third Gilbert probably fought at Agincourt. There was at least one other alliance between the families of Redman and Southworth, that of Brian (vix. 1492), son of Thomas, of Ireby, with Elizabeth, daughter and co-heiress of Richard Southworth, of Gressingham, esquire, and sister of Cecily, wife of Edward, of Gressingham.

The following is the inquisition p. m. on RICHARD, son of Edward, of Thornton, and father of John.—

INQUISITION taken at the Castle of York, 29 July. 21 Eliz., 1579 p m. Richard Redman, who died seized of ⅓ of Manor of Shipton, late parcel of the possessions of St. Mary at York, ⅓ of 9 messuages, 6 cottages and lands in Shipton; ⅓ of 4 messuages, lands, &c., in Gatesalturth, ⅓ of a messuage in Waterfulforth, called Rosehall, with lands belonging late of the Earl of Rutland deceased, ⅓ of 20 acres of meadow in Myton Inges, ⅓ of a messuage with lands in Skipwith, ⅓ of 4 messuages, &c, in Bennyngburge, ⅓ of a rent of 40^s in Northdalton, ⅓ of a mill in Gatesfulfurth, a capital messuage called Upperhall in Grassingham, Co. Lancs, with lands belonging; and the capital messuage in Grassingham, called Netherhall, with lands belonging &c. &c.

And the said Richard Redmayne died 12th June last past, and John Redmayne is his son and next heir, and was of full age at his father's death. (File 266. No. 98).

Richard, who, six years before his death, was executor of the will of his namesake at Thornton, appears to have married a daughter of Christopher Mansergh and to have had, in addition to his heir, John, four daughters:—Margaret, who married a Parkinson (variously called Laurence and John), of Lancashire; Isabel, who married William Robinson, alderman of York; Ellinor, wife of John Tompson or Tompkins; and Agnes, wife of John Metcalfe, probably of the ancient family of Nappa. (About the same time it is interesting to note that another member of this family, Leonard Metcalfe, of Beare Park, Esq , who took part in the Rising of the North in 1569, married a daughter of James Redman of Twisleton).

William Robinson, who married Isabel Redman, was Lord Mayor of York in 1581 and 1594, and twice M.P. for that city. From this union sprang four generations of English statesmen:—Thomas Robinson, first Lord Grantham, who was Ambassador and Secretary of State (died 1770); Thomas, second Lord Grantham, Foreign Secretary (died 1786); Frederick, Viscount Goderich and Earl of Ripon, who was Colonial Secretary and Premier (died 1859); and the present Marquis of Ripon, who has filled several of the highest offices of state.

JOHN Redman, Richard's successor, was succeeded by his son MATTHEW, who was born in 1578; married in 1600, Margaret, daughter and heiress of William Grosvenor, of York (Paver's Marriage Licences); and was knighted by James I., at Windsor, on the 9th July, 1603 (Cotton MS. Claudius c iii.)

The further history of this family of Fulford scarcely calls for special mention. The accompanying pedigree gives its descent down to the latter part of the seventeenth century. It may, however, be well to note the following marriages:—

1626. Jo. Redman, Esq., of Water Fulford, and Jane Claphamson, daughter of Robert Claphamson, notary public of St. Martin, Coney Street, York—at Fulford or St. Martin:

1626. William Waller, of Middlethorpe, and Elizabeth Redman, of Fulford—at Fulford: and in

1627. George Baguley, "clerk," and Mary Redman, of Fulford—at St. Denis, York. (Paver's Marriage Licences).

It is not improbable that the two Redmans, who were Lord Mayors of YORK in the 18th century, were cadets of Fulford.

WILLIAM, the senior of them, married Mary Sotheby, by whom he had

(1) Watkinson Redmayn, who was in America in 1724.

(2) Alice, who married Richard Atkinson. (Familiae Minorum Gentium).

In his will (1728-9), in which he is described as "late Alderman and Lord Mayor of York," the following names occur:—son and daughter, Richard Atkinson and Alice, his wife; Christian Stables; grandsons, Redman Stables and John Redman; and sister, Beatrix Leadall. (Vol. 80. Index to York wills).

The will of CHARLES, the second of the Redman Lord Mayors of York, is dated 1731-2 (Vol. 82, Index to York wills). His sister, Jane, married Samuel Staniforth, of Attercliffe (Fam. Min. Gent.)

Redman of Fulford.

ARMS —Quarterly, 1 and 4 Gules, a chevron, arg between 3 cushions ermine, tasseled or, a crescent charged with a crescent for difference—*Redman* 2 and 3 sable, a chevron between 3 cross crosslets, arg. a crescent for difference—*Southworth*

CREST —On a cushion gules, tasseled or, a horse's head crined of the last, a crescent for difference

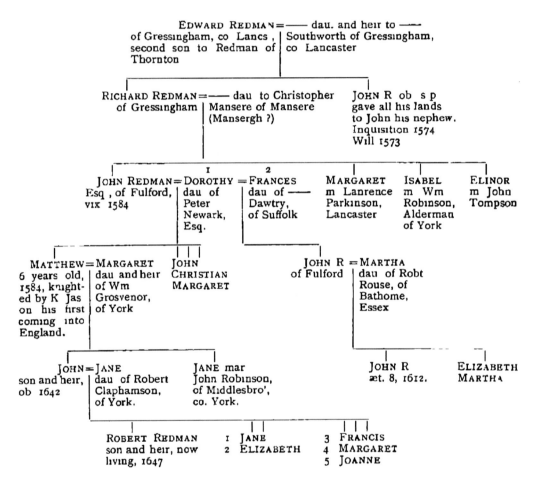

(*Visitation of Yorks, Glover, Somerset Herald, 1584-5, etc*).

LONDON.

Among the more enterprising younger sons of the Redman family who adventured to London in search of fortune, several, no doubt, hailed from this district of Thornton-in-Lonsdale.

The visitation of London in 1568 (G. 10, 76 F 1, 202, College of Arms) discloses one of them in the William Redman, Citizen, of the following pedigree:—

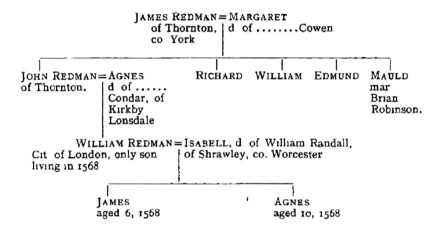

James, of Thornton, who heads this pedigree, was probably born circa 1480, and may have been a great grandson of Thomas, the earliest ascertained member of this colony. Another London Redman, probably also a Thornton descendant, appears in the will of Richard, of Thornton (1573), who directs payment of his debt to William Redman, of London "Stone."

A generation earlier, in 1540, John Redman, who was probably a son of William, of Twisleton, and Margaret Tunstall, and a nephew of Dr. Tunstall, Bishop of London, was appointed Prebendary of Westminster; and eleven years later his body was laid to rest in the Abbey there. In the Letters and Papers, Hen. VIII., vol. xviii.,

OFF-SHOOTS FROM THORNTON COLONY.

pt. 1, among certain property in the Strand granted to one William Lambert, mention is made of "another (tenement) there between Wm. Cholmley's tenement in the East and the gate of the Middle Temple, and tenement within it of Alice, widow of Ric. Redmayn, on the West." (18 Mar., 34 Hen. VIII.) The identity of this Richard, husband of Alice, I am unable to discover.

There is, no doubt, an interesting field in London for students of the history of this family to explore; for it is practically certain that for at least three and a half centuries there has been an unbroken succession of Redmans almost within sound of Bow Bells. One of them lies buried in the churchyard of Stepney, under an altar-tomb, of which Mr. J. T. Page in his "Stepney Churchyard: Its Monuments and Inscriptions," gives the following description :—

An altar-tomb much sunk in the ground, and the upper slab broken. Remains of inscriptions on slab, surrounded by crest and coat-of-arms, but very little of it can now be described correctly.

Crest. A dexter hand, couped at the wrist, apaumée

Arms. Three cushions, impaling a chief ermine

INSCRIPTION
In memory of JOHN REDMAN
. . . . July 176 . .
Aged 75
(The rest quite defaced).

This John Redman of Stepney, Mr. Page tells me, was quite an important man in his day and within his parish. His name is still perpetuated in the district by the well-known street called Redman's Road. John's crest brands him as of Thornton origin; and we shall not probably go far wrong in identifying him as a descendant of the William of the above pedigree, who was a citizen of London town in the sixteenth century.

If I may be pardoned a single personal allusion, the only one I shall presume to make in this book, I should like to be allowed to place on record that my dear mother, born Ellen Redmayne, whose memory has largely inspired such work as I have been able to do on Redman history, spent the closing years of her life in my home in a London suburb, and lies buried in the churchyard of Heston. Of her, as of Margaret Redmayne, of Thornton, it may truly be said.—"She was a woman of generous disposition, courteous to all and kind to the poor."

THE TUNSTALLS OF THURLAND CASTLE.

CHAPTER XX.

Arms—Sable, three combs, Argent.

THE alliances between the families of Redman and Tunstall were so many and extended over so long a period that no history of either family can be considered at all complete without a special and detailed reference to the other; and for this reason I can plead justification for a brief sketch of the family of Thurland Castle, which for nearly three and a half centuries flourished on the border of Lancashire, within a short distance of their Redman neighbours in the district of Thornton-in-Lonsdale.

There were Tunstalls of note in north Lancashire, in the days of the second Edward. HENRY de Tunstall had possessions in Lancaster in 1324; and his son, Sir WILLIAM, in 1373 obtained a grant of free warren in Tunstal, Cancefield, Burgh in Lonsdale, Leeke and Norton. (Rot. chart. 47 Ed. III., n. 14). It was William's son, Sir THOMAS, who appears to have built the castle of Thurland, in the valley of the Lune, which early in the fifteenth century he obtained a licence to embattle. Sir Thomas was a right gallant knight, who with his six men-at-arms and eighteen horse at his back gave a good account of himself on the field of Agincourt. He married Isabel, daughter of Sir Nicholas Harrington, a knightly neighbour

HENRY DE TUNSTAL, 17 Ed II (1324)
SIR WILLIAM DE TUNSTAL = ALICE, daur of Sir Philip Lindsey

├── SIR THOMAS = ISABEL, daur of Sir Nicholas Harrington, temp Ed III
│   │
│   ├── JOHANNA = SIR MATT REDMAN, of Harewood Castle, circ 1416
│   │
│   ├── SIR THOMAS = ELEANOR, daur of Hy., 3rd Lord Fitzhugh, of Ravensworth
│   │   │
│   │   ├── SIR RICHARD, K G, Chamberlain to Hy. VI, Ambassador to France, &c, ob 1493
│   │   │   │
│   │   │   └── William ob s p
│   │   │   THOMAS, ob s p
│   │   │
│   │   ├── SIR THOMAS = ALICE, daur of George Nevill, Archbishop of York, g g, grandson of Edw III
│   │   │   Constable of Conway Castle, Sheriff of Carnarvon
│   │   │   │
│   │   │   ├── (3) CUTHBERT, Bishop of London and Durham, ob 1559
│   │   │   │
│   │   │   ├── (2) SIR BRIAN = ISABEL, daur of Sir Henry Boynton
│   │   │   │   the 'Stainless Knight,'
│   │   │   │   killed at Flodden, 1513
│   │   │   │   Will 16 Aug., 1513   Inq
│   │   │   │   p m 21 Mar. 5 Hen VIII
│   │   │   │   │
│   │   │   │   ├── SIR MARMADUKE = ALICE, d & co-h of Sir Robert Scargill, of Scargill, &c (Will 31 Dec., 1578)
│   │   │   │   │   ob 1566
│   │   │   │   │   │
│   │   │   │   │   ├── FRANCIS = (1) ELIZABETH, daur of Sir William Radcliffe, of Ordsall, Lancs
│   │   │   │   │   │   (2) ANN, daur of Richard Bold, of Bold.
│   │   │   │   │   │
│   │   │   │   │   ├── ISABEL = WILLIAM REDMAN, Esq of Ireby
│   │   │   │   │   │
│   │   │   │   │   ├── ANN = JOHN MIDDLETON, of Middleton Hall
│   │   │   │   │   │
│   │   │   │   │   ├── ELIZABETH = SIR JOHN DAWNAY, of Sessay
│   │   │   │   │   │
│   │   │   │   │   └── ANN = GEORGE MIDDLETON, Esq, of Leighton, co Lancs.
│   │   │   │   │
│   │   │   │   └── BRIAN, of Battersea, Will 2 Aug, 1539
│   │   │   │
│   │   │   └── MARGARET = WM REDMAN, Esq., of Twisleton
│   │   │
│   │   └── MARGARET = SIR RALPH PUDSAY, Kt., of Bolton
│   │
│   └── [children of Sir Thomas & Eleanor:]
│   WILLIAM = ANNE, d of — Parr, Esq
│   ROBERT = — d of Bellingham, Esq
│   MARY = SIR JOHN RADCLIFFE
│   ALICE = SIR THOS PARR
│   ELIZABETH = SIR ROBT BELLINGHAM
│   CATHERINE = SIR JOHN PENNINGTON
│
└── ANNE = SIR ROBT NEVILL, of Hornby Castle

of ancient family, and by her was father of at least eight children, all of whom made excellent alliances and flourished exceedingly.

One daughter, Johanna, was won (circa 1416) by young Sir Matthew Redman, of Harewood, and transmitted her virtues down a long line of descendants; while her brothers and sisters married into the families of Parr, Bellingham, Radcliffe, Pennington and Fitz-hugh. Her eldest brother, THOMAS, the head of his house, found a wife in Eleanor, daughter of Henry, third Lord Fitz Hugh, who, through her mother, brought a strain of Marmion blood into Tunstall veins. The eldest son of this marriage, Sir RICHARD, proved worthy of his Marmion and Tunstall ancestry. It was he who so bravely held the castle of Harlech—Henry VI.'s last stronghold— the defence of which is one of the most inspiring stories in the history of warfare. But Richard's loyalty and valour cost him dearly; for when Edward IV. came to the throne his name figured largely among the one hundred and fifty-three Lancastrians who were attainted by Parliament. His large estates were forfeited and conferred on Sir James Harrington, who held them for a dozen years until, in 1473, Richard came to his own again. He was Chamberlain to the King he risked so much to serve, was Ambassador to France, and filled other high offices with distinction.

Sir Richard had a son, WILLIAM, who died s.p. and was succeeded by his uncle, THOMAS, also a knight, who was constable of Conway Castle, and sheriff of Carnarvon, and who had for wife, Alice, daughter of George Nevill, Archbishop of York, Edward III.'s great-great-grandson. Thus through "time-honoured Lancaster," did a strain of Plantagenet blood mingle with that of Tunstall and of their Redman descendants.

The next generation of Tunstalls produced two men of great repute in their day and of no little honour in our own—one, a brave knight, SIR BRIAN TUNSTALL, "The Undefiled," was one of the most splendid of all the figures that adorned the age of chivalry; and the other, a great churchman, DR CUTHBERT TUNSTALL, was twice a bishop, and friend of Henry VIII.

SIR BRIAN TUNSTALL.

The crown of Sir Brian's too brief life was the glorious episode of Flodden, which was also its close. Scott has given his prowess in that battle the immortality it deserves, and one cannot read his tribute without a thrill of pride that England has produced such men, and that from one of the purest and bravest knights who ever carried a lance have sprung many members of the Redman family. Sir Brian, with Sir Edward Howard, led the van of the English army which sustained the charge of the Scots' advanced column of 10,000 men under Lord Hume. So terrible seemed the impending shock that the English wavered and would probably have broken, had not Tunstall rallied them with brave words and flung himself against the onrushing Scots.

Who, that has read them, does not recall the lines in which Lord Surrey describes to Marmion the disposition of the English forces :—

> The good Lord Marmion, by my life
>   Welcome to danger's hour !
> Short greeting serves in time of strife—
>   Thus have I ranged my power.
> Myself will rule this central host,
>   Stout Stanley fronts their right,
> My sons command the vaward post,
>   With Brian Tunstall, stainless knight.

And again, as Blount and Fitz Eustace "with Lady Clare upon the hill," watched the "battle raging on the plain."—

> Amid the tumult, high
> They saw Lord Marmion's falcon fly;
> And stainless Tunstall's banner white,
> And Edmund Howard's lion bright,
> Still bear them bravely in the fight.

until, when disaster had overtaken the English army, Marmion with his dying breath, bids his squire,

> Fitz Eustace, to Lord Surrey hie;
> Tunstall lies dead upon the field,
> His lifeblood stains the spotless shield
> Edmund is down,—my life is reft,—
> The Admiral alone is left.

Never was braver heart stilled on any battlefield than that of the young Lancashire knight; and it was a fitting tribute to his valour and spotless fame that his body should have a military escort all the way from Flodden Field to its last resting-place in Tunstall. There is still to be seen in Tunstall church a stone figure which tradition says is that of Sir Brian; but, according to Mr. W. O. Roper, F.S.A., it is more probably that of Brian's great-grandfather, Sir Thomas, who built the castle of Thurland.

Sir Brian had married Isabel, daughter of Sir Henry Boynton, of Acklam and Barmston, by his wife Margaret, daughter and co-heiress of Sir Martin de la See, and was succeeded by his son, Sir Marmaduke, of whom later. In his will, which was made on the 16th August, 1513, shortly before his fatal journey to Flodden, he leaves a small legacy to his brother-in-law, William Redman, of Twisleton, whom he appoints one of his executors :—

Item to my Brother Redmayne for my syster marryage XXIII^s... also that my wyff be myne executrix, my broder Wm Tunstall, Wm. Redmayne and Edm. P^{r}Kynsone be myne exors.

Dr. Cuthbert Tunstall,

Bishop of Durham and London,

was brother of Sir Brian and son of Sir Thomas Tunstall and Alice Nevill. At the time of his brother's death at Flodden, Cuthbert was thirty-nine and well on the way to the high dignities he won later. He was educated at Oxford, Cambridge, and Padua, and became in turn rector of Stanhope, archdeacon of Chester, rector of Harrow, Master of the Rolls, dean of Salisbury (1519), Bishop of London (1522) and of Durham (1530). He was sent on several important diplomatic missions—in company with Sir Thomas More, to Charles V. at Brussels, where his long and close friendship with Erasmus began; to France and Germany; and he accompanied Wolsey, with whom he was on terms of great intimacy, on his splendid embassy to France. He also acted as guide and companion to Henry VIII. on one of his royal progresses through England.

Under Edward VI., chiefly through the influence of Northumberland, he was deprived of his rich see of Durham and was sent to the Tower, where he remained in durance until Mary came to her throne and restored him to his liberty and dignities. It is remembered to his lasting honour that during the whole of Mary's reign not a single victim died for heresy throughout his diocese. On Elizabeth's accession he was again deprived, and died six weeks later in Archbishop Parker's house at Lambeth (1559). It should, perhaps, be stated here that there has always been great difference of opinion as to Cuthbert's legitimacy. Surtees thought he was legitimate; but the National Dictionary of Biography gives him the bar sinister.

Margaret Tunstall, sister of Brian and Cuthbert, became the wife of William Redmayne, of Twisleton; and her son, John, probably owed much of his advancement in life to his uncle's influence and counsel

Sir Brian's son and successor in the family estates, Sir MARMADUKE, married Alice, daughter and co-heiress of Sir Robert Scargill, of Scargill and Thorpe Stapleton. He took a prominent part in the suppression of the monasteries; and his name appears on the deed of surrender of Furness Abbey. He narrowly escaped the the fury of the Pilgrimage of Grace rebels, who surrounded Thurland Castle and would have burned it, had not "some more sobre than the residew refreyned them."

Sir Marmaduke had a son, FRANCIS, who succeeded him, and who had for his first wife Elizabeth, daughter of Sir William Radcliffe, a Lancashire knight, and for his second, Ann, daughter of Richard Bold, of Bold, and three daughters—

(1) Isabel, who married William Redman, of Ireby.
(2) Elizabeth, wife of Sir John Dawnay, of Sessay, co. York, from whom the Viscounts Downe derive descent, and
(3) Ann, who married George Middleton, Esq., of Leighton, co. Lanc. (St. George's visitation).

As we have already seen (p. 192) Lady Tunstall, by her will, left small legacies to all her Redman grandchildren, "gotten of the body of my daughter, Isabell."

With later generations of the Tunstalls we have less concern. There was, however, one other alliance with the Redman family of which mention should be made—that of Giles Redmayne, of Ingleton, with Agnes Grace, daughter of Thomas Tunstall, of Thornton, from which union the Redmaynes of Newcastle are descended.

Thurland Castle,

Which was the home of so many generations of Tunstalls and to which at least three Redmans went to woo their wives, stands in its extensive park, near the banks of the Lune, about a dozen miles from Lancaster, and but a short walk from the borders of Yorkshire. When it was being built Levens was probably a century old, and Sir Richard Redman was already established at Harewood Castle; but in its five centuries of existence it has survived many strange experiences.

During the Civil War, when it had passed out of Tunstall hands, it sustained two sieges by the Roundheads—first under Colonel Ashton, and again under Colonel Rigby.

From Manchester, in Lancashire, they wrote that Colonel Ashton hath taken two castles in the north part of that county, the name of one being Hornby Castle and the other Thurland Castle, where he hath taken Sir John Girlington, a strong malevolent in those parts, and also much money and plate, with many disaffected ladies and gentlewomen who were fled for shelter into those castles" (Certaine Information, No 23, p. 181, 1643, Wednesday, June 21).

A month after its surrender Sir John Girlington was back in the castle, and once more the Parliamentary troops,—this time under Colonel Alexander Rigby, presented themselves before its walls. The second siege lasted seven weeks, at the end of which time the castle was delivered to Rigby to be demolished; while its defenders were allowed to "passe away with their lives and goods." A great part of it was destroyed by fire; but fortunately the principal towers were allowed to remain untouched.

More than two centuries after Cromwell's men had worked their will on the castle it was nearly destroyed by fire. The centre tower, containing the entrance hall, was gutted, and a large part of the eastern portion was destroyed.

Of the castle Mr. Roper *(Local Gleanings)* says:—

It is surrounded by a moat of about six or eight feet, supplied by the river Cant The sole entrance is on the west side by means of a narrow bridge, immediately across which are the remains of the old Gatehouse, and a little behind them the ruins of an ancient tower The present castle forms two sides of an oblong, the eastern and a portion of the south side belonging to the ancient building. The western wing has never been completed. The whole castle was restored early in the present century, and it is now somewhat difficult to distiguish the modern additions from the ancient work. The walls of the older part are in very many places more than six feet in thickness.

The Tunstall tenure of Thurland Castle, which lasted nearly two and a half centuries, ceased in 1637, when the castle passed into the hands of the Girlington family, who again alienated it towards the close of the same century to the Welsh family of Leck.

UNIDENTIFIED REDMANS.

CHAPTER XXI.

IN exploring family records which cover so many centuries it is inevitable that one should encounter many names to which a definite place on the family tree cannot be assigned, or which, even if their identity is recognised, do not come into the direct current of the family story. These names, however, are too interesting in many cases to pass by in silence, and I therefore propose to review the more prominent of them in this chapter. They are given in alphabetical and not in chronological order.

In 1331 ADAM de Redman acknowledges that he owes to Robert de Sandford five marks to be levied in default on his chattels and lands in Co. Westmorland (Close Rolls, Ed. III.); and in 13 Ed. III. I also find an Adam de Redeman, holding lands in Raventhwaite, Co Westmorland. He was probably Adam, of Yealand, a younger son of Sir Matthew (II), of Levens, who survived to 1351.

ALAN Redemane, of Whaplode, is mentioned in the Patent Rolls, 1385-9. In the list of Mayors of Kendal the name of CHRISTOPHER Redman appears several times,—as Mayor in 1679-80, 1695-6, and in 1749-50, 1760-1 and 1761-2 (Nicholson's *Annals of Kendal*). There was also a Christopher Redman, whose daughter and heiress Lydia became the wife of James Flavel, of Normanton (d. 1714). The Redman Flavel, of Normanton, who married Ann, daughter of Richard Wordsworth (d. 1700) was probably a son of James and Lydia. Ann was great aunt to William Wordsworth, the poet. (Speight's *Kirkby Overblow*, p. 128). In 11 Richard II (1317-8) there was a grant by William Robinson del Chaumbre de Hencastre to EDWARD de Redmane, of lands at Hincaster (Hist. MSS. Comm. Rep. 10, pt. 4, Levens Hall Papers); and in 1543 Edward Redmayne, LL.B., has a grant of 5th canonry in St Stephen's Chapel, beside Westminster Palace, having been presented by Thomas Deye, draper, and John Deye, pewterer, of London, by virtue of an advowson granted them by William, Bishop of Norwich. GEOFFREY Redman appears in 1335—" Rex cepit fidelitatem Galfridi, fil. Will Redeman, consanguinei Willi Berchand, &c. (Abb. Rot. Orig, vol. ii., p. 96.)

On 20th January, 1456-7, a mandate issued to "Mr. GILES Redman, bachelor of decrees," rector of Bentham, to induct Dom. Oliver Bland to the rectory of Claughton. And Giles Redman figures among the Mayors of Kendal, alternately with Christopher (above), in 1649-50, 1690-1, and 1725-6 (Nicholson's *Annals of Kendal*). In the State Papers for 1692, February 4th, there is a note of a warrant to prepare a bill for the charter incorporating the Company of Pearl Fishers in the rivers Irt and End, and other waters in co. Cumberland. Heads of charter, Thomas Patrickson, gent., to be first governor. In the list of first assistants the names of Giles and Hugh appear.

Among the nobles on the roll of "Humfrey" de Bohun, Earl of Essex and Constable of England, containing offers of service made at the muster of Carlisle in 1300, for the army against Scotland, is John, Lord Greystoke, who offered services due from two and a half knights' fees by

Henry Redman and four others, with five horses fully equipped. And in a cartulary of Cockersand Abbey (circa 1300) among the benefactors are Henry, son of Henry de Redman, and Henry, son of Norman de Redman. The lands given to the Abbey were in Frebank, Newbiggin, Hotone, Lupton, Yeland, &c. A Henry also appears in the Close Rolls, 10th August, 1328, as one of the sureties for Thurstan de Northlegh.

JAMES de Redman was a juror on the inquisition, taken after the death of Philippa, wife of Robert de Veer, Duke of Ireland, 13 Hen. IV. (1412). (Rawl. MS. B. 438, fo. 70b).

In the Ormonde Papers, 5th report, Catholic Chapter of London, is a letter written on 24th November, 1609, by JOHN Redman to Dr. Smith; and another John, in 1485, received a grant for life of an annuity of £10 from the issues of the King's Lordship of Middleham (Pat. Rolls). William, Abbot of York (Wm. Thornton, Abbot of St. Mary's Abbey), writing to Cromwell on 1st July, 1533, says:—"I have sent you the lease to Thomas Whalley and John Redman, of the Parsonage of Rudstone" (Letters and Papers F & D—vol. vi., p. 746), and in the following year (1534) the Abbot sends a letter to Cromwell by John Redman, "who has a little tithe in Kendal granted him by my predecessors" (Letters and Papers, &c., vol. viii.). In the 17th century there was a Dr. John Redman, of Caius College, Cambridge, who was born in 1625. He was a probationer of Merchant Tailors' School, and may have been a grandson of James Redman, of Thornton, who settled in London. A John Redman (of Austwick) also appears in a Roll dated 1st May, 1641 (now at Browsholme Hall), of those who took the oath of protestation

UNIDENTIFIED REDMANS.

MAUD Redman was the second wife of Thomas Leigh, of Isell, co. Cumberland, who gave her the manor of Isell. After her husband's death she married Wilfred Lawson,

And as frankly conveyed over the inheritance to him as she had received it of Leigh, which Wilfred (afterwards Sir Wilfred) having no issue by the said Maud, his wife, settled his estate upon William Lawson, a kinsman of his own, to the great disgust of Mary Irton (heir general of Maud Redman) who had long time before continued in hopes that he would have settled it upon her, but being disappointed so that she attempted to recover it by law against William, pretending that Maud Redman had not made a legal conveyance to Sir Wilfred, and that what she did was the effect of horrible threatenings and violence. But the suit was at last ended by composition, William Lawson giving her for her title the tithes of Blencrake, and the demesne of Threlkeld, worth together about £200 per annum

(Denton's *Cumberland* and Nicolson & Burn, vol. ii., p. 95).

Marmaduke Redman figures in the Lansdowne MSS. (British Museum) :—

The case of Marmaduke Redman, Esq. in the House of Lords, concerning the privilege of Parliament

NORMANNUS le Redeman is appointed, 14th July, 1 Ed. III. (1327), arrayer in the wapentake of Lonsdale, with orders to array all men capable of bearing arms and by forced marches to join the King, then at Carlisle—"Quod omnes homines potentes ad pugnandum in comitatu Lancastriae armentur, et diu, noctuque (sic) iter properent ad Regem Edwardum" (Rot. Scot. I. 218). This Norman had two sons, Matthew and William, both of whom were living in 1357, when they were concerned with John and Robert de Roos in the abduction of the Warton heir.

RALPH de Redmaine appears as witness to a grant (circa 1260) by Anice, daughter of Roland de Thornburgh.

ROBERT Redmayne, LL.D., was archdeacon of Norwich early in the seventeenth century. He is mentioned in the Hist. MSS. Com. 7th report, Appendix, p. 438:— "1618, April 13th, before the Venerable Robert Redmayne, LL.D. for the Commissary of George, archbishop of Canterbury, visiting the diocese of Norwich, the see then being vacant." And in the 9th report he occurs, in 1594, as "Archdeacon" Redman. He was probably the Dr. Robert Redman, who was author of a life of Henry V. (Rolls Publications). Sir Robert Redman, escheator, is mentioned in the Yorks. Arch. Journal, vol. xvi., p. 163 n.

In 1484 there was a grant to the King's servant, RICHARD Redemayne, gentleman, of an annuity of 20 marks out of the King's Lordship of Carnonton (?) Cornwall, (Pat. Rolls Ric. III). We find Richard and William Redman under the Hundred of Lonsdale in the muster list of soldiers in the county of Lancaster in 1574 (Harl. MSS., Cod. 1926, ff. 5-19a, and Baines' *History of Lancashire*, p. 173). Richard is responsible for having in readiness for Her Majesty's service, one plate coat, one long bow, one sheaf of arrows, one steel cap or skull, one caliver, and one morion; while William's contribution is precisely the same.

In 1598 a Richard Redman was living at Kearby, near Leeds, and figures in the following barbarous story recorded by Mr. Speight in his *Kirkby Overblow and District*, (pp. 127-8):—

In 1598 one Elizabeth Armistead, formerly of Kearby, was charged with stealing certain sheets from the house of Christopher Favell, of Kearby, and likewise the same woman did feloniously take certain articles from the house of Richard Redman, at the same place. For these larcenies the poor woman was ordered to be delivered to the Constable of Kearby and "soundlie whipped throwe the said towne of Kearby," and by him next to be delivered to the Constable of Kirkby Overblow, and he was to see to like execution within his town. She was then to be handed over to the Constable of Wetherby and publicly exhibited with her stripe-marks in the market-place; and finally to be again whipped with the cat through the town in manner similar to the foregoing.

Richard Redman, J.P. for the West Riding of Yorkshire, died in 1715. He was the father of Lydia Redman, who, as we have seen, married James Favell, of Normanton.

There is one Redman, knight of the shire, whose place on the family-tree I have hitherto been unable to discover. In 1313 "SIMON de Redman, knight of the shire, returned for Westmorland, obtains his writ de expensis for attendance at the Parliament at Westminster, from the third Sunday in Lent, 18th March, to Saturday next before Palm Sunday, 7th April; and from Sunday in three weeks of Easter, 6th May, to the Wednesday following, 9th May—writ tested at Windsor, 10th May, 6 Ed. II." (Close Roll, 6 Ed. II m. 5^d).

In 1336 there was an assignment out of the vicarage of Kirkby Stephen to THOMAS, son of Thomas Redman, with the consent of the Abbot of St. Mary, York, the patron, and of the Bishop of Carlisle as Ordinary (His. MSS. Com. 9th report. See of Carlisle Papers). A Thomas de Redman was appointed custodian, in 1350, of the lands in "Hoten roef" (Westmorland) which belonged to John of Hoten roef, during the minority of the heir, paying 20 marks for his custody and marriage. (Abb. Rot. Orig., vol. ii., p. 212).

In 1376 Thomas de Redman was one of the jurors on

the inquisition p.m. on Joan de Coupland, taken at Kirkby Kendal on Saturday next after the feast of Corpus Christi, 49 Ed. III. He held of Joan divers tenements in Kirkslack, by homage and fealty, and the service of 3s. and 4d yearly, as of her manor. (Dods. MS. 159, fol. 195^b). It was, by the way, of the same Joan de Coupland, wife of John de Coupland to whom King Edward granted the De Coucy estates in Westmorland for his military services, that the Manors of Levens and Lupton were held. (*Duchetiana*, p. 212).

In 1387-8 I find two demises by Thomas Redman, arch-priest of the chantry of the Holy Trinity, of Yeovil. In 1539 another Thomas was among the gentlemen appointed to assist the Deputy Warden of Carlisle. In 1344 we find a commission of Oyer, &c., on information that Thomas Redman, Roger Redman, William Redman, and others had entered the free chase at Bambrigg, in Wensleydale, in the hands of Queen Philippa, &c. (Pat. Rolls, 18 Ed. III.) Ten years later, Thomas de Redman is a juror on the inquisition on Thomas Sturnell (Dods. MS 70, fo. 148^b); and in 1561 we meet a Thomas who was "late Chaplain to the Bishop of Ely" (Calendar to State Papers). He was also master of Jesus College, Cambridge, and was probably a younger son of William Redman, of Twistleton, and Margaret Tunstall. At some date unknown the assize enquired if Thomas, son of Norman de Redmane, with others named in the neighbourhood of Isell, had unjustly disseised the monks of Holmcultram of a tenement in Blencraik (Harleian MS. 3891, f. 104^b). This would probably be the Thomas who was next heir to Alan de Camberton

WALTER Redman appears early in the sixteenth century, as chaplain and one of the executors of Roger

Leyburn, Bishop of Carlisle (Will, 17th July, 1507. Reg. Test. vi., 58ª).

"... Walterum Redman, veritatis professorem ac magistrum ecclesiae collegiatae de Graistoke—capellanos meos."

On September 21st, of the same year, the chapter of York empower Mr. Walter Redman S.T.P., provost of Graystock and others to collect the Bishop's goods.

In Bishop Nicolson's *Miscellany Accounts of the Diocese of Carlisle* (extra series, Cumb. and West A. & A. Society, 1877), on p. 130, is quoted an inscription at Greystoke naming Walter Readman, 1509. A Walter Redman, of Fulston, is mentioned in connection with the Lincolnshire rebellion (Letters and Papers, Hen. VIII., F. & D. vol. xi).

In the list of Recognizances (1518) occurs William Redmayn, for ward of Thomas Whityngton's daughter (Letters and Papers, &c., vol. ii.).

On the 13th March, 1536, the Letters and Papers (vol. x.) disclose a commission to Sir Thomas Tempest, William Redman and others to make inquisition on certain lands in Northumberland, and a William Redman was witness to the will, in 1558, of Thomas Stanley, 2nd Lord Monteagle (Wills of Archdeaconry of Richmondshire, Surtees Society, ed. Canon Raine).

Among the Duke of Manchester's MSS. (Hist. MSS. Com. Rep. 8) is a petition to promote Captain Redman to be major of the regiment of horse in garrison at Northampton, *vice* Major Lytcott promoted to be Colonel.

This is a typical, but very far from exhaustive list of Redmans whose names I have come across but whose identity it remains to discover. In many cases where several Redmans of the same christian name were living at the same time exact identification is almost impossible.

REDMAN ARMS.

CHAPTER XXII.

THE origin of the Redman Arms still remains a tantalizing mystery. To Guillim, it is true, it presented no difficulties whatever, for he gives an exact description of the romantic circumstances which suggested to some remote Redman the cushion or pillow as an appropriate device with which to decorate the family shield.

This nebulous, though valorous, ancestor "being challenged to combat by a stranger, and time and place appointed as usual, was so intent on the performance that, coming very early to the place, and his adversary not arrived, he fell asleep in his tent; at last, the hour being come, the noise of the trumpets sounded to the battle, whereupon waking suddenly he ran furiously upon his antagonist and slew him."

This pleasing fiction might have been more appropriately woven, one would think, for the three pillows of Wunhale, which, according to Mr. Oswald Barron, hint at some ancient English word for a pillow, allied to *wonne*, a pleasure, and *hals*, the neck; but, however reluctantly, we must dismiss it as a satisfactory explanation of the Redman cushions.

Camden, in the essay on 'Surnames" in his "Remains concerning Britain," says, "And so the three pillows Ermin, of Redman of Northumberland, is the coat of

ARMS OF THE EARL OF STRAFFORD.

TO FACE P. 230.

Ran. de Greystock." It is true that the first Redman who was prominently identified with Northumberland, the fourth Sir Matthew, married Joan, widow of William, fourth Baron de Greystock; but this connection is a very slender peg on which to hang the explanation of arms which Redman knights had borne more than two centuries before Matthew went to woo the Greystock widow.

And yet Camden's conjecture finds some support from no less an authority on feudal hereldry than Mr. Barron, who says, "There must be some connection, feudal or in blood, between Greystock and Redmayne. Greystock's cushions, however, are generally drawn square fashion.

Some plausibility is lent to this suggestion by the fact that the earliest-known bearer of the Redman cushions was the first Matthew, whose wife, Amabel, was not improbably a Greystock, and it is conceivable that he might have adopted the arms of his wife's family

The question is discussed at length in the *Northern Genealogist* (vol. v., p. 53) from which I quote.

In the *Northern Genealogist*, vol. iv., p. 106, it is suggested that the three cushions of the Redmayne Arms were probably derived from the three cushions in the Arms of the Greystocks. This theory was put forth by Mr. Greenwood on my suggestion, and my authority for assigning the "three cushions" to Greystock was Papworth's *British Armorial*. In that work it is stated that the arms of Greystock, baron of Greystock, are *three cushions*, and the authorities given are "Glover's Ordinary" and the "Jenyns Roll" (Harl. MS. 6589), and reference is made to the monument of John de Greystock, in Greystock church. It is, however, also true that this work further assigns *Gules, three lozenges argent*, as the arms of Greystock, again giving as reference the "Jenyns

Roll." It further, on the authority of a Roll, A.D. 1299, gives *Argent, three lozenges gules,* as the arms of John, baron of Greystock.

By the kindness of Mr. Joseph Foster, I am able to reproduce from his interesting work, *Feudal Arms*, two contemporary representations of the ancient arms of Greystock, which show that they should be described as three lozenges, not three cushions.

The first represents an incised monumental slab in Greystock church with the inscription JOHES QODAM BARO DE GRAYSTOK. The second word of the inscription I take to mean QUONDAM, and I presume that the tomb is that of John de Greystock, who died in 1305-6. It certainly appears to me that the oblong rectangle in which each of the three lozenges on the shield is framed, represents the carver's somewhat primitive substitute for carving in relief, but I can imagine that Papworth may have been misled by some such drawing, to suppose that the charges on the shield were intended to represent cushions. In any case, however, the second engraving which represents a seal, clearly exhibits three lozenges. I mistrust a little the accuracy of the engraving, but as far as I can judge, the seal would belong to the end of the thirteenth century, and was therefore the seal of the original John de Greystock.

There was another John de Greystock of the second family, who died in 1436, and was buried at Greystock, but this family seems to have borne for arms *Barry, three chaplets vert.*

It is clear that neither of the Greystock families bore the "three cushions"; and, therefore, the suggestion that the Redmans derived those charges from the Greystocks must be abandoned.—W.F.C.

The whole matter is probably accurately summed up in this expression of opinion by Colonel Parker :—" I do not for a moment think that the Redman cushions owe their origin to any other family. The Greystocks did not bear cushions. The Redman arms are distinct from all their contemporaries, and appear in the most ancient Roll of Arms, and that is quite sufficient evidence of their originality. The Greystock family was not a whit more honourable ; and at the date of their connection with the Redmans bore three *chaplets* for arms."

The Redman arms appear thus in Glover's Roll (1243-6) which blazons two hundred and eighteen coats-of-arms :—

Maheu de Redman,—*de goules, trois horeillers* (cushions) *d'or.*

And thus, whatever may have been their origin, they have now been borne for at least six hundred and sixty years, and are entitled to rank with the very oldest coats in England. The three cushions, it is interesting to note, have been or are borne by the following families :—

The Earls of Moray—*arg. three pillows, gules ;*

Bruce of Annandale—*arg. a saltire sable, on a chief gu, three cushions or ;*

Dunbar—*or, three cushions within the royal tressure, gules ;*

Brisbane, Kirkpatrick, and Hutton.

I have already noticed a large number of cases in which the Redman arms appear, either alone or with those of allied families, from the shields "graven in stone" in Harewood Castle to the stained-glass coat in Thornton church, and from the shield in the Speaker's house at Westminster to the embroidery on a Levens Hall cushion. They were also to be seen quartered with Greystock, *barry of six, argent and azure, three chaplets gules,* in Mr. Aske's house at Aughton (visit. Ebor. 1584);

among the arms found by Mr. Machell at Under Levens Hall (a seat of the Prestons) were Preston, impaling Redman (Nicolson & Burn, p. 209); Redman of Ireby quartered Bellingham—*three bugles sable, garnished and furnished, or;* and Redman of Gressingham and Fulford quartered Southworth, when Edward of Gressingham married an heiress of that knightly family.

In Dodsworth's time (1606) "In a southe windowe" of the church of Kirkby Lonsdale, were to be seen the arms of Redman—*gules, three cushions ermine* (Dods. MS. 49, fo. 30); and the cushions make a brave appearance in the far-famed east window of St. Martin's Church, Windermere. Among the twenty-one coats-of-arms in this window, which include those of Urswick, Harrington, Leybourne, Huddleston or Fleming, of Rydal, Middleton, Wm. Mareschal, Earl of Pembroke, Thweng, &c., are these:—

(16) *gules, three cushions ermine, tasseled or*—a "heurt" (or pomme) in the centre for difference.

In the sixth light —

(17) The arms as above, but without the "heurt."

The date of the arms, which were probably removed from the church of Cartmel, is about 1340. (For a detailed description of this most interesting window, see Chancellor Ferguson's *Bowness and its Old Glass;* Bellasis' *Westmorland Church Notes;* and Clowes's *Description of the great window of St. Martin's Church, Windermere.*)

The following Redman coats are also recorded by Bellasis in his *Westmorland Church Notes,* vol. 1. :—

 p 22   St. Lawrence, Appleby.
      Redman and Musgrave.

(North aisle window), Arms. (1) *gu. 3 cushions, erm., tasseled or,* (Redman), (2) *az. 6 annulets, 3, 2, and 1, or* (Musgrave). (Dugdale 1664, College of Arms, and Hill MSS, 1., 161, citing Machell).

p. 167.   BURTON-IN-KENDAL.
          Preston and Redman.

(Arms in Burton Church, as tricked in Hill MSS. ii., 305) *Ar, 3 bars gu. on a canton quatrefoil or* (Preston, of Preston Patrick); ditto impaling *gu, 3 cushions* (Redman).

The arms of Redman appear with those of Ryther in the east window of the south aisle of Ryther church (Speight's *Lower Wharfedale*, p. 79); and they may be seen with the Aldeburgh arms on a tomb in the church of St. Denis, York, to the memory of "Dorothea, uxor Roberti Hughes, quondam de Uxbridge, Co. Middlesex, armiger, filia Johannis Redman, quae ab antiqua illa Redmannorum familia de Turre Harwood traxit originem..."

Among fifteenth century arms "Rycharde Redmayne, of Yorke chyre" bore *gules, three pillows of silver, with their tassels,* (*Ancestor*, vol. iv., p. 245). William Redman, Bishop of Norwich, had a grant of arms in 1595—*Gules, a crown arg. between four cushions, ermine, tasseled or.* His coat, however, as displayed on a monument against the south-east wall of Great Shelford church, Cambridgeshire, seems to have been *Gules, a cross sable, between four cushions sable, tasseled or.* (*Gentleman's Magazine*, 1799, pt. i., p. 186). Another variant of the paternal coat is the following, from the Harleian MSS., 1396, Vis. Ebor 1584—*Gules, on a fess arg. between three cushions, ermine, tass. or, three fleurs-de-lys of the field.*

Of the Redman shields in Harewood church and castle two bore the label, the cadency mark for the eldest son; and a third bore a chevron. The Redmans of Thornton differenced with a fleur de lys, the cadency symbol for the sixth son; Redman, of Twisleton, with a mullet, for the third son; and the shield of the Redmans of Ireby, Gressingham and Fulford (Vis. Ebor, 1585) bore a chevron. The Fulford Redmans, however, are given the undifferenced arms in 1680 (Add. MSS. 26, 684).

CREST. Redmans of Harewood bore, *out of a ducal coronet or, a nag's head, arg.* Thornton—*a dexter hand, couped at the wrist, gules.* This crest seems to have been peculiar to the Thornton branch. Fulford—*on a cushion gules, tasseled or, a nag's head couped arg.* Bishop Redman of Norwich—*out of a mural coronet, or, a nag's head arg. maned gules;* and another Redman crest mentioned in the Harleian MSS. is, *on a cushion gules, tasseled or, an open book arg., inscribed " odor vitae."*

We have now reviewed, however cursorily, twenty generations of this ancient family. We have followed them down the long course of history from days that were almost within living memory of the Conqueror to the civilized haven of the seventeenth century. We have watched them, from the day when their Norman progenitor gained for them the first family foothold in the north of England, add lands to lands, and wax richer and more powerful as the centuries passed; mingling their blood with that of great families, and sending out their sons to found branches little less flourishing than the parent stem. We have seen them defying a tyrannous King and helping to wrest from him the great charter of our liberties; dealing lusty blows at Scots and French alike, doing sentinel duty on the marches, governing border strongholds, parleying with John of Gaunt at the gate of Berwick, chasing Piers Gaveston to the executioner's block, and bearing arms against their own flesh and blood in the war between King and Parliament.

We have accompanied them with their flag of truce on missions of peace, when proclaiming treaties, and travelling as envoys to foreign courts. We have watched them, generation after generation, ride to distant Westminster to help in the fashioning of their country's laws, and have seen one of their number controlling the counsels of the Commons. They have worn the mitre before us as bishops of four dioceses, have done sheriff's work in as many counties, have owned a score of manors, and counted their acres in many thousands.

For nearly six centuries they have held their heads high before us among the great families of the north; and one by one we have seen the carefully-reared edifices of their fortunes tumble down and their broad acres pass into the hands of strangers. However far the pendulum may swing, it must inevitably return; and with subjects as with Kings the day of great things must sooner or later be merged in night. The wonder is that the Redmans held their own so long, rather than that the hour of their eclipse ever came. They saw many a family rise to power and prosperity as great as theirs, only to sink before them into obscurity; and they might well have thought that their own day of reckoning would never dawn.

We have seen how and when it came; and we need not pursue their history farther. Although the blood of the old Redman knights flows in the veins of many of our greatest nobles of to-day, the bearers of the name no longer fill high places. Many of them, however, are prospering greatly; and it may well be that at no far future "when this darkness is overpast," the sun of the family fortunes may shine again as bravely as ever it did in the days of chivalry.

Redman Quartering Aldeburgh.
In the Great Chamber of Harewood Castle, 1584.

APPENDIX.

WILL OF SIR MATTHEW, III. (p. 56)

In nomine Dei, amen. Ego Mathius de Redmane de Kendall miles condo testamentum meum in hunc modum. Imprimis do et lego animam meam Deo et beate Marie et omnibus sanctis et corpus ad sepeliendum in ecclesia beati Peter de Heversham et melius meum animal nomine mortuarii mei ibidem. Item do et lego omnia bona mea mobilia et immobilia videlicet equos boves vaccas et omnimodo alia averia mea ac eciam oves multones hog gastros (lambs after the first year) meos masculos et femellas, ac eciam omnia blada mea cujus cunque generis fuerint una cum omnibus et omnimodis utensilibus domus mee ubicunque fuerint inventa Margarete uxori mee ita quod ipsa post mortem meam libere ad libitum suum disponat et ordinet de eisdem pro anima mea prout melius viderit expedire. Ad istud testamentum fideliter exequendum Christopherum de Moriceby et Hugonem de Moriceby constituo executores meos.

(Probate not dated, but sometime in April, 1360. Proved before Adam de Salkeld, of Carlisle. *Testamenta Karleolensia*, edited by Chancellor Ferguson).

Reg. vol. ii., fol. 66. *Trans.*, vol. iii., p. 90.

WILL OF MATTHEW DE REDMAN, OF CARLISLE.
(p 56).

In Dei nomine, Amen. Ego Mattheus de Redmane die Mercurii in festo animarum (Wednesday in All Souls—November 2, 1356) condo testamentum in hunc modum In primis do et lego animam meam deo et beate Marie virgini et omnibus sanctis et corpus meum ad sepeliendum in cimiterio praedicatorum Karleoli cum meliori averio meo ad ecclesiam meam parochialem nomine mortuarii.

Item do et lego fratribus predicatoribus Karleoli xxs. et fratribus minoribus ibidem, xxs. Item do et lego fratri Roberto Deyncourt vis. viiid. Item do et lego Symoni clerico vis. viiid. Item lego in cera ad comburendum circa corpus meum unam petram cere. Item in convocationem vicinorum die sepulture mee xxs. Item do et lego Emmoti uxori mei illud Burgagium meum in vico picatorum Karl. Item do et lego dicte Emmoti uxori mee xxix marcas sterlingorum quos dominus Will'us de Graystok michi tenetur pro uno equo et aliis animalibus de me emptis Item do et lego residuum omnium bonorum meorum Emmote uxori mee ut ipsa solvat debita mea si qui (sic) sunt et ad istud testamentum exequendum ordino, facio et constituo meos executores, viz. Gilbert de Hoythwait et Emmotem uxorem meam.

Dat. apud Karl dicto die Mercurii, anno lvi. (Probate in common form. Gilbert renounced).

Reg vol. ii, fo 28

SIR MATTHEW, IV (pp 59-61).
Appointed Governor of Roxburgh.

Rex omnibus ad quos, &c., salutem Sciatis quod cum dilectus et fidelis noster Matheus de Redmane per certam indenturam inter nos et ipsum confectam, penes nos sit retentus custos castri nostri de Rokesburgh a primo die Maii prox' futur' per unum ann' prox' sequentem etc. (Dated 6 March, 4 Ric. ii., A.D. 1380-1).

EXCHEQUER; QUEEN'S REMEMBRANCER MISCELLANEA; 5 RIC. II
MINISTERS' ACCOUNT. (1 MAY, 1381).

Particule compoti Mathei de Redman, militis, nuper custodis castri Reg'. de Rokesburgh, virtute indenturae inter Regem et ipsum Matheum inde fact', videlicit, de receptis et vadiis suis xxx hominum ad arma et i sagittar' equitum, bene et competenter pro guerra, prout ad statum suum pertinet, arraiatorum, de retinentia sua secum commorancium et existentium in eodem castro, super salva custodia ejusdem, videlicit, a primo die Maii, anno Regni Regis Ricardi secundi post conquestum quarto, quo die idem Matheus, custodiam ejusdem castri de comit' Northumbr' per indenturam recepit, usque

APPENDIX. 247

Festum Purificationis Beatae Mariae prox. sequent., anno quinto, quo die idem Matheus custodiam ejusdem castri Thomae Blekansop (Blenkinsop) per indenturam liberavit.

APPOINTED SHERIFF OF THE COUNTY OF ROXBURGH (1 MAY, 1381).

Rex omnibus ad quos etc salutem Sciatis quod nos commisimus eidem Matheo custodiam vicecomitatus praedicti, et mandatum est archiep'is, epis', abbatibus, prioribus etc. baronibus, militibus et omnibus aliis fidelibus suis de com' de Rokesburgh, quod eidem Matheo, tanquam vic' nostro com' predicti, in omnibus que ad officium vicecomitatus pr'd'ti pertinent, intendentes sint et respondentes. In cuj'etc T.R. apud Westm' vi die Martii. P' consilium.

COMMISSIONED TO TREAT WITH THE SCOTS. (20 MAR., 1386).

Le Roy a toutz ceux etc. Confianz au plein de les loialte, seens, avisement, et discretions de les hon'ables piers en Dieu, Wauter, l'evesq' de Bath et Welles et Thomas, evesq' de Kardoille, et nos tres chiers et foialx Henr' de Percy, count de Northumbr' Johan, sire de Nevill, Philip Darcy, Meistre Esmon Stafford, dean de l'eglise cathedrale d' E'vwyk (York), Matheu de Redemane, chivaler etc Don' par tesmoignance de n're gant seal a n're paloys de Westm' le xx jour de Martz l'an de grace mill trois centz quatre vint et sisme, et de noz regnes disme. P le roy et son conseil.

WILL OF SIR RICHARD I. (1425—p 87)

Ricardus Redman miles ordinat testamentum primo die Maii 3 H. VI , de manerio de Levens in com Westm', et de burgagiis et reversionibus cum pertinentiis in villa de Harwode, cum advocacionibus cantariarum in ecclesia de Harwode in hunc modum; Imprimis volo quod feoffatores mei feoffati in manerio de Levens et burgagiis et advocacionibus cantariarum de Harwode, dimittant, et feoffamentum faciant, statim post mortem mei, prefati Ricardi Redman, militis, per cartas indentatas Ricardo filio meo in omnibus predictis manerio et burgagiis, tenendum et habendum eidem Ricardo filio meo, usque ad plenam œtatem Ricardi Redman, filii Mathei Redman militis Ita quod cum predictus Ricardus, filius Mathei Redman militis, pervenerit ad suam plenam aetatem, volo quod omnia predicta maneria et burgag' etc. remaneant predicto Ricardo Redman, filio Mathei, et si predictus Ricardus, filius Mathei Redman, obierit sine herede masculo de corpore suo procreato, predicta manerium et burgag' remaneant Ricardo Redman, filio meo, et heredibus masculis de corpore suo, et si Ricardus, filius meus, obierit sine heredibus masculis, remaneant Johanni Redman, filio Elene Grene, etc. Item volo quod feoffatores mei feoffati in maneriis de Kereby et Kirkby (Kirkby Overblow) teneant predicta maneria cum proficuis etc. ad usum meum et assignatorum meorum, durante minore aetate Briani de Stapleton, filii Briani de Stapleton militis. Et quando prefatus Brianus, filius Briani de Stapleton militis, ad plenam aetatem pervenerit, volo quod predicti feoffatores mei faciant statum et feoffamentum predicto Briano, filio Briani Stapleton militis, et heredibus masculis de corpore etc sub condicione quod si Brianus filius Briani Stapleton militis, seu heredes implacitent, seu intrent vel perturbent me prefatum Ricardum Redman militem, vel heredes meos de corpore Elizabethe, nuper uxoris mee, masculos legitime procreatos, de manerio et castello de Harwode, etc. tunc feoffatores mei intrent in predictis maneriis de Kereby et Kirkeby, et de eisdem statum faciant mihi et heredibus masculis de corpore Elizabethe nuper uxoris mee legitime procreatis, et si contingat me obire sine heredibus de corpore predicte Elizabethe procreatis, tunc volo quod predicta maneria de Kereby et Kirkby remaneant rectis heredibus dicte Elizabethe imperpetuum. Et si contingat predictam Elizabetham obire sine heredibus, remaneant Johanne uxori Willelmi Ingilby, et Isabelle sorori predicte Johanne, filiabus Briani de Stapleton, militis sub condicione et forma predictis, etc.

(Dods. MS. 159, folio 195).

Notes supplied by Colonel Parker, too late for inclusion in the text

YEALAND (See p. 52).

From further information kindly supplied by Colonel Parker, I find that John Redman, who died 24 Ed. III , was not, as I had concluded, the last Redman lord of Yealand. It appears that John's

APPENDIX.

sister, Elizabeth, who, according to his inquisition, was wife of Roger de Croft, became the mother of a John Redman to whom Yealand descended. He was succeeded by his son of the same name, who had a daughter Mabel, wife of Thomas Lawrence

In a manor suit (court of John Multon, knight, of Kingsclere, held at Kendal on Michaelmas day, in 15 Hen. VI.) carried later into the King's Court in 22 Hen. VI, Thomas Lawrence and Mabel his wife, were sued by Thomas Bethom, senior, for common of pasture in Yealand. The fine of 31 Hen. III. between Matthew de Redman, Robert Conyers and Alice his wife, plaintiffs, and Thomas de Bethom, is quoted, as also the following pedigree:—

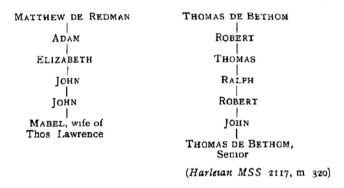

```
MATTHEW DE REDMAN        THOMAS DE BETHOM
       |                          |
      ADAM                      ROBERT
       |                          |
   ELIZABETH                    THOMAS
       |                          |
      JOHN                       RALPH
       |                          |
      JOHN                      ROBERT
       |                          |
  MABEL, wife of                 JOHN
  Thos Lawrence                   |
                           THOMAS DE BETHOM,
                                Senior
```

(*Harleian MSS* 2117, m 320)

The Redman pedigree, it will be observed, is wrong in omitting two generations (Henry II and Matthew II.) between Matthew and Adam.

It is thus clear that the lands at Yealand did not pass finally out of Redman hands on the death of John, in 1351, but remained in the family, with an interval of Croft occupation, until someway into the fifteenth century, when Mabel Redman became the wife of Thomas Lawrence.

WIVES OF SIR RICHARD I. & II

Colonel Parker is convinced that it was the second and not the first Sir Richard Redman, of Harewood, who had for wife Elizabeth Gascoigne, and although many students of Redman history, in addition to myself, had arrived at a different conclusion, Colonel

Parker's opinion is of such weight that I am bound to give his views on the matter.

First, he says, we have the statement in the Gascoigne pedigree that Sir William Ryther and Sir Richard Redman (grandsons of Sibilla and Elizabeth Aldeburgh respectively) married two sisters, granddaughters of Sir William Gascoigne; we have (ii) the tomb of Sir Richard Redman and Elizabeth Gascoigne, his wife, in Harewood church; and (iii) a pedigree quoted in a case Coram Rege in 1516, where the succession to Harewood, &c, was in dispute between Joan, wife of Marmaduke Gascoigne, and Richard Redman, her uncle.

In this case one of the jurors was objected to on account of his relationship to Richard Redman, which is stated thus:—(Thomas Leigh) son of Roger, son of Margaret, daughter of Anne, daughter of Sir William Gascoigne, father of Elizabeth, mother of Edward, father of the said Richard Redman.

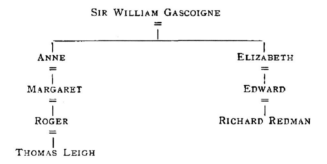

The only point I may mention is that I have come across "Ellen," wife of this Sir Richard, on more than one occasion, e.g., Plea Roll, Lanc^r. Palatine, Lent 3 Ed. IV. But this and the other references may be only clerical errors for Elizabeth. Possibly there may have been two wives, though I doubt it; yet a second marriage with a Croft or a Betham might explain the difficulty of the relationship of William (his son) to Margaret Strickland, who were related in the fourth degree, although I cannot trace the kinship.

APPENDIX.

DESCENDANTS OF CUTHBERT, OF HAREWOOD.

By Elizabeth Wilstrop, Cuthbert had at least two sons and one daughter, and the Richard Redman, gent, who in 1602 was plaintiff in a fine re Newham Grange, may have been a third son. Wilstrop Redman, Cuthbert's son and heir, sold the manor of Borrowby in 1597, and is found dealing by fine with other land in Newton in 1599 He was of Newton in the parish of Lythe, and married as his first wife, Jane, second daughter of Roger Radcliffe, of Mulgrave Castle, by Margaret, his second wife, daughter of John Ryther, of Ryther She was party to fines in 1597 and 1599, and was living in 1603. Wilstrop appears to have had issue by her two sons—Thomas, born 1596, styled (1627) " of Ughthorpe, gent," a recusant; he is styled "Thomas Redman, Junior, gent," in a List of Recusants in 1616.

Wilstrop's second son, Cuthbert, occurs as a recusant "of Lythe, gent," in 1634. Jane, wife of Wilstrop, died before 1608, when her husband, then of York Castle (a prisoner ?), wed Grace Leadbitter. Cuthbert's second son was Thomas Redman, of Newton, par. Lythe. He married Isabel Radcliffe, third daughter of Roger Radcliffe, of Mulgrave, and sister of Jane, wife of Wilstrop Redman He was born in 1569, and occurs last as "Thomas Redman, Senior, gent," n a list of recusants in 1616 His wife (born 1573) occurs in 1603, and in 1608, 1611, and 1614. Thomas and Isabel had issue, Ralph, a recusant 1611, and also Cuthbert (vix 1633).

WILLS PROVED—PREROGATIVE COURT OF CANTERBURY, 1383—1585.

1505	Redman,	Richard, Bishop of Ely, &c.	...	38 Holgrave.
1516	,,	Thomas, Calais and Kent	...	22 Holder.
1540	,,	Robert, London	...	15 Alenger.
1552	,,	Ann, Kent	...	29 Powell
1557	,,	John, Prebʸ of Westminster	...	3 Noodes.
1557	,,	Thomas, Bucks.	...	11 Noodes
1565	,,	Edward, London, &c.	...	20 Morrison.
1565	,,	George, Cambridge	...	12 Crymes.
1572	,,	John, London	...	9 Peter.

WILLS IN THE YORK REGISTRY.

(This list, down to 1618, is taken from the Record Publications of the Yorkshire Arch Socy.)

	Marion Redemane, buried St. Andrew's, York, June 16, 1428,
1514	Thomas Redeman, Probate act Bulmer.
1543	Dorothy Redman, rel. Richard Redman. of Harewood, esquire, to receive inventory, Ainsty.
1538	18 July, Charles Redman (buried St. Oswald's, Arncliffe), 27 June, 1537.
1517	23 February, Lionell Redman (buried at Flyntham).
1524	14 July, Richard Redman (buried at Kirby Overblawes), 7 October, 1523.
1540	11 March, Robert Redman (Kerebie), 11 April, 1540.
1551	30 September, Walter Redman. Regilston, par. Sandal Magna.
1561	21 June, Arthur Redman, Holcottes (buried at Arncliffe).
1562	16 April, Richard Redman, Hoton Robert, August 7, 1561.
1573	27 January, John Readman, Gaitfulfurthe, gentleman, 13 December, 1573
1579	7 May, John Readman, Losco Grange, parish of Featherstone, gent^{n.}
1580	17 March, Richard Readmayn, Arncliffe, 1579
1586	27 July, Isabell Readman Gaitfulfurthe, wo
1586	15 February, Janet Readman, Losco Grange, parish of Featherstone.
1586	1 December, Richard Readman, Losco Grange, parish of Featherstone.
1591	19 February, Thomas Redmane, Carleton, otherwise of Cotes, parish of Snaith
1586	15 November, Isabella Readman, Keirby, Ainsty (Admōn)
1591	20 April, Thomas Readman, Heslewood, Ainsty (Admōn).
1596	8 November, John Readman, Kerebie, Ainsty (Admōn).
1599	Janet Redman, Castleford (Admōn).
1600	18 August, John Redmayne, Waterfoulforth

APPENDIX.

1602	6 August, John Readman, Arnecliffe, Craven.
1606	3 May, William Redman, Stowpebrowe, parish of Fylinge.
1607	25 May, Dorothy Redman, Carleton City (Admōn).
1607	1 October, Janet Redman, alias Shepperd, Leeds, Ainsty (Admōn).
1610	12 September, Jane Readman, Greenhead in Sawley.
1613	16 February, Gabriel Readman, Maltby, Cleveland (Admōn).
1615	5 October, Isabell Readman, Stowpebrowe, parish of Fylingdales, wo
1617	8 September, John Redman, Yarome.
1617	8 May, Mary Skipton, wo. of Jo Redman, of Ashton, gent^n. April 20, 1615
1618	3 February, Richard Redman, Kingston-upon-Hull
1660-1	Robert Readman, of Normanton.
1662-3	Simon Redman, of Andebuthill.
1663-5	John Redman, of Horton-in-Ribblesdale.
1666-7	Edward Readman, of Whitby.
1666-7	Richard Redmayne, of Meare.
1668-9	Dorothy Redmayne, of Beverley.
1670-71	Edward Readmond, of Hull.
1672-73	Thomas Redman, of Gisborough
1678-80	Elizabeth and John Readman (two wills).
1678-80	Wm. Readman of Sinington.
1681-82	Marie Readman, of Wighill.
1681-82	John Readman, of Whitby.
1681-82	Marie Redman, of Sinington
1683-84	Ann Readman, of Whitby
1688-90	William Redman, of Weyton-on-Swaile
†1687-8	Elizabeth Readman (ibd).
†1687-8	William Redman (T)
†1687	March, Christopher Redman, 168⅞ (Ad.).
†1688	April, Elizabeth Redmaine (T.)
†1661	Dennis Readman, of Good Madham (Ad.).
†1728	Robert Redman, Clerici of St. Michael's, Berefide, will of.
†1683-86	William Redman, of Wadsworth.
1705-6	Sarah Readman, widow, of Rosedale

† Dean and Chapter vacancies

1709-10   Hannah Redman, late of Moorgate.
1712-13   Edward Readman, of Whitby.
1714-15   Thomas Readman, of Stockton-on-Tees.
1714-15   Richard Redman, gentⁿ·, of Normanton.
1718-20   Elizabeth Redmayne, of Linton.
1718 20   Emma Readman, of Stockton
1719-20   Anna Redman, widow, of Dean Field.
‡1692   Richard Redmayne, armʳ of Linton, Elizabeth, his widow.
‡1695   Admōn of goods of Robert Rydman, of Dean Field
‡1704   24 October, Mr. Milo Gale, clerk, testament of Jonathan Redman, of Wadsworth—Admōn of goods to Simon Redman.
‡1706   October, Admōn of goods of Ann Redman, spr., of Dean Field, parish of Keighley, to Ann Redman, wo, and mother.
‡1718   17 December, testament of Elizabeth Redman, wid., of Linton, to Robert Whittell, gen.
‡1719   July, testament of Anna Redman, widow, of Dean Field, parish of Keighley—Admōn of goods to Peter Heaton.
1719-20   Anna Redman, wid., of Dean Field.
1728-29   William Redman, civitate Ebor, armiger; John Redman, of Whitby.
1729-31   John Redman, of Rosedale.
1731-32   Caroli Redman, civ Ebor, armiger.
1735-36   John Redman, late of London.
1736-37   Leonard Redmain, of Halton Gill.
1738-39   Francis Redman
1748-49   Simeon Redman, of Upper House in Wadsworth.

RICHMONDSHIRE WILLS—(SOMERSET HOUSE).

Lonsdale Deanery.

8 May, 1553,   Redmayn, Richard, Ingleton.
30 Jan., 1556.   Redmayne, Giles, Ingleton
3 Jan, 1561.   Redmayn, Wm, of Thornton.

---

‡ Craven with Ripon Act Books, 1684 to 1721.

APPENDIX.

1573.	Redmayn, Richard, of Thornton, Esq, (Inv. 2).
12 June, 1582.	Readmane, Wm , of Ingleton.
Mar., 1582.	Redmayne, Alexander, par of Thornton.
19 Nov., 1585	Redmayne, Edmond, of Burton-in-Lonsdale
1592. 17 Dec., 1591.	Redmayne, Elizth., par. of Thornton.
Sep., 1598.	Redmayne, Francis, gent^n, of Burton
10 Feb , 1600.	Redmayne, Agnes, par. of Thorneton.
7 Feb , 1604	Redmayne, Nycholas, par. of Thorneton
5 Oct., 1607	Redman, Marmaduke, of Thornton Hall.
9 Mar., 1609	Redmayn, Jeffray, par. of Thornton.
27 Jan , 1611.	Redman, John, of Newbie, par. of Clapham.
27 Jan., 1611.	Redman, John, alias Jenkine, of Ingleton.
25 Feb , 1612.	Redman, Edward, of Ingleton
7 July, 1614.	Redman, Leonard, par. of Ingleton.
	(Tuition Bond, 11 Feb , 1618)
4 Aug , 1614.	Redman, Thomas, of Callcotes, par. of Ingleton.
30 Jan., 1614.	Redman, Richard, of Ingleton.
29 June, 1615	Readmaine, Elizth of Ingleton.
11 Jan., 1615.	Redman, William, par. of Thorneton.
6 June, 1616.	Redman, William, of Thorneton.
30 Oct , 1616.	Redman, Richard, par of Thorneton
31 Oct., 1616.	Redman, Marmaduke, of Westus, par. of Thorneton.
21 May, 1618. 6 Nov., 1619.	James Redman, par. of Thorneton.
1620.	Bond by Redman, Thomas, of Callcoats, Ingleton.
12 May, 1625.	Redman, William de Parkefoote.
8 Sep , 1625.	Redman, Jacobus de Wrayton.
5 Feb., 1628.	Redman, Agnes, of Midleton.
26 June, 1629	Redman, Joseph, of Kirkby Lonsdale
29 Oct , 1629	Redman, Isabella, par of Ingleton.
6 May, 1630.	Redman, Ch^r , of Ingleton.
13 Jan., 1630	Redmayne, Francis, pa of Thorneton.
3 Feb , 1630.	Redman, Leonardus de Ingleton.
21 Apl , 1631	Redmayne, Marmaduke de Caldcold, par of Ingleton.
6 Dec., 1632	Redman, Jane de Ingleton.
10 Jan , 1632.	Redman, Alice, par. of Thornton
6 Feb., 1633.	Redman, Jennetta de Wrayton.

11 Sep., 1634. 20 Aug., 1635	Redman, Alexander, of Ingleton.
6 May, 1639.	Redmaine, Marmaduke, of Westhouse, par. of Thornton.
23 June, 1642	Readman, Dorothie de Ingleton
7 May, 1646.	Redmaine, Thomas, ,,
20 Jan., 1647.	Redmaine, William, of Thornton.
1661.	Redman, Bryan, of Twisleton.
1662.	Redmaine, Jane, of Callcoats
23 June, 1664.	Redman, Alice, of Wennington, widow
2 Mar, 1664	Readman, Isabella, of Ingleton.
17 Jan, 1666.	Readmaine, Jas., of Westhouses, par. of Thornton.
22 Apl., 1669.	Readman, John, of Couldcoates.
20 Nov., 1670.	Redmaine, John, of Ireby.
2 Mar., 1670	Redmayne, Chr., of Moregarth
29 June, 1676.	Redmaine, Thos. de, Couldcoates.
7 Sep., 1676	Readmaine, John, of Westhouse.
10 May, 1677.	Readmaine, Thos., par. of Clapham
25 July, 1679.	(Lady) Sarah Redmaine, of Thornton.
5 Apl, 1680.	Giles Redmaine, of Moorgarth.
25 May, 1680.	Redmaine, Thos., of Mewith
1 Apl, 1681.	John Redmaine, Armiger, of Thornton Hall
3 June, 1685.	Redman, Miles, de Graystongill.
13 Oct., 1685	Redmond, Agnes de ,,
29 May, 1689.	Wm. Redman, of Westhouse
19 Apl, 1692	Redman, Jenetta, of Ingleton.
10 Sep, 1696.	Giles Redman, of Grastongill.
12 Aug, 1697.	Redman, George, of Mooregarth.
22 Jan., 1697.	Redman, Agnes, of Greystonegill.
29 Apl., 1700	Redman, Richard, of Austwick
30 Mar, 1703.	Redmayne, Ralph, of Halsteads, Armiger.
16 Aug., 1705.	Wm Redmayne, of Slaitenbergh, par. of Bentham.
21 Apl., 1709.	Redmayne, Wm, of Austwick.
20 Apl, 1710	Richd. Redmayne, of Austwick.
17 Apl, 1712	Redmayne, Wm., of Ireby
26 Feb., 1712.	Redmayne, Jenetta, of Mooregarth, Ingleton.
27 May, 1714	Redmaine, Wm., of Lawkland.
29 June, 1719.	Redman, Eliz., of Helmside, in Dent.
4 Feb., 1719.	Isabella Redman, of Lawkland.

APPENDIX. 257

4 Feb.,	1719.	Redmayn, Miles de Maysongill.
3 Feb.,	1720.	Marg^t. Redman, of Austwick.
	1721.	Admōn with will annexed of Richard Redman, late of Thornton (Holme Head).
10 Feb.	1721.	Admōn of Thomas Redmaine, of Ingleton.
15 Jan.,	1723.	Proof of will of James Redmaine, of Ingleton.
	1725	Proof of will of Thomas Redmaine, of Ingleton.
26 Aug.,	1727.	Admōn of goods of John Redmaine, of Ireby.
21 Dec.,	1727.	Michael Redman, of Ingleton.
	1728.	Admōn of Thos Redman, of Ingleton.
	1728.	Probate of will of Thos. Redman, of Hill, par. of Bentham
	1730	Tuition of Margaret and Ellen, daughters of Thomas Redman, of Seedhill.
9 June,	1730.	Probate of will of Alexander Redmayne, of Lowerfields, par of Thornton.
17 June,	1732.	Probate of will of Giles Redmayne, late of Coldcotes, par of Bentham.
11 July,	1732	Probate of will of Thos Redmayne, of Austwick
7 Mar.,	1732.	Probate of will of Leonard Redmayne, of Woodlease, in Ingleton.
5 Apl.,	1737.	Curation of person, &c., of Ellen Redman, daughter of Thos. Redman, late of Ingleton.

AMOUNDERNESS DEANERY.

23 Sep,	1578	Edmund Redmayne, of Lancaster.
	1729.	Thomas Redman, of Cockerham.

KENDAL DEANERY.

7 July,	1582.	John Redman, of Holm, Westmorland.
23 Oct.,	1577,	Christabel Redman, Kendal.
6 Oct.,	1592.	Nicholas Redman of Skelsmergh, Westmorland
27 Nov	1593	William Redman of Skelsmergh, Westmorland.
July,	1594.	William Redman of Kendal.
29 Jan,	1611	Christopher Redman of Skelsmergh
9 July,	1636.	Thomas Redman of Skelsmergh.
3 Sep,	1670	Giles Redman de Kendal.
26 Apl.,	1689.	Christopher Redman de Kendal.

EASTERN DEANERIES

       1524. Jacobi Redman, par. Hornby.
       1584 Robert Readman de Arkende (O B. 72 A.W.)
       1593. Thomas Readman of Usborne (O.B. 72 A.W.)
6 Mch., 1681. Ellen Readman, of Richmond.
              Ad. Act fo 31, A B 1680-84
14 Sep., 1699. Christopher Readman de Surneside.
              p. Coverham   Ca.

WILLS PROVED WITHIN THE PECULIAR OF THE MANOR OF HALTON AND NOW IN PROBATE REGISTRY, LANCASTER.

      1660. William Redmayne, of Halton.

INQUISITIONS POST MORTEM.

"Calendarium Inquisitionum post mortem sive Escaetarum."

VOL. II.

p. 163. Escaet' de anno vicessimo quarto Ed III.
       Joh'es fil Ade de Redmane de Yeland,
          Yeland Maner' due partes. Lancast

p. 301. Ed. III. (1369-70)
       Matheus de Redeman de Allerdale alienavit diversis personis.

          Kirkoswald maner'
          Laisingbye maner'
          Glassonby 20 acr' ter'   } Cumb^r.
          Lamanbye maner' due partes
          Karholl' un' ten'

VOL IV

p. 108 5 Hen. VI.
      Ricus Redman, Miles.
            Harwode maner
            Estcarleton.
            Donkeswike
            Heltwayte.

APPENDIX. 259

p. 153. 12 Hen. VI.

    Elizabeth, who was wife of Richard Redman, chevaler.
        Rughford maner' extent . . . Ebor.

p. 186. 17 Hen. VI.

    Matheus Redman, miles qui obiit A° 7 Hen. V.
        Harrewode medietas maner' . . . Ebor.
    Rici Redman filii et heredis Mathei Redman militis filii Richardi Redman et Elizabeth uxoris ejus.
        Probat' aetat . . Ebor.

p 375. 16 Ed. IV.

    Ricūs Redmayn, miles.
        Harewode medietas manerii
        Otteley ten' voc Kayle

p. 411. 22 Ed. IV.

    Will'us Redman, miles.

Harewode maner Ottley ten' voc' Kyell Denton	Ebor.
Levens maner' Kendale baron' membr' Lupton Mess' et ten'	Westmerland.

INQUISITIONS FROM HEN. VIII. TO CAR. I.

Chancery Escheators and Court of Wards

    Redman Redmayne.

        Edward, 2 Hen. VIII., Yk & Westrd., C. Vol. 25, No. 3, 117.
            (14 Jan. taken at Kirby in Kendal) Esch. File 116, No 3.
            (14 Nov., taken at Wearby, co. York) Esch File 217, No 18.

   ,,   Edward, 4 Hy. 8, York.   C. Vol, 79, No. 199.
                                  E. File 218, No. 13.
        (and see Cal. State Papers, Hy. VIII, F. & D. Vol. I.)

Redman, Edward, 6 Hy 8, York,		C. Vol. 79, No. 172.
(10th June, taken at Harewood).		
" Elizabeth, 22 Hy. 8, York,		C. Vol 51, No 63.
" Richard, 36 Hen. 8, York,		C Vol 70, No. 62.
		E. File 241, No. 29.
" Richard, Westmorland,		C Vol 71, No. 75.
		E. File 137, No. 3.
		W & L. Vol. 1, No. 130a.
" Thomas, 6 Hen. 8, York,		C Vol 29, No. 25.
[of Bossal]		E File 219, No 13.
" William, 30 Hen. 8, York,		C. Vol. 60, No. 90.
		E. File 237, No 21.
Redman, John, York, 16 Eliz.,		C. Vol 169, No. 47.
[Gressingham & Fulford]		E. File 261, No 2.
		W & L Vol. 15, No. 34.
Redman, Richard, 21 Eliz.,		C Vol 185, No 72.
[Gressingham & Fulford]		E. File 266, No. 98.
Redman, John, 43 Eliz ,		C. Vol 263, No. 14.
Redman, William, York, 5 Jas. 1.,		2 pt. 17.
(of Thornton in Lonsdale)		W & L. Bun 8, No 154.

MISCELLANEOUS INQUISITIONS.

Redman, Chris (no county), 16 Jas. I ,		10' pt 152
" William, York, 22 Jas. I.,		" 188.
(of Highleys, Ingleton)		
" Marmaduke, York, 6 Car I ,		19 pt. 163.
(of Coldcotes, Ingleton)		

DUCATUS LANCASTRIAE CALENDARIUM INQUISITIONUM POST MORTEM, &c.

3 Hy. VIII Edmundus Redmayn,
Yreby ut de maneriis de
Tateham, Hornby, Wray   Messuag'
ton, Clayhton, Tunstall   et terr.

27 Hy. VIII Thomas Redmayn
Ireby, Tunstall, Horneby,
Wratton infra Mellyng dominium Claghton.

APPENDIX. 261

28 Hy. VIII   Will'us Redmayn.
    Parva Urswyke maner'
    Ulverstone in Fourness
    Claghton   } Messuag' terr'
    Overkillet   bosc' ect.
    Gressyngham

CHANCERY PROCEEDINGS BETWEEN 1647 AND 1714.

Date	No			
1694	302	Atkinson	vs	Redman & Atkinson
1705 to 1710	333	*Redman*	—	*Redman*
		Redman	—	Cocke
		Redman	—	Barell
		Redman	—	Sands
1650		Redmaine	—	Dodsworth
		Redmane	—	Fairbank
		Readman	—	*Redman*
	370	*Readman*	—	*Redman*
1690 to 1700	284	Redman	—	Hutchinson
		Redman	—	Hutchinson
		Redman	—	Hutchinson

                                                       } Vol. 3

Date	No			
1701	215	Foster	—	Redman
1691		Manning	—	Redman
1691		Redman	—	Keck
1691		Redman	—	Manning
1698		Redman	—	Spencely
1698	136	Scaife	—	Redman
	183	Speight	—	Redman
1695	119	Wigg	—	Redman
1694	433	Wigg (Thomas)	—	Redman
	543	Redman	—	Raye
		Redman	—	Kocke
		Reedman	—	Emerson
Before 1714	317	Archer	—	Redman
	313	Audley	—	Ridman
	337	Condon	—	Redman

                                         } Vol. 2

		No.			
		388	Kirkley — Redmane		
		523	Speight — Redman		
		559	Redman — Hutchinson		
	In Vol. 7	13	Burraston — Redman		

Michaelmas, 1681.

		239	Redman — Ffizer	
1699		314	Redman — Hanham, Bart.	
1709		21	*Redman — Redman*	
		30	*Redman — Redman*	
		54	Redman — Pritt, Bart.	
		61	Redman — Muston	
		91	Redman — Greenwood	
		96	Redman — Durdant	
		467 (32)	Redman — Traheron	
		471 4	Redman — Hanham	

Vol. 9 of Index Bills & Answers before 1714. Collins. No. 3

582 (5) Readman — Metcalfe

Vol. 10.

Depositions before 1714.   Collins. No. 4

159. 45. Redman — Redman
160. 30 Redman — Redman

Vol. 11. Bills & Answers before 1714.   Hamilton No. 1

292 15 Redmayne — Pinckney

Vol. 12.   Hamilton No. 2

293. 44 Redmayne — Chetwynd
295. 31 Redman — Ffizer
296. 85 Redman — Rawlings

Vol. 13.					
1662		64 } 456	Readman — Edkins		
1664		462. 70	Redman — Edkins		
			Redman — Fizer	Page 285	
1680		164 556	{ Redmayne — Chetwynd { Redman — Waterer	Page 311	
1681	4th Pt.	No. 168	Redman — Duck		
		„ 560			

Vol. 14 } Vol. 15 } Nil.

	Vol. 16	Bills & Answers before 1714.		Milford No. 1	
	3rd Part, No. 85	Readman — Ridall			
	6th ,, ,, 78	Readman — Culverell			
	24th ,, xxvii. 28	Redman — Oglander	} 105		
		Redman — Leigh			
	Vol. 17	B. & A. before 1714.		Milford No. 2	
	85th Pt., 59	Redman — Kempson			
	91st ,,	Redman — Talbot			
153		Redman — Hassell			
	110 Pt. 48	Readman — Seaster			
CCC iii. 213th ,, 48		Redman — Kecke			
	Vol. 18.	B. & A. before 1714.		Milford 3	
	Hilary Term. 1685				
CCC. lxxxii. 33		Redman — Darby			
	Vol. 19.			Milford 4	
	No.				
DCXLI. 140th. Pt. 20		*Redman — Redman*			
	Vol 20 Nil.			Milford No. 5	
	Vol. 21.	Depositions.		Milford No. 6	
	698 1st Pt.	*Redman — Redman*			
	703	*Redman — Redman*			
	Vol. 22 } Nil.				
	Vol. 23 }				
	Vol. 24			Reynardson No. 4	
	No. 80. Michaelmas 1682.				
	28.	Redman — Lake			
	Bundle No 86.				
	101.	Redman — Hornby			
	102	*Redman — Redman*			
	Vol. 25. Nil.				
	Vol. 26.			Reynardson No. 6	
1693.	306 7.	*Redmayne — Redmayne*			
1696.	305	Redman — Pockley			
	Vol. 27.	Depositions bef 1714.		Reynardson No. 7	
No. 1000. 47th Pt.		Redman — Hutchinson			
		Redman — Spenceley			
	Vol 28.	Single Bills. From 1659 to 1660.			
		Bills & Answers before 1714.		Whittington No. 1	

Single Bills from 1670 to 1671, inclusive
No. 478 — Henry Redman — Stanton
No. 517   Single Bills in 1709   Mr. Barnard & Smith
            Redman — Redman & others
1652. No. 15   Allerton — Redman Michaelmas
1655. 1st Pt. No. 34.
            Redmaine — Middleton
            Redmayne — Ackroyd
            Redmaine — Paler
1655 No. 46,
            Redman — Wilson
   Vol, 29,   Bills & Answers before 1714.   Whittington No. 2
1667 No 101.
            Redmaine — Maude
   Vol. 30.   Bills & Answers for 1688.   Whittington No. 3
        No. 335.   Redman — Horfall & others
        No 351. (Ralph) Redmayne — (Eliz[th.]) Redmayne,
                              widow & others
1698 to 1707. No. 448.   Redmaine — Marshall
            Rodman — Oddy
   Vol. 31.   Depositions of Chas. II., James II. & Wm. 3 & A.
                              Whittington No. 4
1648   Jenkins — Redman
1669. No. 820.   Redmaine — Dodsworth
     903.   Lowther — Redman
   Vol 31. No. 920. Redman — Horsefall
   Vol. 32. Miscellaneous Bills & Answers and Depositions
           before 1714.   Nil.

REGISTER OF GUILD OF CORPUS CHRISTI.
(SURTEES SOCIETY)

1526 Magister Oswald Wylstrop et uxor.
(Wife Ann or Agnes, d & co-hr of Thos. Redman of Bossall).
Oswald's will proved 2 Apl., 1584, directs that he shall be buried at Hammerton.

1478. Magister Gilb. Redman, Rector.

APPENDIX.

1545. Magister Joh. Redman et uxor.
(John Redman of Waterfulford, gentⁿ. His wife was Isabel, sister of Rd. Vavasour. She was living in 1576 Will 27 July, 1586. (Yorks. A S Record Series)
1490. Dom. Johnnna Redeman.
1498. Dom. Job Redeman.
1418. Magistra Maria Redeman.
1429. Dom. Thom. Redeman.

LIST OF ROMAN CATHOLICS IN THE COUNTY OF YORK IN 1604

(ED.: Edward Peacock, F S.A., London, 1872. Rawlinson MSS. B. 452).

THORNTON.

1. Marmaduke Readman, Esqre,, Ann, his wief; ffrancis Readman Margaret his wief; Richard Battye, Anne, wief of William Readman, Jeffery Readman, Avelyn, wief of William Readman.

HORTON (IN RIBBLESDALE).

Anne Readman, a recusant; Ellin, wief of William Readmayne (Ingleton).

LYTHE.

Isabell, wife of Thomas Readman, a "poore gentleman."

LIST OF AUTHORITIES CONSULTED.

Records of the Heralds' College.
Manuscripts—Addison, Ashburnham, Cotton, Dodsworth, Harleian, Lansdowne, Ormonde and Rawlinson.
      „   Parker, at Browsholme Hall.
Charters at Levens Hall.
Assize Rolls
Close Rolls.
Charter Rolls.
Patent Rolls.
Pipe Rolls
Parliamentary Rolls.
Placita de Quo Warranto
Proceedings in Chancery.
Rotulorum Originalium Abbreviatio.
Rotuli Scotiae
Documents, &c., illustrating the History of Scotland.
Abbey Chartularies and Coucher Books
Historical MSS. Commission's Reports.
Calendars of State Papers.
Parliamentary Writs and Writs of Military Summons.
Cartae Miscellaneae
General and Special Liveries.
Calendarium Genealogicum
Exchequer Accounts.
Wills and Inventories (Surtees Society).
Durham Records
Ducatus Lancastriae.
Fines
Inquisitions post mortem.
Wills at Somerset House, York, Lancaster, Richmond, &c.

LIST OF AUTHORITIES CONSULTED.

Parish Registers—Thornton in-Lonsdale, Ingleton, Bentham, Melling, Kirkby Lonsdale, Giggleswick, &c.
Inscriptions on Brasses and Tombs
Domesday Book
Rymer's Foedera.
Heralds' Visitations.
Monasticon Anglicanum (Dugdale).
Ancient Rolls of Arms.
Familiae Min. Gentium.
Miscellanea Genealogica et Heraldica.
Royalist Composition Papers.
Lancs. & Yorks. Wills and Inventories (Surtees).
Cheshire Families (Harleian Society)
Paver's Marriage Licences.
Register of the Guild of Corpus Christi in York.
Calendar of Documents, France (Round)
The Ancestor
Remains concerning Britain (Camden)
Duchetiana (Duckett)
Collectanea Genealogica, &c
Testamenta Vetusta (Nicolas).
National Dictionary of Biography.
Red Book of Exchequer.
Testa de Nevill.
Gentleman's Magazine
Chronicles of Froissart, Grafton and Ridpath.
Battle of Agincourt (Nicolas).
Battle of Otterbourne (White).
Historic Peerage of England (Nicolas)
Extinct, Dormant, &c., Peerages (Burke).
Extinct, Dormant, &c., Baronage (Banks).
History of the Commoners (Burke).
Transactions of Cumberland and Westmorland Antiquarian and Archaeological Society
The Yorkshire Archaeological Journal.
Lancashire and Cheshire Historic Society's Journal.
The Genealogist.
The Northern Genealogist

Histories of Cumberland (Nicolson & Burn, Hutchinson, Housman, and Ferguson.
An Accompt, &c., County of Cumberland (John Denton)
Description of the County of Cumberland (Sir D. Fleming).
Allerdale-above-Derwent (Jefferson).
Workington Hall (Curwen).
The Gosforth District (C. A. Parker).
Bowness and its old Glass (Fergusson).
Histories of Lancashire (Baines, Fishwick).
Lancashire Pipe Rolls, &c. (Farrer).
Lancashire Fines (Farrer).
Lancashire Assize Rolls (Col. Parker)
Lancashire Halls (Phillips)
Furness Annals (Beck).
Furness and Cartmel (Jopling)
Lancashire Families (Harleian Society)
Local Gleanings—Thurland Castle (Roper)
Pedigrees of County Families—Lancashire (Foster).
History of Westmorland (Ferguson)
Description of County of Westmorland (Sir D Fleming).
Annals of Kendal (Nicholson).
Levens Hall (Curwen).
Colonel Grahme (Bagot).
Sizergh Castle (Lady Edeline Strickland)
Shappe in Bygone Days (Whiteside)
Westmorland Church Notes (Bellasis).
History of Yorkshire (Fletcher).
History of Craven (Whitaker).
History of Richmondshire (Whitaker).
Ducatus Leodensis (Whitaker)
Loidis et Elmete (Whitaker).
Craven and N. W Highlands (Speight).
Lower Wharfedale (Speight).
Kirkby-Overblow (Speight).
History of Harewood (Jones).
History of Harewood (Jewell).
Ingleton (Balderstone).
Pedigrees of County Families—Yorkshire (Foster).

LIST OF AUTHORITIES CONSULTED.

Yorkshire Families (Harleian Society).
The Stapletons of Yorkshire (Chetwynd-Stapleton)
Sieges of Pontefract Castle (Holmes)
Yorkshire Genealogist (Turner).
Yorkshire Notes and Queries (Turner).
Wills in York Registry (Record Series, Yorks. A. S.)
Testamenta Eboracensia (Surtees Society)
Archbishops' Marriage Bonds (York)
&c., &c.

INDEX OF PERSONS.

Abingdon, Sir Thos, 62
Adam, "the Dean," 5, 15, 16, 17, 18
Addison, 59
Adingham, The Lady, 33
Agnes, relict of Ralph, 67
Albemarle, Earl of, 128, 131
Albini, De, 21, 23, 71
Aldeburgh, 133-5
——— Catherine, 135
——— Elizabeth, 68, 74, 80, 81, 87, 88, 117, 119, 134, 135, 155
——— Ivo, 133, 134, 135
——— Maria, 135
——— Sibyl, 80, 81, 134, 135, 136
——— William, 80, 81, 134, 135, 142, 143, 145, 148
Aldgitha, 47
Algar, Earl of Mercia, 46, 47
Amabel (? Stuteville), 32, 33, 34, 35, 237
Andover, Viscount & Viscountess, 76
Andrewe, Thos, 162
Anne of Cleves, 200
Anselm 2
Appleyard, Richard, 113
Archer, Lord, 58
Argyll, Duke of, 94
Arneys, 80
Arundel, 15, 28, 99
Ashton, Col, 226
Aske, 107, 108, 164, 239
Atherton, Robt, 113
Atkinson, 114, 203, 204, 214
Avranches (Averenge), Adam, 3, 4, 5, 9, 11, 48
——— Hugh, El Chester, 6
——— Robt, Lord of Okehampton, 6
——— Roland, Lord of Folkestone, 6
——— Vicomtes, 6
——— William, 23

Babthorpe, L, 196, 205
BAGOT, COL JOSCELINE, 28, 67, 73, 75, 76
——— Richard, 76
——— Sir Walter, 76
Baguley, George, 214
Baines Robert, 192
Baliol, John, 47, 92
——— Edward, 133, 134, 145, 149

Banes, Thomas, 55
Barberouse le Grand, 91
BARROW, MR OSWALD, FSA, 90, 236, 237
Barton, Thomas, 162, 196, 199
Bateman, Thomas, 182
Bath & Wells, Bishop of, 61
Beauchamp, Sir Walter, 85.
Beaumont, 76
Beckwith, Adam, 97
Begham, Abbot of, 120
Bellasis, Henry 114
Bellew, John, 10
Bellingham, 71, 74, 77, 220
——— Alan 74, 75, 112, 113
——— Sir Robert, 75, 90, 220
——— Sir Roger, 93, 100
Benson, 175
Bentley, George, 113
Berchand, 229
Berkshire, Earl of, 75, 76
Bethom (Bethun, &c), 3, 15, 23, 31, 49, 195
Bindlos, 203
Birkbeck, Thomas, 170
Birton, John, 46
Blackburn, 163, 164
Blackhouse, R, 204
Bland, Oliver, 229
Blenkensop, Thomas, 51
Bohun, Humphrey de, Earl of Essex, 37, 229
——— William de, Earl of Northampton, 53
Bold, 220, 225
Bolling, Ed, 113
Bolton, Prior of, 143
Boteiler, 30, 51
Boulter, Sir John, 141
Bower, 206
Boynton, 220, 223
Brackenbury, John, 170
Breant Full de, 128, 131
Brethy William, 26
Bromflete Sir Henry, 159
Brown, Agnes, 113
——— Sir Anthony, 109, 112
——— Sir Humphrey, 113
Browne, John, 204
——— It, 168
Bruce, Robert, 42, 43, 44, 92, 134
Brus, De, 10, 88

INDEX OF PERSONS.

Buckingham, Henry, Duke of, 98
Burgh, Richard, 69
Burn, 74
Burton, 15, 23
Bussel, 19, 20
Bussey (Busay), 20, 23,
Butler, Pierce, 209

Caisneto, Matilda de, 128
Calverley, Isabel, 124, 125, 126
Camberton, 26, 46, 47, 234
Camden, 142, 150, 236
Cansfield, 161, 191
Carburie, 160
Carew, Sir George, 210
Carlisle, Bishop of, 54
Carrick, Earls of, 208
Catreton, Thomas de, 59
Chamberlin, Robert, 114
Chambre, Ed, 123
Chartres, Abbess of, 122
Chaucer, 85
Chester, Ranulph, Earl of, 21, 129
Chichiley, Thomas, 140
Cholmley, Elizabeth, 163, 164, 210
——— Sir Richard, 163
——— Sir Roger, 163
——— William, 217
Christiana 10
Clancarty, Earl of, 206
Claphame, George, 164
Claphamson, 214, 215
Clement, Pope, 61
——— Vincent, 94
Clifford, Robert, 41, 43, 44, 53
——— Roger, 58, 59, 61
——— Thomas, Lord, 69
Cobham, Lord, 62
Cockersand, Abbot of, 35
Colewell, 37, 124, 126
Commynge, Robert, 185
Condar, Agnes, 216
Constable, Kathe, 163
——— Sir Robert, 163
Conyers, Chris, 190
——— Isolda, 39, 49
——— James, &c, 192
——— Richard, 191
——— Robert, 4, 5, 30, 31, 39, 49
Conyston, Ralph, 114
Cornthwayt, Roger, 35
Cornubia, John de, 40, 45
Cornwall, Earl of, 50
Coulton, Posthumas, 191
Coupland, 3, 24, 29, 67, 234
Courcy, Alice, 128, 130, 131, 132, 152
——— Robert, 128, 130, 152,
——— William, 128, 130
Courtney (Courtenay), 23, 24, 128
Cowen, 216
Cowper, William, 103
Crinan, 47
Croft, 2, 39, 51

Cromwell, 197, 230
——— Henry, 208
——— Oliver, 110
——— Richard, 110
Croxton, Abbot of, 162
Cumberland, Henry, Earl of, 111
——— Elizabeth, daughter of, 111
Curthorpe, William, 82
Curwen (Culwen), 26, 34, 41, 47
CURWEN, MR, F S A, 72, 76
——— Elizabeth, 160
——— John, 160
——— Sir Patricius, 172
Cutler, Elizabeth, 141
——— Sir John, 139, 140, 141, 150

Dacre, Hugh de, 58
D'Aincourt (D'Eincourt, &c.), 12, 23, 30, 56
Dake, William, son of, 40
Danby, 191
Darcy, Sir Arthur, 164
——— Lord, 106, 107, 108
Dawnay, Sir John, 192, 220, 225
Dawson, Roger, 92
Dawtry, Frances, 215
Daynes, William, 140
Denethwayt, Thomas de, 59
Denhay, Prioress of, 122
Denton, John, 33, 34
Derby, William, Earl of, 167
Derwentwater, Thomas, 27
Devon, Earl of (De Redvers), 128, 131
Devonshire, Duke of, 94
Devorgil, 47
Deye, 229
Diks, 102, 103
Dodsworth, 152, 170, 171.
Downe, Viscounts, 225
Downes 176, 184
Drake, Nathan, 167, 168
Duckett (Duket), Elizabeth, 93
——— Sir George, 89, 91, 101, 119
——— Henry, 123
——— Sir Lionel, 101
——— Richard, 89, 91, 159
——— Thomas, 93
——— William, 101
Duncan, King of Scotland, 47
——— Earl of Moray, 47
Durham, Bishop of, 64, 65

Edward IV, 69
Edwin, Earl, 10, 46
Egremont, Boy of, 128, 129
Eldred, 10, 47
Elfieda, 47
Elgyfa, 47
Ellel Grimbald & Sueneva, 5
Eltham, John de, Earl of Cornwall, 50
Ely, Bishop of, 234
——— (Dr Redman), 119-123
——— Prior of, 122

Erasmus, 224
Etheldreda, 47
Ethelred II, 46, 47
Everingham, Eleanor, 118
—— Sir Henry, 118
Ewyas, John de, 40
Exeter, Bishop of, Dr O King, 122
—— Dr Redman, 119-123
Eyre, Ann and Thomas, 165.

Fairfax, Col , 169
—— Lord, 168
Falconberge, W de, 10
FARRER, MR W , 2, 4, 33
Favel, 228, 229, 232, 233
Fenwick, John, 182
Fergus, Lord of Galloway, 47
Ferrers de Earls of Derby, 92
—— Matilda, 81, 135
Fitz Adam, William, 40
Fitz Duncan, Alicia 128
—— William, 47, 128, 129
Fitz Geoffrey, Robert, 23,
Fitz Gerald, Alexander, 128
—— Henry, 128
—— Margery, 128, 131
—— Warine, 128, 131, 132, 152
Fitz Hall, Thomas, 40,
Fitz Hugh, Eleanor, 159, 220, 221
—— Henry, Lord, 67, 159, 196, 197, 220 221
—— Joan, 67, 68
—— Sir John, 66
—— William, Lord, 159
Fitz Reinfrid, Christina, 23
——Gilbert Fitz R , 10, 15, 19, 20, 21, 22, 23, 24, 28, 29, 48
——Roger, 21
Fitz Simon, Simon, 23
Fleetwood, 209, 210
Flemyng, John, 198
Fletcher, 109, 165
Forbes, Col William, 168, 169, 171, 207
Fortibus, de, 131, 132
Fossa, Michael de, 23
Foxcroft, 173, 190
Froissart, 62, 63
Furness, Abbot of, 33, 161, 198
—— Michael de, 24

Gamel, son of Levin, 18
Gardener, 160
Gardiner, Bishop, 200
Gargrave, Thomas, 110
Garnett (Gernet), 15, 16, 17, 29, 190
Gascoigne, 106
—— Bridget, 114,
—— Elizabeth, 86, 88, 102, 103, 104, 105, 109, 110, 156
—— Margaret, 137
—— Marmaduke, 101, 137
—— Sir William, 86, 95, 101, 102, 103, 106, 109, 114, 137, 156

Gaunt, John of, 58, 60, 197
Gaveston, Piers de, 44
Gernat(e), 13
Gerrard, Sir William, 182
Gibbonson Thomas, 161
Giffard, Osbert, 23
Gilbert 10, 19
Girlington, Sir John, 226
Glendower, Owen, 122
Gloucester, Duke of, 95,
Glover, 147, 154
Goderich, Viscount, 213
Godith(a), 10, 46
Godwin, Earl, 70,
Gospatric, 30, 47
Grace, 47
Graiton, 60
Grahme, 75, 76, 77
Grantham Lord, 213
Greenbancke, Robert, 203,
Gregory, 60, 114
Grene, 87, 160
GRENSIDE, REV W B , M A , 187,
Gresley, Robert de, 48
Grey, 62, 65, 66
Greystock (Graystock, &c) Amabel, 34,
—— Sir Herbert, 95
—— Joan, 237
—— John, 34, 37, 229, 237, 238
—— Sir Ralph, 67, 87
—— Ranulf, 34
—— Thomas, 33, 34
—— William, 33, 34, 56, 67, 237
Grindal, Archbishop, 124,
Gros, Wm le (Earl of Albemarle), 128.
Grosvenor, 69, 213, 215,
Guarinus, 8
Guillim, 236,
Guldiftre, 128, 130
Gundreda, 10
Gunilda, 46, 47
Gynes, Ingelram de, 45

Haliburton, William, 80
Hammerton, John, 164
—— Henry, 162, 164
—— Margaret, 164
—— Richard, 164
—— Sir Stephen, 95, 162, 164,
Hardye, R , 165
Hardyng, John, 65
Harewood, Lords of, 128
—— Earl of, 142
Harold, the Englishman, 70
Harrington, 33
—— Isabel, 219, 220
—— Sir James, 221
—— John, 34, 58
—— Sir Nicholas, 219, 220
—— Robert, 34, 47
—— Thomas, 100
Hastings, Thomas de, 30
Hebblethwaite, Sara, 209.

INDEX OF PERSONS.

Helton, Sir Thomas, 62
Henry III , 119
——— VIII, 224
Heton (Heaton), 17, 18, 19
Hewitt, Elizabeth, 175, 177, 178, 179
Heysham, Richard, 30
Hieland (see Yealand)
Hobart, Sir James, 123
Holme, Canon of York, 84
Holond, Robert de, 42
Honorius, Archdeacon of Richmond, 19
Hornby, Prior of, 162
Hotspur, 62, 79, 80, 83
Houlme, Christopher, 194
Howard, Earl of Berkshire, 75
——— Sir Edward, 222, 223
Huctred, son of Osulf, 12
Huddleston, Sir John, 101, 103, 104, 105
——— Richard, 198
Hugh, the Hermit, 11
Hughes, 241
Hume, Lord, 222
Hungerford, Sir W , 85
Hutton, 171

Icconshaw, 55
Ikerrin, Viscount & Viscountess, 208, 209
Ingleby, John de, 82
Insula, de (see Lisle)
Ireby, 15, 47, 55
Irton, 110, 231
Isolda (de Croft), 39, 49

Jackson, H , 124, 126
Jeonar, E, 209
Jewell, 144, 151
Joan, 47
Johannes Clericus, 2
Johnson, 191
Jones, 22, 154
Jordan, 2

Kellet, 15, 16, 19
Kendal, Barons of, 2, 3, 10
Kent, Earl of, 114, 133
Ketel, 10, 14, 15, 16, 47
King, 142
Kirkby, 23, 25, 30
——— Irleth, 11
Kirkebrid, Richard, 83
Knolles, Sir Robert, 58
Knowles, John, 181

Lacy, Roger de, 20
Lambert, Aveline, 110, 111, 190, 191, 192
——— Benjamin, 111
——— Elizabeth, 111
——— Genl , 110, 111, 190, 208
——— John, 110, 111, 190, 192

Lambert, Josias, 111
——— Samuel, 111, 190, 192
——— William, 217
Lamplugh, 165, 197
Lancaster, Earl of, 44
——— Duke of, 60, 132, 221
——— Dean of (Adam), 17, 18
——— de, Alice, 10
——— Gilbert, 2, 3, 10, 15, 20, 24
——— Helwise, 2, 10, 19, 21, 22
——— John, 41, 50
——— Jordan, 10
——— Roger, 3, 10, 36
——— Serota, 10
——— Warinus, 9, 10
——— William I, (Baron of Kendal), 3, 8, 10, 39
——— William II, (Baron of Kendal) 2, 3, 10, 11, 19, 21, 71
——— William III, (Baron of Kendal), 10, 23, 30, 31, 41
Langleys, William, 51
Lascelles, 141, 142
Latham, 31
Laud, Archbishop, 138
Lawson, Sir Wilfrid, 231
——— William, 231
Layton, Anthony, 108
——— Dorothy, 109, 110
——— Edward, 187
——— Grace, 109, 137, 202
——— Richard, 109
——— William, 109, 187
Leadall, B , 214
Leadbitter, Grace, 116, 118
Leake, 206
Leck, 227
Leeds, Duke of, 94
Leigh, Elizabeth, 101, 104, 105, 106
——— Thomas, 231
Leighfield, John, 114
Leinster, Duke of 94
Levin, 18
Lewis, Sir John, 139, 140, 150
Leybourne (Leyburn), 23, 41, 43, 190, 235
Lindsay, 10, 63, 64, 65
Lisle, (De Insula), 15, 81
——— Elizabeth, 133, 134, 135, 142, 143
——— John, Lord, 132, 135, 143, 153
——— Robert, Lord, 132, 133, 135
Lowther (Lowdar), 12, 198
Lucia, daughter of Algar, Earl of Mercia, 10, 46, 47
Lucy, 53, 67, 68, 69
Lulls, George, 140
Lullson, Jennet, 191
Lumley, 62, 69

Machell 240
Malcolm II , King of Scotland, 46, 47

Malcolm III, King of Scotland, 47
Maldred, 47
Mansergh, 15, 206, 213, 215.
March, Earls of, 47
Mariota, 46
Marmion, 221, 222, 223
Marshal, John, 23, 92
Mary, Queen of Scots, 115
Maude, 141
Maulay, 23, 148, 149
Mawde, Edward, 113
Mayer(s), 182, 183, 209
Mayler, 211
Memecester, David de, 15
Mercia, Earl of, 46, 47
Meschines, William, Earl of Cambridge, 128, 129
Metcalfe, 196, 211, 213
Middleton (Midelton), 3, 92, 93
——— Christopher, 159, 160
——— Sir Geoffrey, 162
——— George, 220, 225
——— John, 162, 198, 199, 220
——— Leonard, 123
——— Margaret, 92, 93
——— Sir William, 101, 114
Monk, Gen., 208
Monteagle, William, Lord, 167
Montgomery, Roger, 70
Moray (Murray), Earl of, 47, 129
Morcar, Earl, 10, 46, 70
More, Sir Thomas, 224
Moriceby (Morisbe, &c.), 1, 12, 55, 56
Morland, 12
Morley, 162, 189, 192
Morris, 140, 169
Morville, Hugh, 10, 12, 19
Mountenay, Thomas de, 43
Mowbray, Sir Alexander, 156
——— Elizabeth, 154, 156
——— Nigel, 49, 71, 86
Multon, 10, 23, 34
Musgrave, 92, 93
Mustel, Robert de, 2

Nevill, Alice, 197, 220, 221
——— Edmund, 35
——— George, Archbishop of York, 197, 220, 221
——— John (of Raby), 61
——— Margaret, Lady, 119
——— Ralph, Earl of Westmorland, 119
——— Sir Robert, 220
Newark, Bishop, 235
——— Dorothy and Peter, 215
Newton, Thomas, 203, 204
Nicholson, 183, 235
Norfolk, Duke of, 69, 94, 95, 108
Northumberland, Earl of, 59, 60, 61, 65, 68, 84
——— Duke of, 91
Norton, John, 198

Norwich, Bishop of, 61, 229
——— Dr W Redman, 123-126
Nyandsergh, John de, 54

Ogales, 168
Ogle, 62, 66
Oglethorpe, 114
Oley, Rev B., 173
Orme, 46, 47
Ormond, Earl of, 91
Osulf, 12
Otway, 206, 207

Paganel, William, 128
PAGE, MR J T, 217
Palton, 54
PARKER, COL JOHN (of Browsholme), 12, 32, 120, 157, 159, 202, 239
——— Christopher (Radholme), 187
——— Edward, 175
——— Robert (Marley), 211
——— Dr, Archbishop Canterbury, 200, 225
Parkinson, 211, 213, 215, 224
Parr, 90, 98, 220
Patric (son of Gospatric), 30
Patrickson, 165, 166, 183, 229
Pennington, 1, 90, 220
Pepin, Roger, 30
Percy, 42, 62, 79, 91, 95
Philip, the Marshal, 25
Pickering, 154, 160
Pigott, 111, 114
Pilkington, Alice, 101, 103
Pipard, Gilbert, 128
Plantagenet, 69, 132
Pleysington, John, 113
Plumpton, William, 114
Poictou, Roger of, 70
Pointon, Alexander de, 23
Poplington, Hugo, de, 15
Premontre, Simon of, 120
——— Hubert, of, 121
Preston, Elizabeth, 96
——— John, 94, 96, 161
——— Richard, 54
——— Thomas, 94, 102
Proctor, Thomas, 161
Pudsay, Sir Ralph, 220

Radcliffe, Elizabeth, 220, 225
——— Sir John, 90, 220
——— Sir William, 220, 225
Radnor, Earl of, 141
——— Elizabeth, Countess of, 141
Randall, Isabel, 216
Ranulph, Earl of Chester, 21, 129
Rede, Robert, 103
Reder, Thomas, 163

REDMAN, REDMAYNE, &c
 Abigail, 209
 Adam, 42, 45, 46, 48, 50, 51, 52, 228.

INDEX OF PERSONS.

REDMAN, REDMAYNE, &C
Afra, 124, 125
Agnes, 35, 161, 194, 211, 213, 216
Alan, 228
Alice, 103, 118, 165, 194, 214, 217
Ann, 110, 111, 118, 124, 126, 192
Aymé, 97
Benedict, 5, 23, 24, 25, 29
Brian (of Bossall), 118
—— (of Gressingham), 186
—— (of Ireby), 187, 212
—— (Captain), 235
Catherine, 163, 184
Charles (York), 214
Christian, 215
Christiana, 212
Christopher, 191, 192, 228
Cuthbert, 109, 110, 115-116, 118, 119
Daniel, Col , 207, 208, 209
Dorothy, 118
Drew, 124, 125
Edmund, 159, 186, 187, 216
Edward, Sir, 74, 93, 96, 97, 98-106, 113
Edward (Gressingham), 211, 212, 215, 240
Edward, 229
Eleanor, 118
Elena, 51
Elizabeth, 51, 82, 83, 84, 86, 94, 96, 102, 118, 119, 124, 125, 175, 176-9, 208, 209, 214, 215
Ellen, 161, 192, 211, 218
Ellinor, 116, 208, 209, 213, 215
Emmot 56
Felicia, 69
Frances, 190
Francis, 109, 110, 118, 163, 164, 165, 215
Francis, (Ireby), 190, 191, 192
Gabriel (Ireby), 191, 192
Geoffrey, 161, 162, 196, 199, 229
George, 96
—— (Borwick), 196, 202, 203, 204, 210
George (Ireby), 188, 189, 190, 191, 192
Giles, 160, 183, 197, 226, 229.
Grace, 110
Hardres, 124, 125
Helen, 22, 101
Henry I , 4, 5, 13, 14-28, 48, 73, 79, 179
Henry II , 32, 35, 36-37, 39.
Henry (Harewood), 101, 102, 103, 104, 105, 137
Henry, 37, 45, 46, 230
Hugh, 172, 183, 229.
Ingram, 35
Isabel, 116, 118, 125, 206, 211, 213, 215
James (Kirkby Lonsdale), 206, 208.
—— (London), 216

REDMAN, REDMAYNE, &C.
James (Thornton), 162, 193, 216, 230
—— (Twisleton), 196, 199, 204, 213
James, 230
Jane, 115, 116, 118, 214, 215
Jason, 192
Jennet, 162, 185, 190, 191
Joan (Fitzhugh), 67, 68, 78, 215
—— (of Harewood), 89, 101, 102, 104, 105, 106, 137
John, 26, 51, 87, 96, 124, 125, 126, 214, 217, 230, 241
John, Doctor, 124, 196, 198, 199-201, 216, 226
John (Fulford), 211, 212, 213, 214, 215
John, Sir (Thornton), 166, 167, 169, 170, 171, 174, 177, 178, 183, 207
John (Thornton), 158, 159, 161, 162, 163, 164, 165, 170, 173, 174, 175, 177, 185, 216
John (Twisleton), 195, 196, 197
Juliana, 35
Lucy, 67, 78, 212
Lydia, 228, 233
Magdalen, 101, 102, 103, 104, 105
Margaret, 51, 55, 56, 96, 97, 110, 124, 126, 162, 163, 164, 179, 184, 185, 194, 204, 206, 211, 212, 213, 215
Marie, 163
Marmaduke, 231
Marmaduke (Borwick), 196, 202, 203, 204, 210
Marmaduke (Ireby), 191, 192, 210
Marmaduke (Thornton), 163, 164, 165, 166, 185, 200, 210, 211
Martha, 215
Mary, 124, 125, 168, 169, 171, 178, 191, 192, 214
Matilda (Maud), 110, 162, 196, 199, 216, 230
Matthew, 44, 45, 56 (Carlisle), 68, 231
Matthew, Sir (I) (Levens), 3, 4, 5, 19, 20, 27, 29-34, 79, 237,
Matthew, Sir (II) (Levens), 31, 32, 37, 38-47, 228
Matthew, Sir (III) (Levens), 46, 53-56, 97, 158
Matthew, Sir (IV) (Levens), 46, 53, 56, 57-69, 76, 78, 79, 134, 237
Matthew, Sir (V) (Harewood), 83, 84, 89, 90-1, 92, 96, 159, 220, 221
Matthew (VI) (Harewood), 74, 109, 110, 112-114, 137
Matthew, Sir (Fulford) 212, 213, 215.
Matthew, Sir (Batt Sark), 90, 91
Matthew (Thornton), 159
Nicholas, 13, 35.
Norman (I) (Levens), 3, 4, 5, 8-13, 15, 16, 17, 48, 73
Norman, 25, 26, 159, 230, 231, 234

REDMAN, REDMAYNE, &c
  Oswald, 185
  Ralph, 8, 174, 175, 176, 177, 178, 179, 180-2, 232
  Randle, 35
  Rebecca, 171, 178, 206
  Richard (I), Sir (Harewood), 69, 74, 78 89, 92, 96, 117, 119, 134, 135, 155
  Richard (II), Sir, 87, 90, 91-94, 96, 117 119
  Richard (III), 101, 102, 103, 104, 105, 107-111, 190, 192
  Richard (Bossall), 83, 84, 87 89, 92, 117, 118
  Richard (Bishop of Ely), 117, 119-123
  ——— (Fulford), 211, 212, 213, 215
  ——— (Thornton) 160, 161, 162, 163, 164, 166, 174, 175, 176, 177, 178, 183, 198, 210, 211, 216
  Richard, 93, 96, 109, 110, 164, 217, 232, 233, 241
  Robert, 215, 232
  ——— Sir, 232
  Roger, 53, 194, 234
  Sarah, 124, 125, 206
  ——— (Lady), 169, 170, 172, 173, 174, 176, 177, 183
  Simon, Sir, 233
  Thomas, 233, 234
  ——— B D, 196 202
  ——— (son of Henry I), 25, 26, 27, 54
  ——— (Borwick), 202, 203, 204
  ——— (Bossall), 115, 117, 118
  ——— (Fulford), 176
  ——— (Ireby), 109, 186, 187, 188, 202, 212
  ——— (Newton), 116, 118
  ——— (Thornton), 91, 159, 160, 162, 163, 165, 186, 195, 211, 216
  Waldeve, 26
  Walter, 93, 96, 234
  Watkinson, 214
  William, 22, 26, 45, 46, 50, 96, 110, 116, 163, 231, 232, 234, 235
  ——— Sir, 56, 93, 94-97, 98, 100
  ——— II, (Harewd), 113, 114
  ——— (Great Shelford), 124, 125, 126
  ——— (Ireby), 108, 110, 111, 187, 188, 189, 190, 191, 192, 193, 202, 210, 220, 225
  ——— (London), 216
  ——— (Bishop of Norwich), 123-126, 241, 242
  ——— (Thornton), 159, 160, 166, 167, 168, 169, 170, 171, 185, 216
  ——— (Twisleton) 102, 104, 195, 196, 197, 198, 199, 202, 204, 205, 220, 224, 226, 234
  ——— (York), 214
  Wilstrop, 115, 116, 118

Redvers, De, 128, 131
Richard I, 22
——— II 35
——— III, 98, 99
——— Duke of York, 95
——— son of Alard, 2
——— son of Waldieve, 17
Richmond, Duke of, 94
Rigby, Col, 226
Ripon, Lord, 213
Rither (see Ryther)
Robinson, 211, 213, 215, 216, 229
Rockingham, Marquis of, 89
Roger, 16, 19
——— Archbishop 152
Rohaise, 21
Rokesby, Sir Thomas, 84
Romelli, Alice, 47, 128, 129, 130
——— Avice, 128, 129, 130, 152
——— Cecily, 128, 129
——— Matthew, 128, 129
——— Ralph, 128, 129
——— Robert, 127, 128, 129, 151
Roos, 10, 69, 82, 87, 231
Rosse 191
Rougemont, Lisle de (see Lisle)
Rouse, 215
Rushworth, John, 140
Rysheworthe, Alexander, 113
Ryther (Ryder, Rithre), 106, 107, 114, 135, 136
——— William, 80, 81, 82, 87, 113, 114, 134, 135, 136

St Asaph, Bishop of, 119-123.
St Radegund's, Abbot of, 120
Sandford, Robert, 50, 228
Savage, Archbishop, 103
Saville, J, 192
Scarborough, Earl of, 69
Scaigill, 188, 220, 225
Scots, Mary, Queen of, 115
Scrope, Archbishop, 86
——— (of Bolton and Masham), 69, 98, 115, 117, 118, 205
See de la, 223
Selby, 172, 176
Selside (Sillcet), 12
Seymour, Jane, 101
Shap, Abbot Redman of, 120, 121
Sherman, Robert, 103
Shyreburne, Robert de, 35.
Simuel, Walter, 122
Simon of Prémontré, 120
Skelton, Adam de, 35
Sopham, Prioress of, 122.
Sotheby, Mary, 214
Southaic, Gilbert, 47
Southworth, 187, 211, 212
SPEIGHT, MR H, 142, 146, 152, 193, 232
Spencer, Sir Thomas, 58
Stables, 214

INDEX OF PERSONS.

Stanes, John, 108
Staniforth, Samuel, 214
Stanley, 186, 222, 235
Stapleton, Sir Brian, 80, 81, 84, 87, 88, 95, 134, 135
——— Christopher, 164
——— Elizabeth, 150
——— Joan, 101, 162, 164
——— Sir John, 101
——— Sir Miles, 101
——— Robert, 114
Staveley, Dorothy, 206
Stiveton, Elias de, 20
Stodelay, John, 103
Story, Dr, 144
Strafford, Earl of, 89, 127, 137, 139, 140, 150, 154
Stray, Thomas, 102, 103
Strickland, 1, 3, 94, 96, 161
——— Cecily, 195, 196, 197
——— Sir Thomas, 94, 96, 97, 195, 196
——— (Sir) Walter, 23, 30, 45, 54, 80, 94, 100, 108, 161
Sturnell, Thomas, 234
Stuteville, Amabel, 32-35
——— Hawisia, 12
——— Helwise, 10, 34
——— Joan, 33, 35
——— Nicholas, 12, 33, 35.
——— Robert and William, 12
Sulby, Prior of, 121
Surrey, Lord, 222, 223
Sutherland, Duke of, 94
Sutton, 134, 135, 148
Syngelton, Gilbert, 35

Tailbois, Ivo, 10, 46, 47
Talbot, Thomas, 183
Tatham, 17, 18, 20, 179, 182, 183, 194
Tempest, Sir Richard, 101
——— Sir Thomas, 235
Terham, Abbot of, 123
Thirkekeld, William, 79
Thirlby, Dr, Bishop of Ely, 202
Thomas, 47
——— Son of Gospatrick, 11, 47
Thoresby, 141
Thornburgh, 54, 95, 123, 232
Throckmorton, Dr, 198
Thwaites, William, 118
Thweng, 10, 118
Tocotes, Roger, 99
Tompkinson (Tompson), 211, 213, 215
Topping, Thomas, 181
Torenthorn, Thomas, 15
Torrell, Christopher, 124, 126
Tosti, Earl of Northumberland, 70
Traches, William, 128
Travers, Richard, 110
Trimble, 11
Tunstall, 219-227
——— Agnes Grace, 226

Tunstall, Alice, 90, 220
——— Anne, 220, 225
——— Brian, 220
——— Brian, Sir, 108, 188, 197, 198, 220, 222, 224
——— Catherine, 90, 220
——— Cuthbert, Dr, 188, 197, 198, 201, 204, 220, 224-6
——— Elizabeth, 90, 192, 220, 225.
——— Francis, 188, 220, 225
——— Henry, 219, 220
——— Isabel, 111, 188, 189, 190, 191, 192, 210, 220, 225
——— Johanna, 90, 159, 220, 221
——— John, 42, 109
——— Margaret, 196, 197, 202, 204, 220, 226, 234
——— Marmaduke, 108, 162, 188, 192, 220, 223, 225
——— Mary(ie), 90, 192, 220
——— Richard, Sir, 220, 221
——— Robert, 96, 220
——— Thomas, Sir, 42, 90, 159, 196, 197, 219, 220, 221, 223
——— William, 159, 219, 220, 221, 224
Twisleton, John, of, 55, 158
Twysday, Thomas, 93

Ughtred, 14, 15, 16, 47
Ulest, Philip de, 49
Ulverstone, Waldeve of, 17-18
Umphreville, 62, 65, 66
Urban, V, Pope, 134

Vavasour, 82, 196, 200, 205
Veer, de, 230
Venour, John le, 26, 27
Vescy, Lord, 159
Veteripont (Vipont), 19, 25, 34, 43, 47.

Wake, 33, 34, 35
Waldieve, 17, 18, 179
Walker, Roger, 191
Wallace, 41, 91
Waller, William, 214
Waltheof, 47
Warren, de, 8, 10, 41, 128
Warwick, Earl of, 10
Watson, 164
Welbeck, Abbot of, 120
Wentworth, 95, 137, 139, 198
——— Sir Thomas, 89, 137, 198.
West, Lord de la Warr, 203
Westminster, Duke of, 94
Westmorland, Ralph, Earl of, 119
Weston, Canon, 72
Whalley, Thomas, 230
Wharton, 162, 171
Whitaker, Dr, 153, 154
Whittington, 196, 202, 204, 210, 235
Wildman, 176, 184
Wile, 178, 179

William, I., 21, 70
——— Son of Waldeve, 18, 20
WILSON, REV JAMES, M A., 34, 55
——— Richard, 204
Wilstrop, 115, 118
Windsor (Wyndesore), 20, 23, 25, 68
Wodehouse, Robert, 53
Wolsey, Cardinal, 106, 197, 224
Wood, John, 189
Wordsworth, 129, 130, 229
Wrythe, 88
Wycliffe, Richard, 205
Wyndham (Wymondham), Abbot of, 123
Wyntown, Androw of, 66.
Wythes, Edward, 116

Yealand (Yeland, &c), 4, 5, 29, 40, 49, 67
——— Adam, 3, 4, 5, 20, 23, 31, 39, 48, 49, 51
——— Alice, 4, 5, 49
——— Norman, 3, 4, 5, 48, 71
——— Roger, 4, 5, 13, 15, 20, 48
Yetts, Thomas, 181
Ykleton, Prioress of, 122
York, William, Abbot of, 230
——— Archbishop of, 107
——— Roger, Archbishop of, 152

Zouche, 115, 118

GENERAL INDEX.

Acreynges, 115
Agincourt, 85, 94, 195, 212, 219
Aldeburgh Church, 135
Allerdale-below Derwent, 129
Altar-plate, Thornton, 181
Alwoodley, 127, 141
Amounderness, 17
Ancestor, The, 34, 90
Angerton, 67
Appleby, 25, 109, 240
Appleton Nunnery, 135.
Arms —
    Aldeburgh, 144, 145, 147, 149, 154, 241
    Baliol, 144, 145, 146, 147, 149
    Bellingham, 240
    Bindloss, 203
    Bordesley, 147.
    Brisbane, 239
    Bruce, of Annandale, 239
    Clavell, 155
    Constable, 147
    Daincourt, 147
    Dunbar, 239
    Ellis, 155
    Ely, See of, 123
    Exeter, See of, 123.
    Fleming, 240
    Franke, 155
    Galloway, 147
    Gascoigne, 154, 155
    Grauncester, 147
    Greystock, 236-9
    Harrington, 240
    Heaton, 155
    Huddleston, 147, 240
    Hutton, 239
    Kirkpatrick, 239
    Leybourne, 240
    Lisle, De, 153 4
    Lucy, 68
    Manston, 154-5
    Mareschal, Earl of Pembroke, 240
    Mauley, 148-9
    Middleton, 240
    Moray, 239
    Mowbray, 154
    Musgrave, 240
    Nevill, 155
    Percy, 68
    Pickering, 154

Arms —
    Preston, 240 1
    REDMAN, 36, 73, 85, 123, 126, 147, 154, 155, 162, 184, 210, 217, 236-242
    Ross, 147
    Rylstone, 155
    Ryther, 136, 147, 154, 241.
    Selby, 172, 174
    Southworth, 240
    Stapleton, 154
    Sutton, 145, 147, 149, 154.
    Thwayts, 154-5
    Thweng, 147, 240
    Tillsolf, 149
    Tunstall, 219
    Urswick, 240
    Vipont, 146 7
    West, 203
    Wunhale, 236
Arnside, 72
Arthington, Convent, 131
Assepatrick (Aspatria), 27, 67, 68
Attercliffe, 214
Austwick Manor, 162

Ballilinck, 209,
Ballinabole, 208
Bannockburn, 44
Baugy, Battle of, 69
Bennyngburge, 212
Bentham, 108, 160, 191, 205, 229
Berwick, 43, 60, 61, 78
Biddleston, 172
Birthwaite (see Braythwayt)
Black Friars, Church of (York), 88
Blencogo, 79, 87, 93, 117
Blencrake, 231, 234
Bolton Priory, 130, 153
—— Church, St Mary, 131.
Bondgate, 114
Borrowbye, 115, 116
Borwick (Bewick), 199, 202, 203
—— Hall, 203, 204
Bossall, 89, 115, 116, 117-119
Bosworth, Battle of, 99
Bourbourg, 61
Bramham Moor, 84
Braythwayt, Brythwaith, &c, 55, 67, 74, 109, 112
Brittany, 58

Broad Elves, 141
Broughton Church, 162
Brygster, 109
Burgh-in-Lonsdale, 219
Burgundy, Duchy, 57
Burneside, 71, 72, 74
Burton-in-Kendal (Church), 241
―――― Lonsdale, 167, 171, 177, 190, 191, 198, 205
Byland, 20, 79

Caldre, 21, 34
Caldwich, 210
Caley, 101
Calton, 110, 111
Camberton, 26, 46
Cambridge Castle, 132
Cambus-Kenneth, 41
Cancefield, 219
Canterbury, 124, 125
Carlaverock, 135
Carleton, 12, 32, 33, 34, 81, 112
Carlisle, 37, 54, 58, 79, 80, 82
―――― Castle, 54, 79
Carnarvon, 221
Cartmel, 20
Carucate, 70
Charter, Great, 22
Chester, 19, 20, 21, 224
Chideoke (Shideoke), 99, 100
Claughton, 187, 198
Claxton, 115, 116
Clifford, 191
Cockersand, 4, 30, 37, 121, 230
Coleshill, Battle, 130
Coneswic, 19
Conishead, 19
Coniston Manor, 198
Conway Castle, 221
Copeland, 129
Coroner (Lancashire), 31, 32
Crecy, 54, 132, 136
Crests, Redman, 174, 242
Crosthwaite, 15
Crusades, 8
Cunswick, 190

Dalmain (Dalemayn, &c), 109, 187
Denis, St (York), 241
Domesday, 70, 127
Drigg (Dregg), 12, 32, 33, 34
Dumfries, 81, 127, 140, 141
Dunfermline, 133
Dunkeswick, 81, 127, 140, 141
Durham, 22
Dyghton, 82
Dymouthe, 46

Earle, 172
Edinburgh, 134
Egremund (Egremont), 67, 68
Ely Cathedral, 122, 123
Embleton, 55

Embsay Priory, 129
Ewecross, 158

Falkirk, 41
Faringley, 43
Ffostwayts, 109
Fleetwood Colony, 210
Flintham, 101
Flodden, 108, 110, 163, 186, 197, 222, 223
Foxholes, 115, 116,
Frebank, 230
Friar Preachers' Church (York), 88, 149
Fulford, 176, 211, 215
Fulston, 235
Furness, 21, 30, 33
Furness Abbey, 20, 32, 33, 225
Fylinge, 116

Galloway, 145
Gallows Hill 146
Garter, Knights of, 132
Gatesalfurth, 212
Gatesfulfurth, 212
Gawthorpe, 86, 101, 114, 141
―――― Hall, 137, 138, 140, 141
Glanmagorn, 209
Grace, Pilgrimage of, 107, 164, 225
Grayrigg, 91, 93
Graysouthen, 26
Great Shelford, 124, 241
Gressingham, 109, 205, 211, 212
Greta Bridge, 121
Greystoke, 109, 235, 238

Haddington, 134
Hailinethait, 11
Halsteads, 179, 180, 182
Halton, 206
Hamerton, 164
Hampton Court, 76
Harewood Castle, 74, 80, 82, 104, 106, 110, 112, 113, 114, 139, 140, 142-151
―――― Church, 102, 141, 151-6
―――― House, 137
―――― Manor, 68, 80, 81, 84, 87, 88, 97, 104, 105, 107, 110, 112, 113, 114, 127-142
―――― Village, 150, 151
Harfleur, 195
Harlech Castle, 221
Harrow, 199, 224
Hartley Castle, 93
Haslewood, 82
Hazelslack, 72
Hawthornthwayt, 18
Healthwaite, 131
Helicourt Castle, 145
Hellifield Manor, 164
Helsington, 45, 113
Hencaster (see Hincaster)
Henshill, 104

GENERAL INDEX

Heppa (see Shap)
Hetherwood, 114
Hetherycke, 113
Heversham, 16, 56, 80, 95, 97, 108, 113.
Hexham (Battle), 89
Hildriston, 4
Hincaster, 92, 104, 113, 117, 229
Hind Castle, 74, 109, 112
Hinton, 104
Holehows, 55
Holmcultram, 234
Holmescales, 41
Holynhall (Hollyng Hall), 104, 105, 140
Hornby, 187, 190
——— Castle, 162, 186, 220, 226
Horsforth, 81
Hotone, 230
Hospital of Jerusalem, 8, 13
——— St Peter, York, 19, 30
Hospitaller Knights, 8
Huby, 81, 141
Hull, 107
Hutton (Old), 41
——— Roof (Ruff), 80, 109, 115, 233
Hynd Castle (see Hind Castle)

Illubruar, 99
Ingleton, 74, 194
Iugmanthorp, 82
Inishmay, 209
Ireby, 17, 181, 187, 189, 190
——— (Over) Hall, 193, 194
Irt (River), 183, 229
Irton, 110
Isell, 100, 101, 231

Jerusalem (Hospital and Temple), 8, 13, 181
Jesus College, Cambs, 202, 234

Kearby, 232
Kellet (Kellote), 198, 205
Kendal, 19, 20, 21, 30, 69, 70, 74, 79, 83, 96, 98, 104, 108, 109, 112, 230.
Kentmere, 72
Kereby, 87, 141
Keswick, 112, 113
——— East, 81, 127, 140, 141
Kildeholm, 12, 20
Killclogher, 209
King's Hall, Cambs, 200
Kirkabia, 16
Kirk Andres, 50
Kirkoy-Kendal (see Kendal)
——— Lonsdale, 206
——— ,, Church, 208, 240
——— Overblow, 87
Kirk Diomed, 12
Kirkham, 16, 17
Kirk Levyngton, 50
Kirkslack, 234
Knights Hospitaller, 8

Knight of Shire—
 Cumberland, 40
 Lancashire, 40, 42
 Westmorland, 44, 55, 92, 233.
 Yorkshire, 83
Knolsmere, 164

Lancaster, 16, 17, 18, 29, 70
——— Castle, 48
Langele (Langeley), 67, 68
Layfield, 164
Layton, 112
Lecke, 190
Leeds, 116
Leeke, 219
Leicester, 30
Lesgyll, 109
Levens Hall, 2, 28, 71-77
——— Manor, 2, 9, 13, 14, 16, 27, 29, 30, 31, 36, 67, 70-77, 87, 96, 97, 98, 104, 109, 112, 113, 234
——— Nether, 14, 94, 240
——— Over, 14, 82
Liddell Castle, 172
Linlithgow, 134
Linton-in-Craven, 175.
Lofthouse, 81, 114, 141
Lonsdale, 17, 83, 158
Loughmarash, 209
Lowther, 11,
Lund, 160
Lupton, 16, 20, 27, 30, 42, 45, 46, 100, 104, 109, 230, 234
Lyme, 48
Lythe, 115, 116

Magna Charta, 22
Malynghall, 74, 109, 112
Manserghe, 165
Mainecester, 48
Masongill, 177, 198, 193
Medlar, 20
Melling, 162, 187
Merton, 51
Mewith, 190,
Middleham, 230
Middle Temple, 217
Middleton, 99, 206, 207
Millom Castle, 101
Morlaix, Siege of, 136
Munster, 209, 210
Myton Inges, 212

Nantes, Siege of, 132
Natelunt (Natland), 30
Nawmger, 115
Neatby (Nateby), 110
Nesbit Moor, 133
Netherlands, 167, 190
Newbiggin, 230
Newcastle, 62, 64, 66, 171n, 174.
Newhall, 114
Newton, 115, 116, 117

Norham Castle 163
Norman origin of Redmans, 1-7
Northampton, 42, 85
North Dalton, 212
Norton, 219
Nottingham, 25
Niby, 141
Nutgeld (Noutegeld), 28

Oakham Castle, 134
Okeland, 198
Oosburne (see Ouseburn)
Otley Pole (Poole), 104, 105
Otterbourne, 62, 65, 66, 78
Ouchy le Chasteau, 58
Ouseburn, Little, 115, 116
Overlands, 164, 166, 167
Overton, 27
Ovington, 124

Parke, 182
Parker MSS, 211, 230
Pearl Fishers' Company, 239
Pecquigny, Treaty of, 95
Penwortham, 20
Penyerhocke, 133
Percy Rising, 83
Pickering—Lythe, 116
Pilgrimage of Grace, 107, 164, 225
Pontefract Castle, 107, 167, 168
Portugal, King of, 58
Preston Hall, 94, 161
Pulton, in Lonsdale, 160

Quinfell (see Whinfell)

Ravensworth Castle, 197
Raventhwaite, 228
Rawden, 153
Redman (Manor), 7, 13, 26, 27, 205
——— Chapel, 102, 151
Redman's Road, 217
Redmayne Hall 195, 205
Registers, Thornton, 185
——— Ingleton, &c, 194
Rigton-in-the-Forest, 81, 141
Rising of the North, 213
Rochester Castle, 23, 24, 29
Rouen, 195
Rougemont, 43
Roxburgh Castle, 59, 60, 61, 78
——— Siege, 133
Rudstone, 230
Rughford, 88
Runnerthwayt, 50
Rutland, 134
Ryther Castle, 80, 134
——— Church, 241
——— Manor, 135

St Asaph Cathedral, 122
— Mary Acte's Church, 125
— Mary and Holy Angels, York, 152

St Mary of Kildeholm, 12
— Mary and St Sepulchre, 152
— Sauveur Castle, 59
Sark, Battle of, 91
Selside, 9, 15, 16, 67, 95, 109, 112
Seneschal of Kendal, 19, 28
Seton, 117
Shadwell, 141
Shap Abbey, 19, 20, 25, 117, 120, 122
Shelford Great, 124
Sheriff of Cumberland, 54, 80, 100
——— of Dorset, 100
——— of Du mines, 38, 42
——— of Lancashire, 22, 31, 48
——— of Roxburgh, 59, 60
——— of Somerset, 100
——— of Westmorland, 22
——— of Yorkshire, 19, 22, 82, 83
Shipton, 212
Shrewsbury, Battle of, 83
Silverdale, 3 20, 29
Sizergh, 3, 72, 91, 108, 195
Skelesbolt, 30
Skelsmergh, 41
Skipton-in-Craven, 127, 129, 131
Skipwith, 212
Sleddall, 54
Sluys, Battle of, 136
Snaythe, 110
Spain, 58
Speaker's House, 85
Spurs, Battle of, 89
Stamford, Statute of, 43
Stanhope, 224
Stepney, 217
Striklanketill, 55
Stirling Castle, 133, 134
Stockhouse, 81
Stockton, 81, 114
Strid, The, 129
Stuteville Fee, 33
Sutton-in-Holderness, 134
Swindon, 141
Synderbarrow, 109

Tatham, 17, 187
Tebay (Tibbeie), 51
Thornton-in-Lonsdale, 8, 55, 74, 110, 166, 167, 191, 198, 205
——— Church, 163, 173, 174, 179, 181, 184
——— Hall, 171, 175, 177, 184
Threlkeld, 231
Thurcroft, 97
Thurland Castle, 90, 159, 188, 219, 225, 226, 227
Todgill, 190
Tournay, Siege of, 136.
Trantherne (Tranton, &c), 11, 12, 20, 36
Trimbe, 12
Trinity College, Cambridge, 200
Tyrrebanke, 165

GENERAL INDEX.

Tunstall, 187, 190, 219, 223
Twisleton, 55, 94, 102, 158, 205
Tyndale, 134

Ulvedale, 67, 68
Ulverstone, 17, 18, 19, 198.
Urswick, 21, 199
——— Little, 195, 198
Usburne (see Ooseburn)

Vaunes, Siege of, 136
Vironfosse, Battle of, 132

Wardeley, 113
Warwick Castle, 44
Waterfulforth, 212
Waverton, 26
Wearby, 106
Weardley, 81, 127, 140, 141
Weeton, 81, 127, 140, 141
Welbeck, 120
Welford, 49
Wescoe Hill, 141
Westhouse, 177, 190, 191, 205
Westminster Abbey, 172, 200
Westwick, 116

Wheatley, 145
Whinfell, 30, 54, 67, 95, 113
Whitby, 115, 116
——— Strand, 117
Whittington, 160
Wigglesworth, 164
Wight, Isle of, 132
Wigton, 127, 140, 141, 153
Wike, 127, 140, 141
Windermere, St Martin's Church, 240
Workington, 26, 46
——— Hall, 172
Wrayton, 167, 169, 187, 190.
Wynsdale, 198

Yeadon, 81
Yealand, 3, 4, 5, 16, 27, 29, 30, 35, 36, 48-52, 71, 230
——— Conyers, 39, 52
——— Redmayne, 31, 32, 39, 51, 52, 71
Yeovil, 234
Yewcross, 108
York, 19, 30, 88, 107, 108
——— Castle, 116
——— Cathedral, 152.

PRINTED BY TITUS WILSON, KENDAL

CPSIA information can be obtained at www.ICGtesting.com
224028LV00001B/173/P